IMAGES
*of America*

# STANLEY

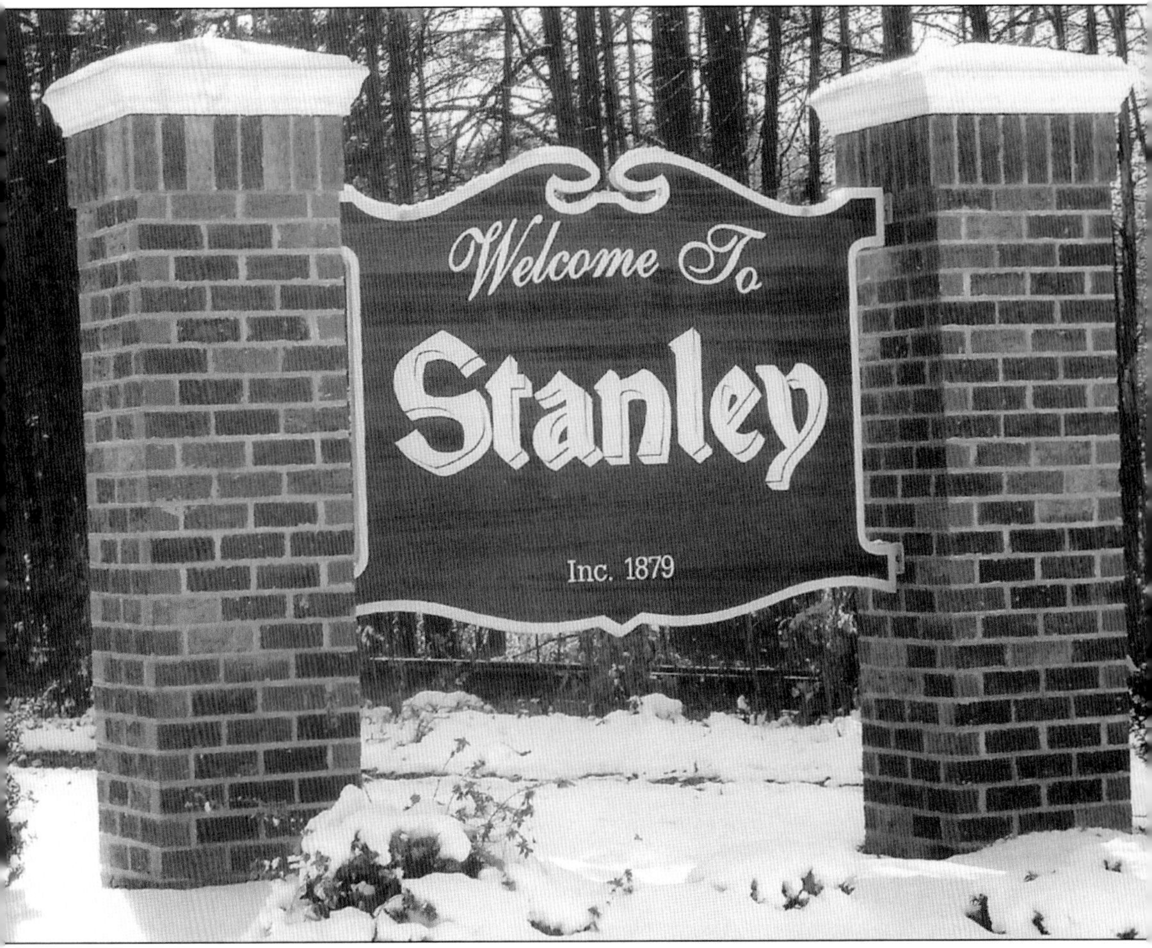


Prominently displayed on the north and south ends of town on Highway 27 are signs erected through the generosity of the members of the Stanley Home and Garden Club. The city limits of Stanley encompass approximately three square miles, and the elevation is 863 feet. The population in 2010 was 3,556. The 28164 zip code borders Mount Holly, Dallas, and Spencer Mountain, and extends north to Lake Norman in Lincoln County. (Courtesy of Joyce Handsel.)

**On the Cover:** In this photograph from the early 1940s, Stanley Mills employees are shown standing beside the mill building. Stanley Mills, located on North Main Street, began as Stanley Creek Cotton Mills in 1891. Over the years, the name was changed to Lola Mills, Katterman & Mitchell, Stanley Mills, J.P. Stevens and Company, and JPS Converter Yarns. It closed in 2000 as Belding Hausman Inc. (Courtesy of Ronnie Lineberger.)

IMAGES
*of America*

# STANLEY

Joyce Handsel, Pat Smith,
and Ruth Wood

ARCADIA
PUBLISHING

ISBN 978-1-4671-1642-8

Published by Arcadia Publishing
Charleston, South Carolina

Printed in the United States of America

Library of Congress Control Number: 2016941244

For all general information, please contact Arcadia Publishing:
Telephone 843-853-2070
Fax 843-853-0044
E-mail sales@arcadiapublishing.com
For customer service and orders:
Toll-Free 1-888-313-2665

Visit us on the Internet at www.arcadiapublishing.com

*This book is dedicated to Joyce Joy Handsel, curator and administrator of Brevard Station Museum.*

# Contents

# Acknowledgments

We wish to thank all the caring people who donated the many photographs and other artifacts to Brevard Station Museum that became the foundation for this book. Our thanks also go to the museum volunteers who have helped in preserving this precious history. Bill Carangelo, Nancy Dukes, Joyce Joy Handsel, Freida Long Robinson, Keith Quillen, Pat Cantrell Smith, and Ruth Campbell Wood have all been instrumental in this effort. Wood served as a full-time volunteer for 15 years and used the knowledge she gained there to help author this book. These volunteers worked side by side with Joyce Handsel, current administrator of the museum, whose service without salary for 25 years has made this local museum one of the finest in North Carolina. This book is dedicated to her in honor of her enduring devotion. With Ruth Wood and Sarah Grissop she coauthored a cookbook, *Echoes and Images of Magnolia Country Cooks*, and was the principal author of two other books, *Echoes and Shadows of Two Centuries, 1750 to 1950* and *Handsel Family Heritage*. Many articles on local history and genealogy in newspapers and on www.brevardstation.com bear her signature. Undoubtedly, Handsel is the driving force for the preservation of the history of Stanley. She was the go-to person on this project and without her strong commitment, this book about the town called Stanley would not be the excellent one it is.

We wish to thank the members of the Brevard Station Museum Board of Directors—Michael Bradshaw, Allison Clippard Cobb, James Flanders, Barry Frady, Joyce Handsel, Judith Dellinger Johnson, William Barry Smith, and Pat Cantrell Smith—for their support.

Our deepest appreciation goes to retired teachers Kitty Smith Saunders and Freida Long Robinson for the daunting task of proofreading the captions.

The authors will donate their royalties from the sale of this book to the Brevard Station Museum, a nonprofit volunteer organization. Unless otherwise noted, the images in this book appear courtesy of the Brevard Station Museum.

# INTRODUCTION

Stanley, North Carolina, had its beginnings in the mid-1700s when the first pioneers, the majority of whom were of German and Scots Irish heritage, began arriving in the wilderness of the Catawba River region. Some of the early settlers made their first homes along the banks of a small creek that emptied into a larger creek before reaching the Catawba River. This small creek was named for a gold prospector who had ventured into the area, stayed a while searching for gold, and then moved on farther south. The exact identity of the gold prospector, a Mr. Stanley, has been lost to time. The area quickly began being referred to as the Stanley's Creek Community.

In the middle to late 1700s, France sent to this country a botanist named André Michaux to record, document, and send back to France samples of plant life in America. Michaux kept a journal in which he made note of stopping several times in the area that is now Stanley. His notes tell of staying at the home of Peter Smith, an ancestor of many people now living in Stanley. While at Smith's home, Michaux noted he had discovered a new and different magnolia, the Magnolia macrophylla. Smith's son, David, transplanted some sprouts from the tree to his beautiful new brick home in Lincoln County and named the place Magnolia Grove. These trees are still located in Stanley, and the surrounding area contains one of the largest collections in North Carolina. The tree itself has the largest leaves and flowers of any tree in North America.

Peter Eddleman, a skilled furniture craftsman who came to the Stanley area with his family while very young, had apprenticed with furniture makers in Pennsylvania and built many pieces of furniture for local folks using that style. Today, one of his pieces remains, in the 1799 Rhyne home, which is still occupied by descendants of Thomas Rhyne, who built the house.

Gold was excavated in the area after being discovered near Charlotte in the late 1700s. Several mines in the Stanley area were quite profitable, especially the Moore and Smith gold mines. From 1804 to 1828, all domestic gold coined by the US Mint came from North Carolina. However, gold mining waned in the area after the 1849 California Gold Rush.

The Wilmington, Charlotte, & Rutherfordton Railroad reached the area in December 1860 and was the first east-to-west railroad through the interior of North Carolina. A depot was built and named Brevard's Station in recognition of the Brevard family, who owned a large portion of the surrounding land.

When Christ's Lutheran Church was built on the property of the Brevard family, a few people settled around the church, but the greater population developed when the railroad ran its tracks through the area. During the Civil War years, the depot was a rallying point for soldiers leaving for camps and for sending supplies to troops. The community that developed around the railroad was combined with the Stanley Creek Community and eventually incorporated in 1879 as Brevard Station Community, later Stanley Creek, and then Stanley.

On April 17, 1891, Jacob Jenkins, J.T. Abernethy, August Farley, N.M. Rutledge, Edgar Durant Thompson, Henry Michael Summerow, and D.C. Finger began Stanley Creek Cotton Mills. A few years later, the mill changed owners and became the Stanley Manufacturing Company. Another change of ownership came in 1918, when the mill became the Lola Manufacturing Company under the proprietorship of John C. Rankin, S.M. Robinson, and Robert Fulton Craig. Lola Gingham Mill was established at that time, with William P. Hornbuckle as plant superintendent. Hornbuckle and Craig are credited with inventing and receiving a patent for a new type of dyeing machine when the machine they had imported from England for the gingham mill was insufficient for their needs. This shortly led to the beginning of Gaston County Dyeing Machine Company, an international company. In 1930, a silk mill, the Katterman and Mitchell Mill, was begun with the purchase of Lola Gingham Mill.

Around 1928, the United States established an air mail route from New York to Mexico. Being directly in the line of the southern route, Stanley was chosen as a stopover site to build an airport for pilots carrying the mail. The caretaker of the field was Luther J. Sherrill. The airport remained in Stanley until 1932 when the field was discontinued, and the tower and beacon light were shipped elsewhere.

The first pioneers were educated, but their children lacked in schooling because their help was needed in establishing homes and farmland in the new country. However, that generation as adults recognized the growing demand for their own children to receive a formal education, and schools were established. In 1845, there were two schools in the Stanley Creek area: one for children on the east side of Tuckaseege Road and one for children on the west side. The first schools in the new community of Brevard Station were perhaps established in 1881: one at the Petersons', one at Mary Smith's home, and one in the Springfield section. In the outlying area, there were the Five Forks School and Rankins School. Brevard High School began in 1883 and had as principal a Professor Brower, who was a graduate of Trinity College (now Duke University). The Methodist Conference chose Stanley as a location for one of its schools, and construction on the building was begun in 1900. This was where many of Stanley's children attended school until the North Carolina Compulsory Attendance Act was passed in 1913. Shortly afterward, public schools were built under control of the state board of education.

Stanley is the home of the 2002 National Junior Pee Wee Pop Warner Football champions. The town's 10- and 12-year-olds' football team went to Florida to play in the Disney World Super Bowl, where they defeated a team from Connecticut.

Dr. Graham Weathers, a native of Stanley, was an accomplished sculptor with works displayed not only locally, but in the Smithsonian Institution and worldwide. Stanley is the home of numerous talented and accomplished people, such as doctors, lawyers, artists, politicians, sports figures, inventors, and other visionaries.

Stanley maintains its small-town image while being a part of the greater Charlotte metropolitan area and provides a pleasant mixture of housing, including charming older houses, subdivisions, and affordable homes. These are located close to great schools and the new Harper Park. There is easy access to medical care. Excellent accommodations are available at Stanley Total Living Center for seniors, with all levels of care available. With a population of around 3,500, the town is comprised of several banks, many churches, good restaurants, a park, a shopping district, and a museum. Brevard Station Museum is a unique small-town repository with a genealogical research area and a display of thousands of artifacts. Visitors come from numerous states and countries.

# *One*

# Early Settlement

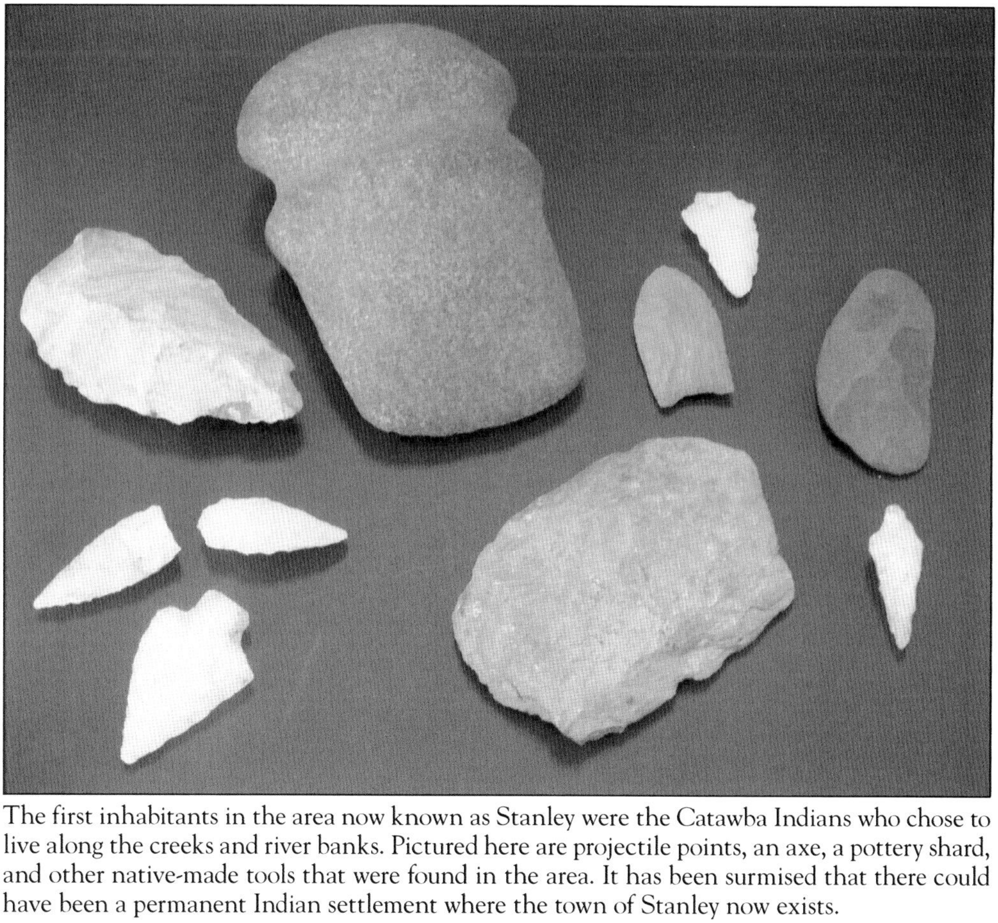

The first inhabitants in the area now known as Stanley were the Catawba Indians who chose to live along the creeks and river banks. Pictured here are projectile points, an axe, a pottery shard, and other native-made tools that were found in the area. It has been surmised that there could have been a permanent Indian settlement where the town of Stanley now exists.

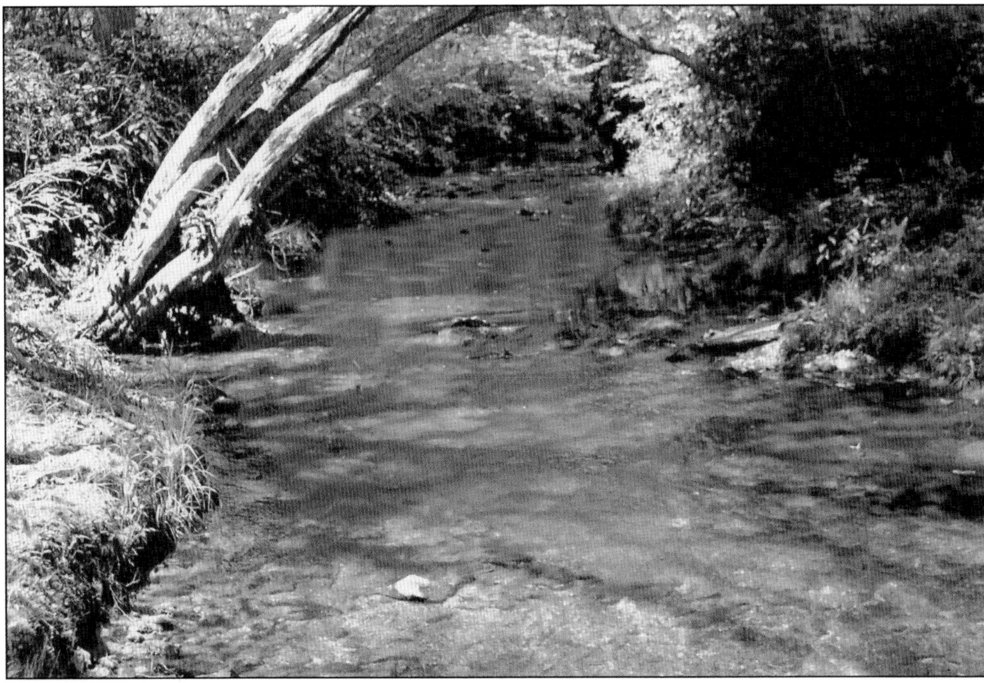

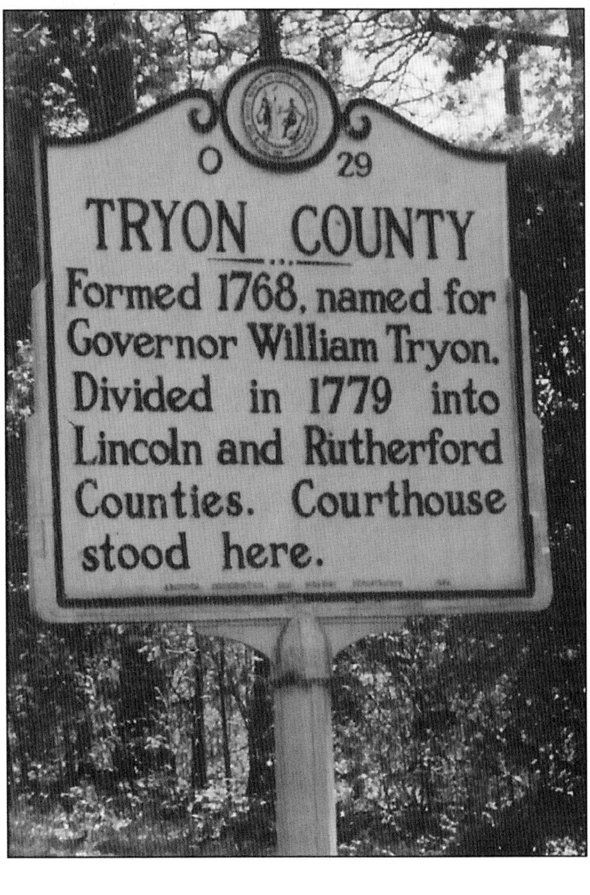


Stanley Creek, a tributary of Dutchman's Creek, which runs into the Catawba River, was named for a gold prospector in the mid-1700s. The first settlers made their homes along this creek and began the original community of Stanley Creek. Names of some of the early settlers in the area were Abernethy, Armstrong, Cloninger, Eddleman, Hansel, Hoffman, Leeper, Rankin, Rhyne, Rutledge, Seitz, Smith, and Wills, among others. (Courtesy of Jacob Walley.)

Tryon County was formed in 1768 and named for the intensely disliked William Tryon, a North Carolina governor appointed by King George. Farmers in the county, including the area that would become the town of Stanley, were taxed to pay for a palace for Tryon. In response to taxation without representation and the brutal battle at Lexington, Massachusetts, the outraged farmers revolted and declared their independence from British tyranny in the 1775 Tryon Resolves.

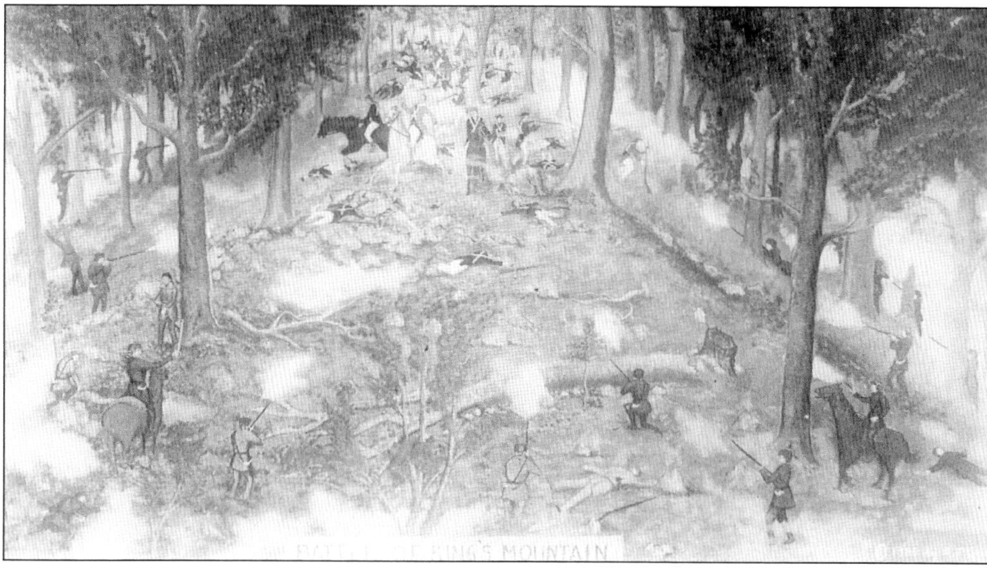

Robert Cope's depiction of the Battle of Kings Mountain, seen here, was painted in 1930. The battle has been called the turning point of the Revolutionary War by many historians. A number of Stanley area men fought as Patriots, and some died on the mountain in that fierce battle. (Courtesy of Doris Cope Rhyne.)

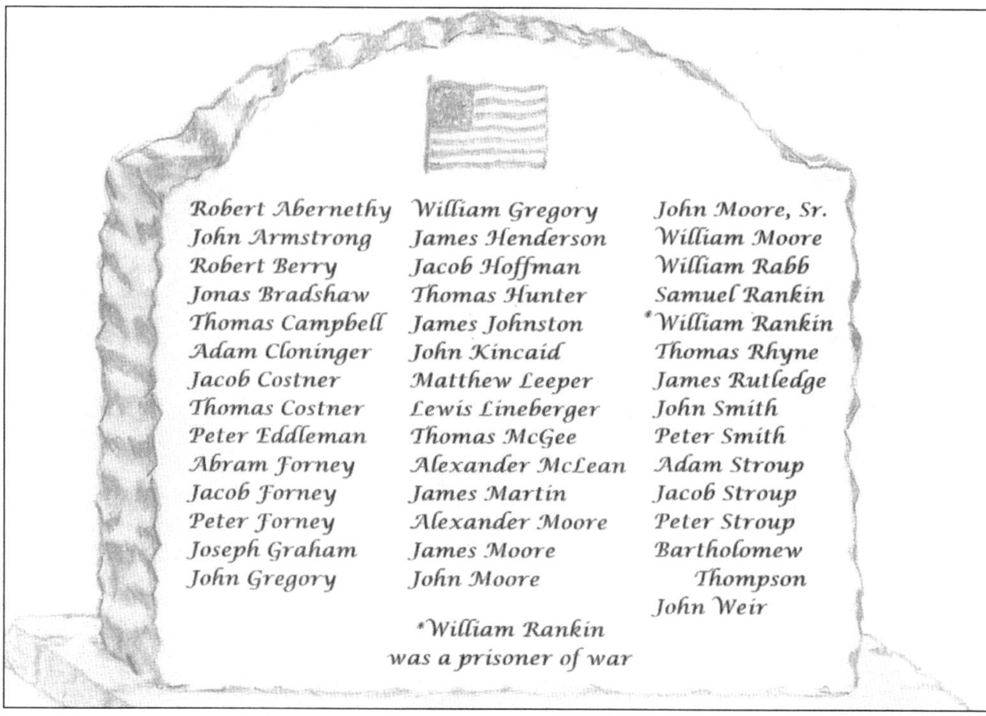


Listed here are some of the names of Stanley area men who participated in the Revolutionary War, either as regular members of the Continental army or as local militia. Some fought at Kings Mountain and others at the Battle of Ramsour's Mill near present-day Lincolnton, while still others like the Stroups made guns, gun powder, and other provisions for the Patriot army. (Courtesy of Ruth Wood.)

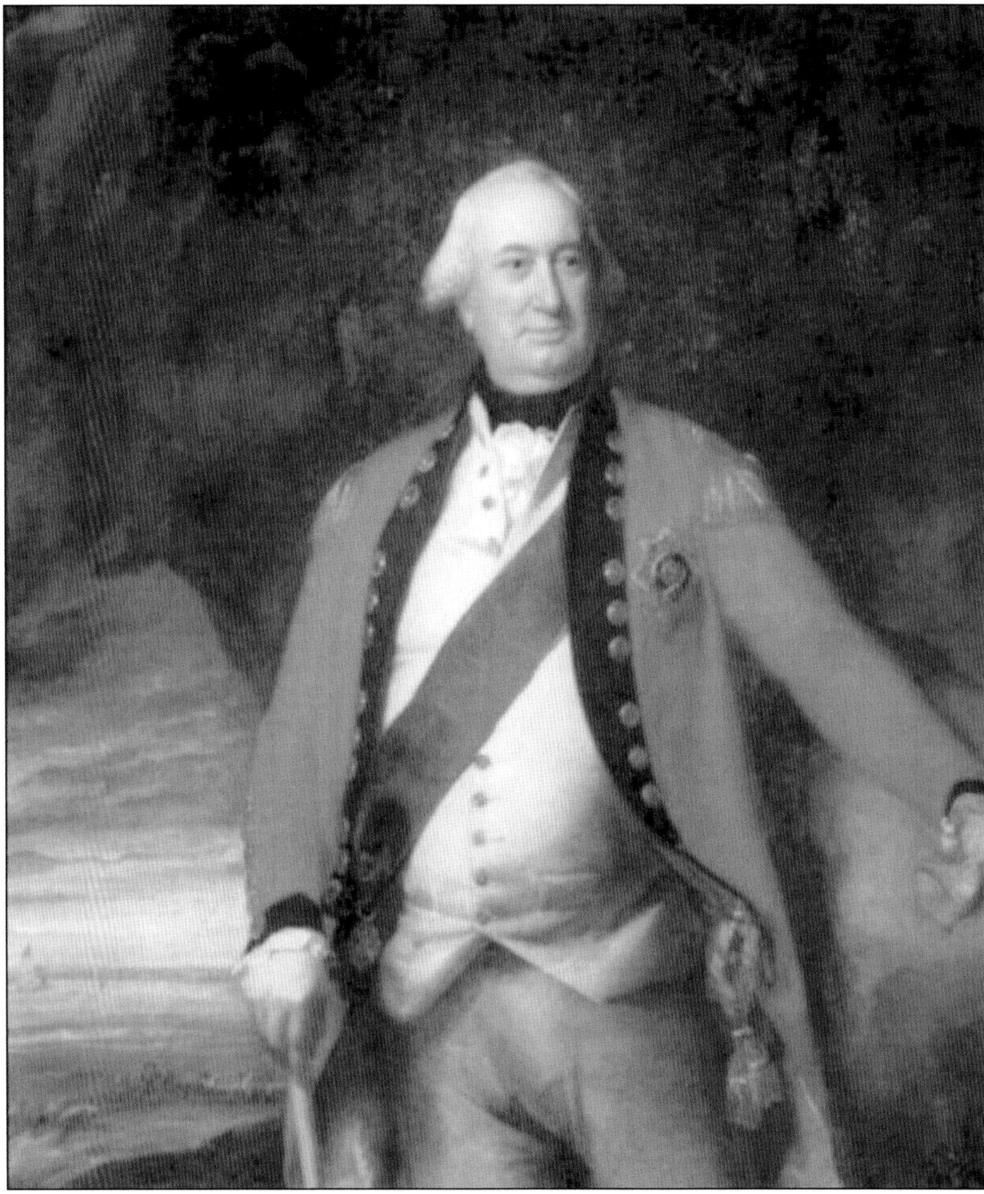

After a stinging defeat of the British army in Cowpens, South Carolina, Gen. Charles Cornwallis moved his army of 2,550 men into North Carolina. His army marched into Lincoln County and waited for the rain to stop before crossing at Cowan's Ford in an attempt to capture the American general Daniel Morgan. The local militia was called up to stall the British. Five hundred local men turned up to fight, while many families fled for their lives, hiding their cattle and valuables. Cornwallis made his headquarters at Forney's plantation. At midnight on February 1, 1781, the British troops began wading into the Catawba River at Cowan's Ford under fire from the militia. Many soldiers drowned with their heavy packs of ammunition. Cornwallis's troops moved on toward Greensboro to meet the patriots at the Battle of Guilford Courthouse, where General Cornwallis defeated Maj. Gen. Daniel Greene. Heavy British casualties forced Cornwallis to march to Yorktown, Virginia, where he surrendered to Gen. George Washington after the Battle of Yorktown.

Peter Eddleman, a Revolutionary soldier, was born in 1763 and died in 1847. He migrated to the Stanley area after the war. He married Dica Swanson Clippard, and they had two sons, David and William. Eddleman was a skilled cabinetmaker in the Pennsylvania style. One piece, a fine hand-carved china cabinet, was made for the 1799 Rhyne family house and is still there. Another cabinet that survived the years was made for the Rankin family of Willowside.

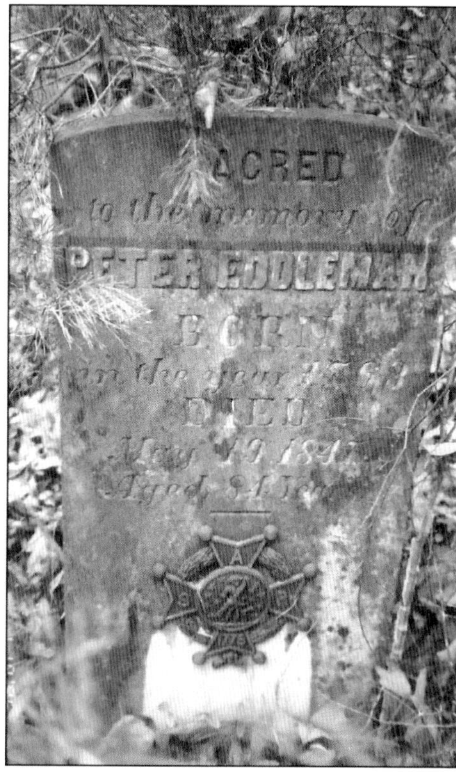


Peter Eddleman's cherry desk was donated by his great-grandson William Roseman Eddleman to the museum of the National Society, Sons of the American Revolution, in Louisville, Kentucky. In a secret compartment of the desk was found an original document dated 1798. It indicated that Peter Eddleman's father, before his death, had provided for care of Peter's mother. Also found in the desk was an 1817 bill of sale for the purchase of a horse. (Courtesy of Bob Bowen.)

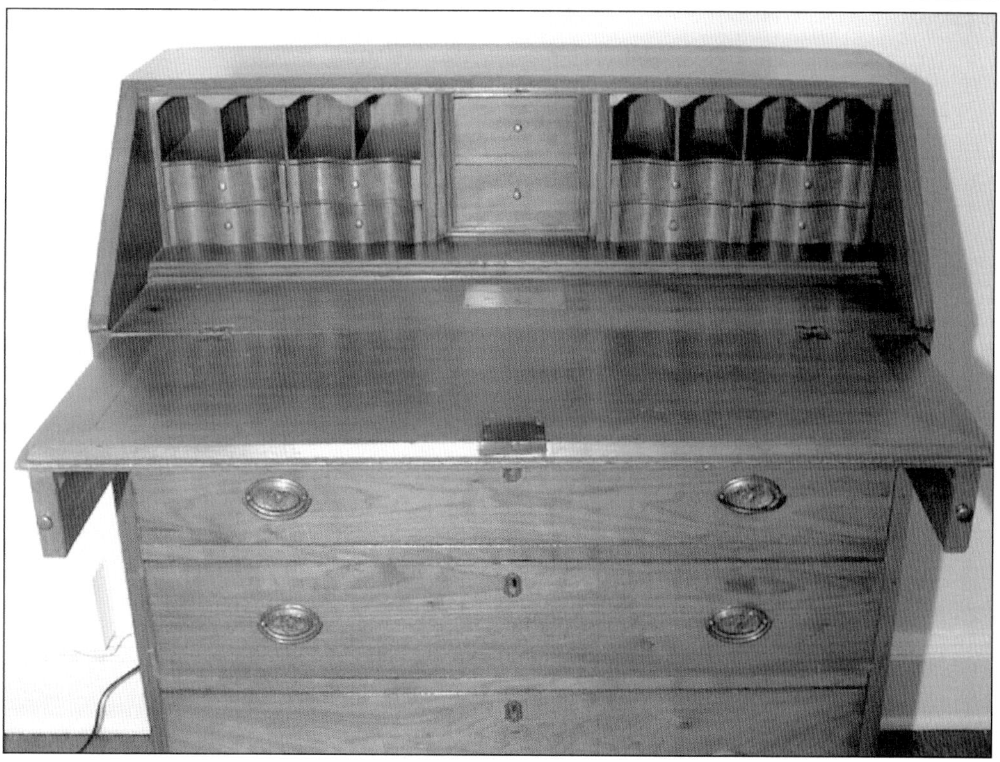

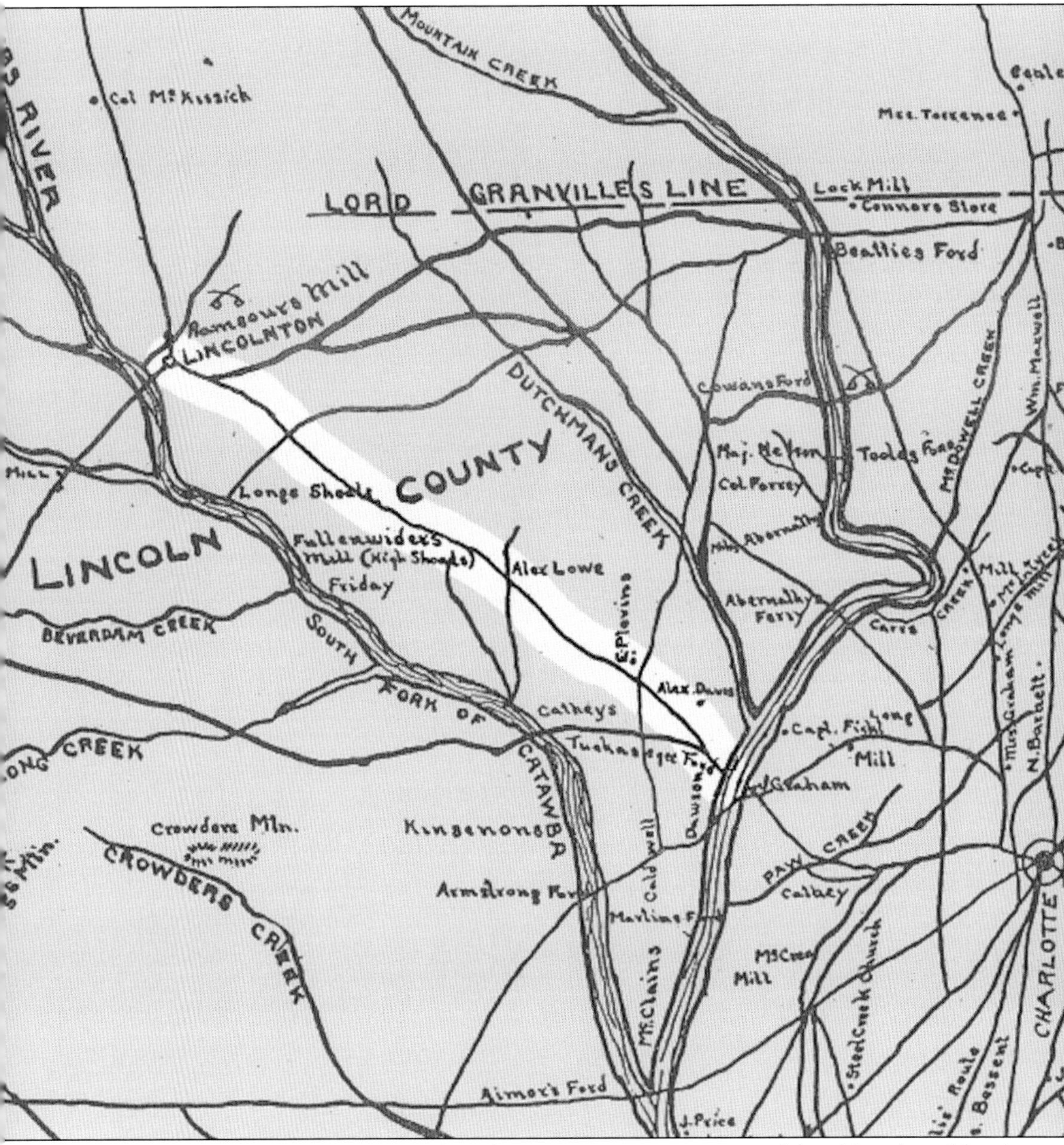


The Tuckaseegee Trail, highlighted on this 1789 map, was a portion of the old trail used first by the Native Americans and later by hunters, prospectors, and settlers as they wandered down into North Carolina from Pennsylvania, Maryland, and Virginia. The trail crossed the Catawba River near present-day Mount Holly and meandered through the Stanley area on into Lincolnton and beyond to the Blue Ridge Mountains. Along this trail in the late 1700s came André Michaux, a botanist from France, to collect plant specimens for his country. His journal mentions his travels along the Tuckaseegee Road. He and his son, Francois André, stayed at the homes of Peter and Bennett Smith in the Stanley area. The Smith property was located near the Tuckaseegee Road. After Michaux, records indicate other botanists traveling along the Tuckaseegee Road and through the Stanley area. They included John Lyon, Elisha Mitchell, and highly respected botanist Moses Ashley Curtis. (Courtesy of D.A. Tompkins Co.)

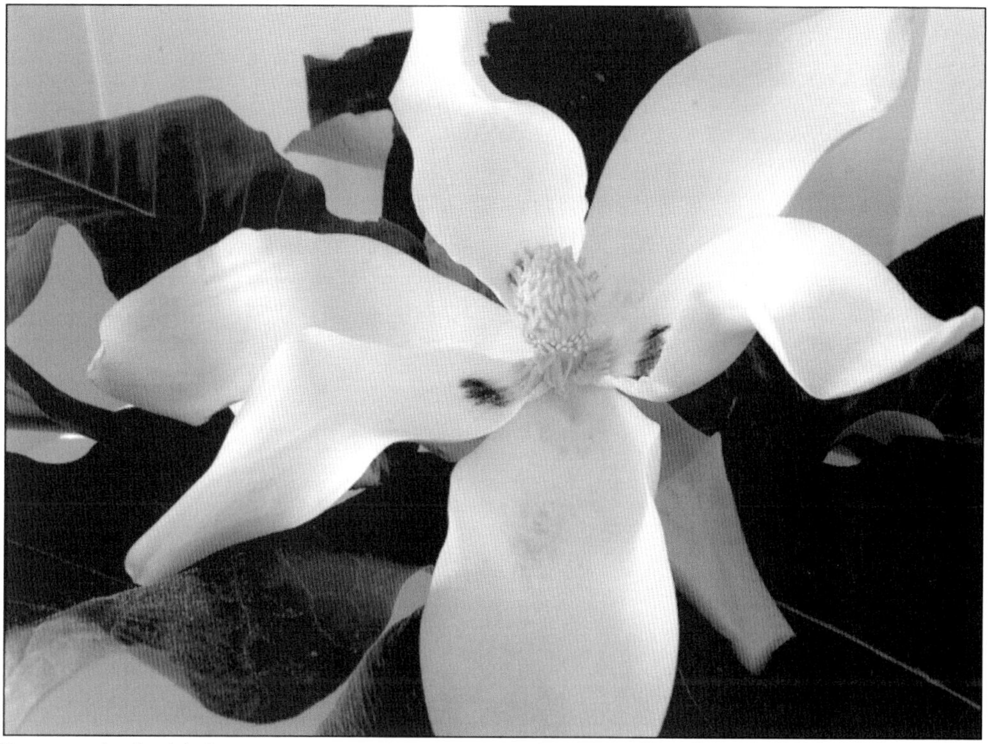

Botanist André Michaux was sent to America to explore and study its native plants and trees. As he usually did when in the Stanley area, he and his 19-year-old son Francois André stayed with Bennett and Peter Smith, on whose property he discovered the big leaf magnolia in 1789 and named it Magnolia macrophylla. The beautiful, fragrant, and creamy white flowers have purple triangular markings near the base of every other petal and are the largest found growing on any North American tree. They can measure 18 inches from tip to tip. The leaves can often measure three feet in length and a foot wide. Botanist John Lyon also visited the Peter Smith property and recorded shipping more than 4,000 Magnolia macrophylla plants from there, suggesting an abundance growing on the Smith property.

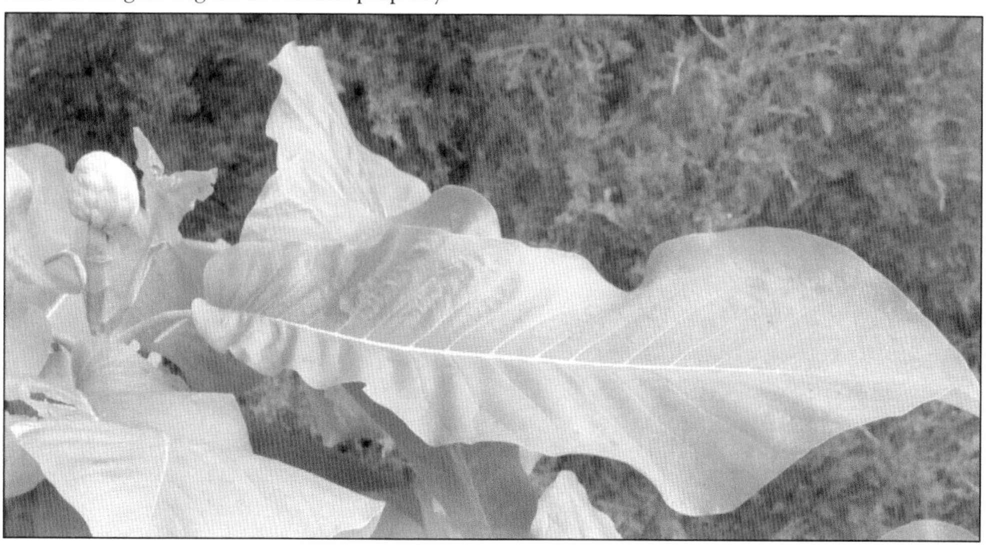

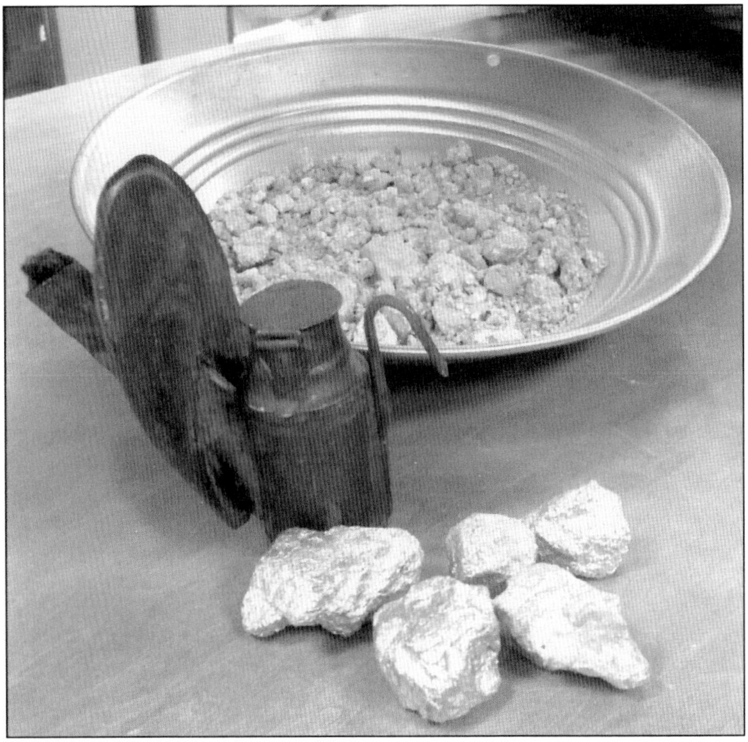

Gold mining became a major industry in North Carolina beginning around 1800. Stanley area farmers also mined for gold, and some extractions were quite profitable, especially from the Moore Gold Mine. Early settler Peter Smith had a profitable mine, as did William Richards, Samuel Rankin, Thomas Rhyne, and a few others. Local gold mining waned after the 1849 California gold rush.

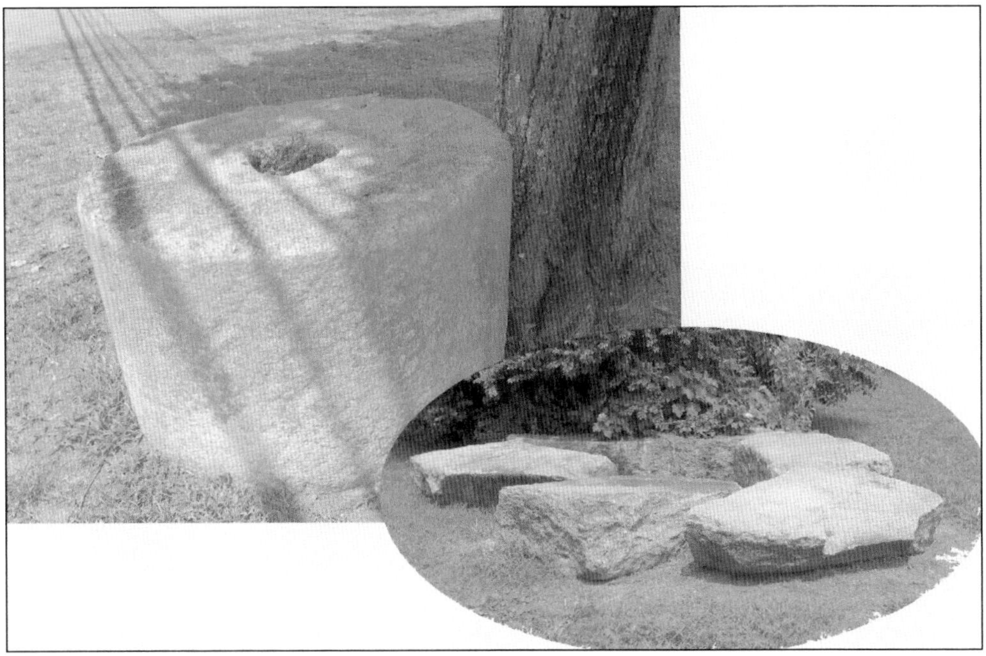

The Moore Gold Mine was located on the Alexander Moore property southwest of Stanley. Moore's mine implemented the arrastre method of mining, which uses a rock-lined pit in which broken ore is pulverized by large stones attached to horizontal poles, fastened to a central pillar. The stones are dragged around the pit by a mule. The mine, though profitable, was eventually sold to Cabarrus Gold Mining Company.

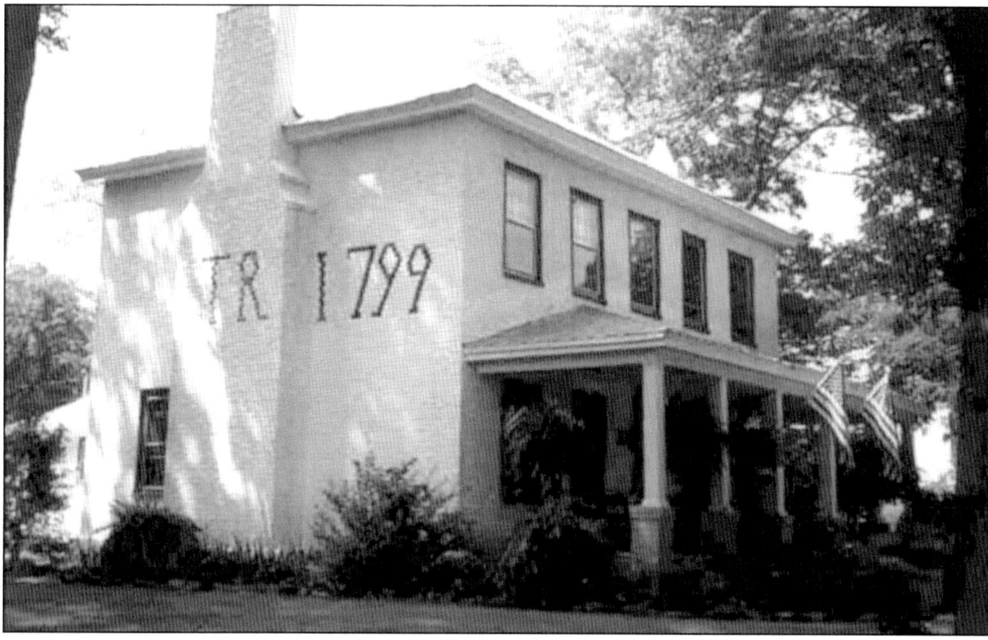


The 1799 house, as it is known in the Stanley area, was built by Thomas Rhyne and his wife, Barbara Wise, on a section of their vast acreage. From its completion, this house has been passed from one generation of the family to the next. In 1988, it was recognized as a National Bicentennial Farm for being farmed while owned by the same family for its 200-year lifetime.

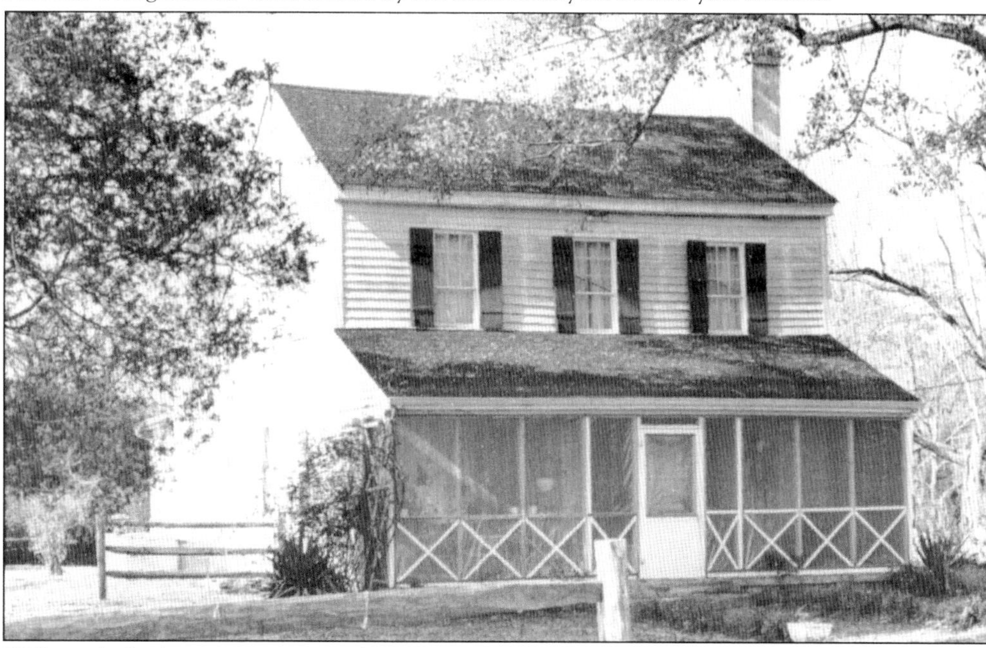

Willowside, built in 1800 near Stanley on 300 acres along Stanley Creek, was the home of William Rankin, who fought in several battles of the Revolutionary War. Rankin is thought to be the last Revolutionary War soldier to die in Gaston County. At his death, Willowside passed to his son Richard, who attended the meeting in 1842 that created Gaston County. He also served several terms in the North Carolina legislature.

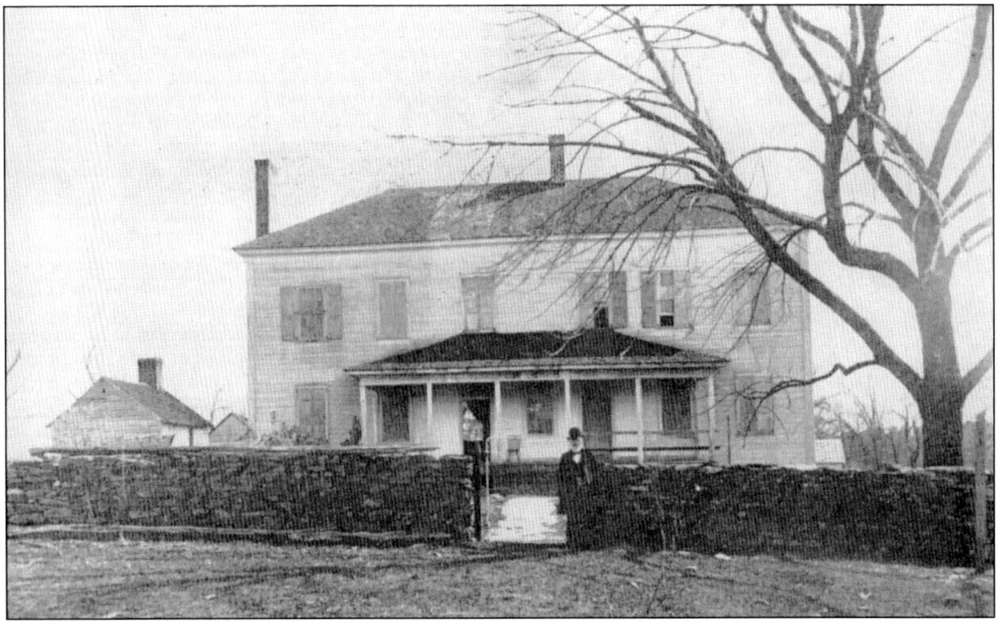

Mount Tirzah, when built by Robert Alfred Brevard sometime in the early 1800s, was the largest plantation house in the Catawba River region. His son Alexander Franklin Brevard resided at Mount Tirzah until his death on October 22, 1909. The house then became a tenant dwelling and farm, after which it sat empty until vandals burned it in 1968. (Courtesy of *State Magazine*.)

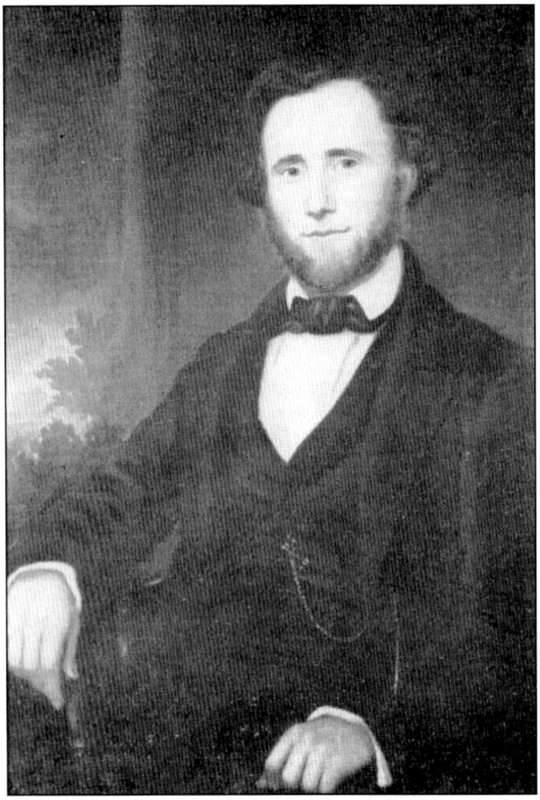

Shown here is Alexander Franklin Brevard, born at Mount Tirzah on October 3, 1825. He attended Davidson College and the University of North Carolina. A lawyer by profession, Brevard never married. He owned a considerable amount of property that included the area where the town of Stanley is located. The railroad depot, built on the Brevard property, was named Brevard's Station, which became the first official name for the town. (Courtesy of *State Magazine*.)

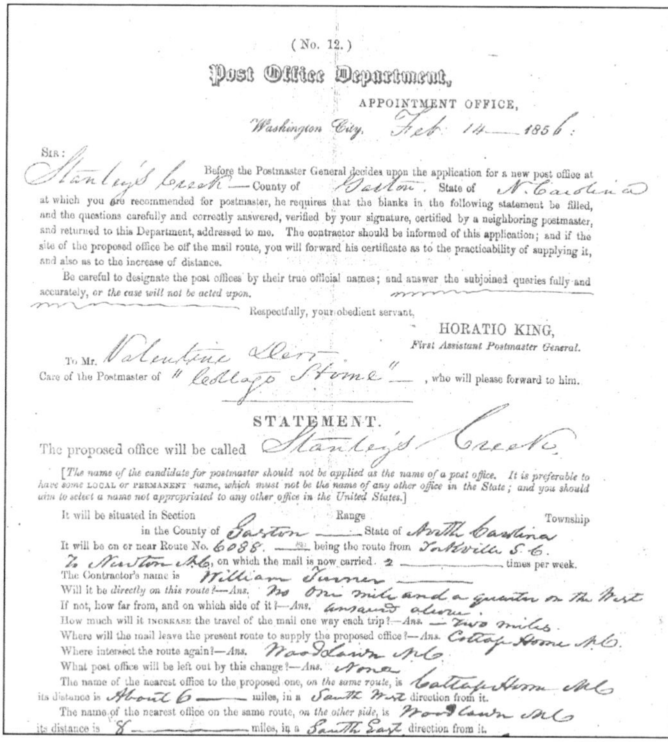

( No. 12. )

**Post Office Department,**

APPOINTMENT OFFICE,

*Washington City,* Feb 14 — 1856:

SIR:

Stanley's Creek — Before the Postmaster General decides upon the application for a new post office at — County of Gaston. State of N. Carolina at which you are recommended for postmaster, he requires that the blanks in the following statement be filled, and the questions carefully and correctly answered, verified by your signature, certified by a neighboring postmaster, and returned to this Department, addressed to me. The contractor should be informed of this application; and if the site of the proposed office be off the mail route, you will forward his certificate as to the practicability of supplying it, and also as to the increase of distance.

Be careful to designate the post offices by their true official names; and answer the subjoined queries fully and accurately, *or the case will not be acted upon.*

Respectfully, your obedient servant,

HORATIO KING,
*First Assistant Postmaster General.*

To Mr. Valentine Derr
Care of the Postmaster of "Cottage Home" — , who will please forward to him.

**STATEMENT.**

The proposed office will be called Stanley's Creek.

[*The name of the candidate for postmaster should not be applied as the name of a post office. It is preferable to have some* LOCAL *or* PERMANENT *name, which must not be the name of any other office in the State; and you should aim to select a name not appropriated to any other office in the United States.*]

It will be situated in Section Range Township
in the County of Gaston — State of North Carolina
It will be on or near Route No. 6088. — being the route from Yorkville S. C.
To Newton N.C., on which the mail is now carried. 2 — times per week.
The Contractor's name is William Turner —
Will it be *directly on this route?—Ans.* No One mile and a quarter on the West
If not, how far from, and on which side of it?—*Ans.* answered above.
How much will it INCREASE the travel of the mail one way each trip?—*Ans.* — Two miles.
Where will the mail leave the present route to supply the proposed office?—*Ans.* Cottage Home N.C.
Where intersect the route again?—*Ans.* Woodlawn N.C.
What post office will be left out by this change?—*Ans.* None
The name of the nearest office to the proposed one, *on the same route,* is Cottage Home N.C.
its distance is About 6 — miles, in a South West direction from it.
The name of the nearest office on the same route, *on the other side,* is Woodlawn N.C.
its distance is 8 — miles, in a South East direction from it.

Having bought a plantation with slightly over 500 acres of land along Dutchman and Stanley Creeks, Valentine Derr, known also as Felty Tarr, became postmaster in the Stanley Creek Community in 1856. He operated the post office initially from his home before it was moved to the railroad depot at Brevard Station in 1861. He served as a captain in the state militia for a time, and in 1857, he became a justice of the peace in Gaston County.

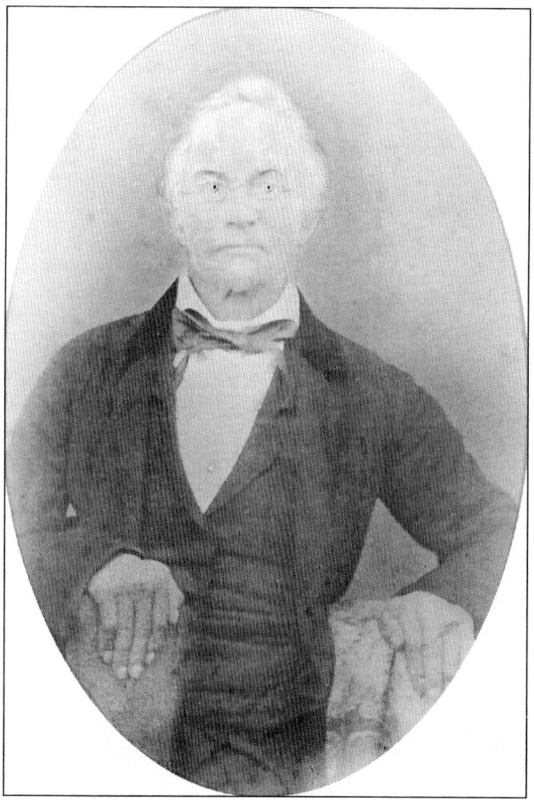

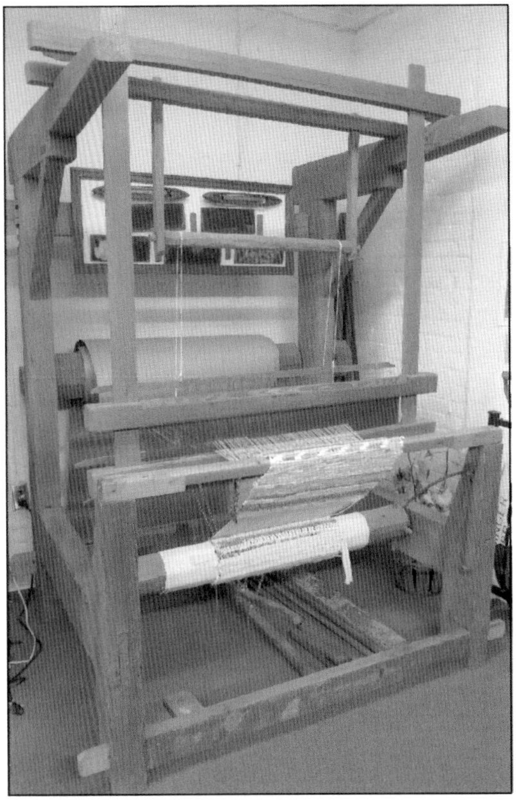

In colonial North Carolina, many people wove cloth from locally produced fibers. Wool, cotton, flax (linen), and hemp were the most common fibers used. This loom was used in Stanley and has been dated to the 1800s. It is on exhibit at Brevard Station Museum.

The heart of the earliest homes was the hearth. Originally, all cooking was done in and over the fire in iron pots. Some fireplaces had brick ovens beneath or beside the fire for baking. Many kitchens were enclosed in a separate building to avoid the heat and danger of fire. (Courtesy of Pat Smith.)

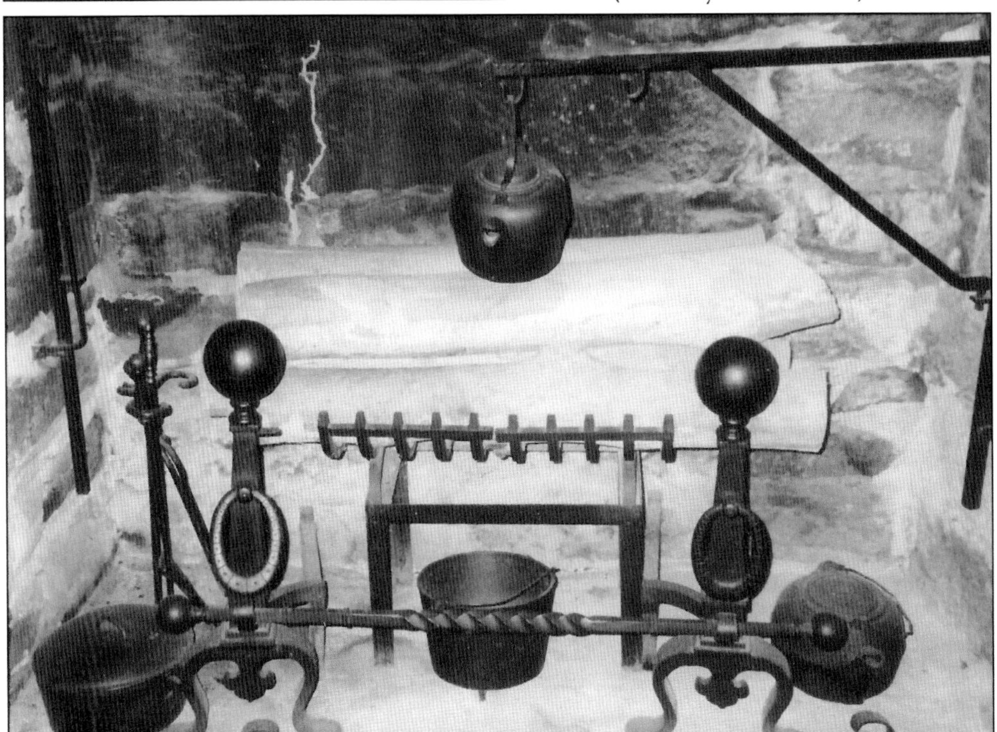

# *Two*

# Coming of the Railroad

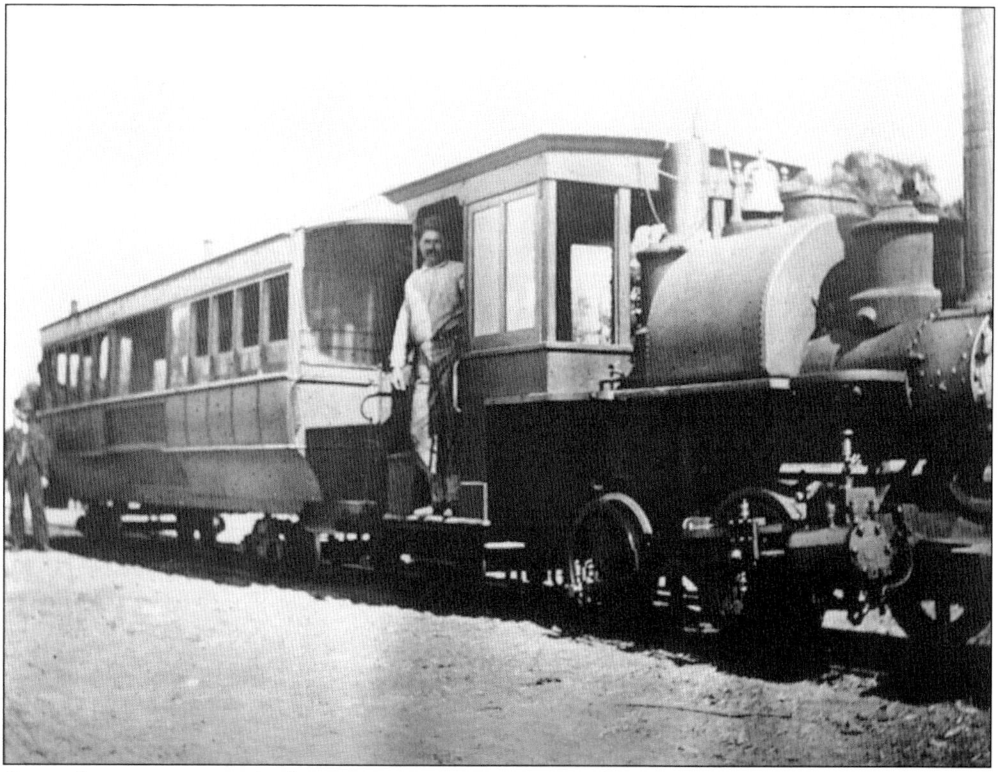

Great changes came to the farming communities surrounding Stanley Creek in December 1860, when the first railroad crossed the Catawba River and a station was built on Brevard property. The early trains were similar to the one pictured here. The western section of the Wilmington, Charlotte & Rutherford Railroad consisted of two engines, *Wilmington* and *Bladen*, two passenger cars, fifteen boxcars, and seventeen flatbed cars.

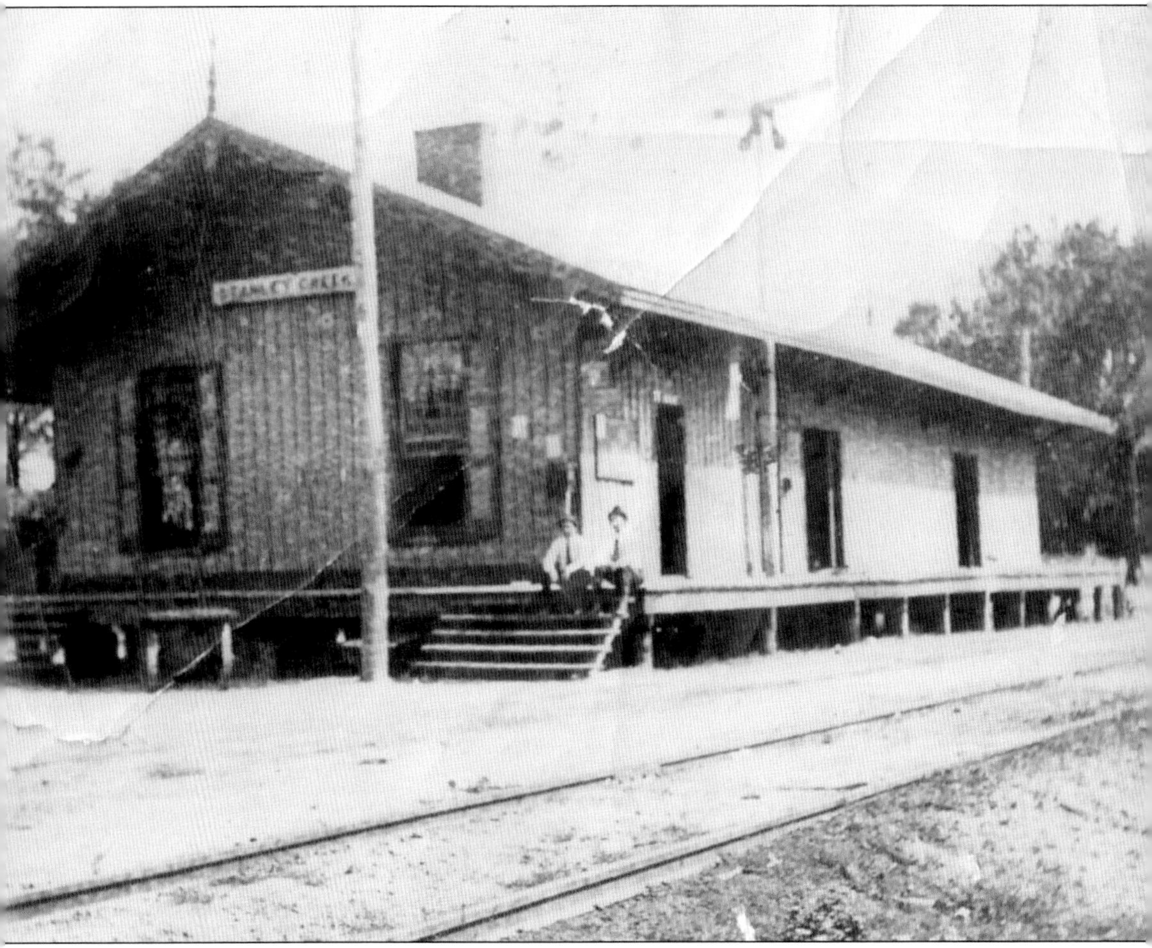

The Brevard railroad station was built in 1860 in the Stanley area and was designated Depot 13. Trains were stopping here only one-and-a-half hours after leaving Charlotte. For a few months, westward passengers were transported to Lincolnton, North Carolina, and Abingdon, Virginia, by four-horse post coaches three times a week. During the Civil War years, the depot was a rallying point for all men who were leaving for training camps or to battle. It is said that a cheering crowd of people gathered around the depot to see the first troops depart. The railroad was also used to send supplies to the battlefields during the war. W.H. Abernathy was the railroad's agent at the depot in 1864. By 1865, the weary soldiers began returning to their homes to begin the difficult period of Reconstruction. A community began to build up around the railroad station, and in 1879, a village of 15 families was incorporated as Brevard Station. In 1893, the names of the town and the depot were changed to Stanley Creek.

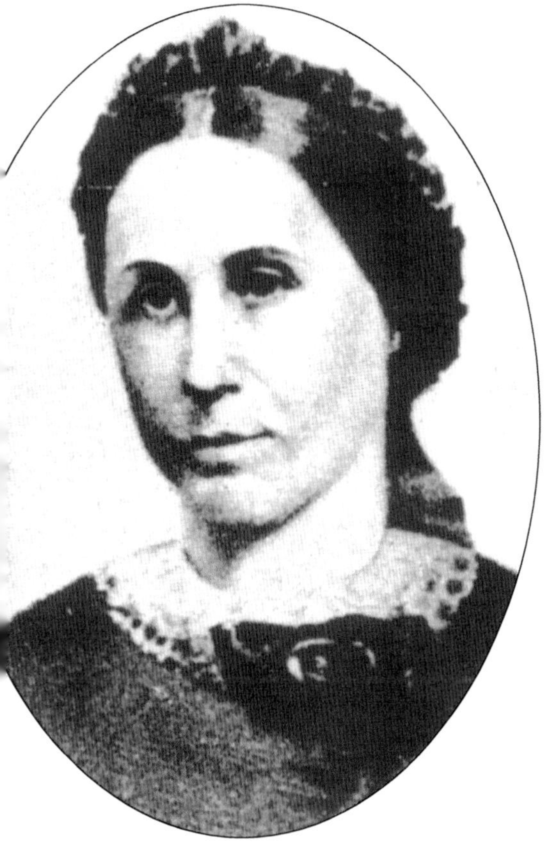

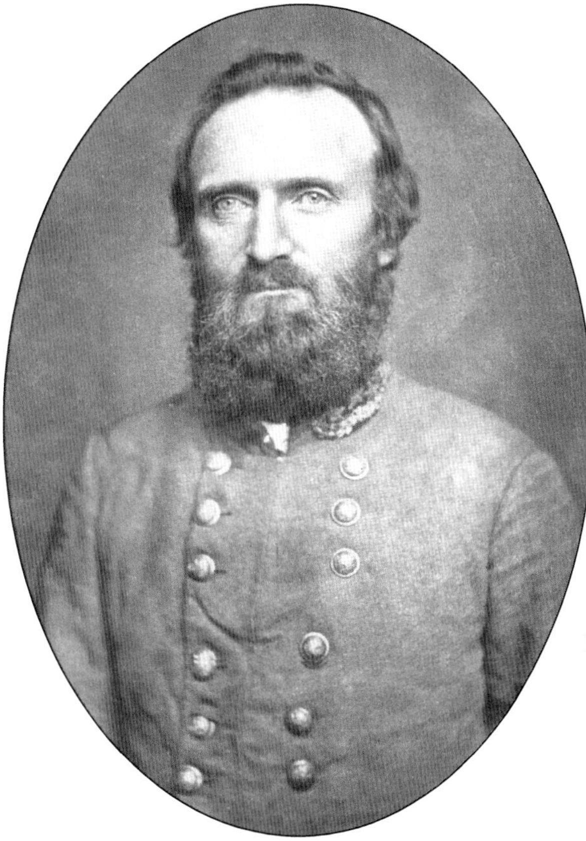

Mary Anna Morrison was the daughter of Rev. Robert Morrison, a Presbyterian minister educated at the University of North Carolina and Princeton and founder and first president of Davidson College. Reverend Morrison's wife, Mary, was the daughter of Revolutionary War general Joseph Graham, and she inherited a 600-acre farm where she and her family built Cottage Home, a 12-room house on Plank Road. This home was a popular and hospitable place where education, religion, music, art, and good manners were abundant. In 1857, Mary Anna married Thomas Jackson, later known as Gen. Stonewall Jackson, at Cottage Home.

Richmond, Va. October 19th, 1862

Dier Wife and family all, I once more embrace the opertunity of writing you a few lines to let you know that I am in tollarabl good health, with the exception of Rheumatism in my legs. I expect it was occasioned by hard marching. All though I can walk about well enough, I hope these lines will find you all well. I would have wrote to you sooner, but I have been whear I could get no paper. I have not heard from the boys cince I wrote to you-and a good while before, and I have not heard from home cince Wm. Beatie was at our camps. I was at Staunton nearly five weeks, the Smallpox broke out their and we was sent back to this hospital incampment. We landed hear yesterday evening, but we found the Smallpox hear as bad as it was at Staunton. So I suppose that we will have to stand our chance anyhow. I wrote you a letter when I was hear before and I also wrote you one at Staunton. I want to know if you got them or not. I want you to wrote soon and let me hear from you all. I want to know how you are getting along for I don't know when I can come to se you.

I send my best respects to all the friends but there is none of them thinks worth while to waste paper and ink on me. If you have heard from the boys I want you to write to me how they are and whear they are, and then if I am able I will write to them. I don't expect that we will go to our regiment any more until the Smallpox is out of danger. I want to know how you are managing your business and afairs. Write soon, and direct your letter to Richmond, Va., Winder Hospital, 1st division Ward L, If there is any one passing I would like to have a pair of socks, or two, but I can get them hear at one dollar a pair, and if they will cost you near that, you had better not send them. I am not well collected for writing this morning. So I will stop for the present, but I will try to write again the course of a week or so.

So nothing more but remember your loving husband untill death.

David H. Wallace

to Nancy R. Wallace

This is a transcription of a letter written by David Henry Wallace, who married Nancy R. Williams. In 1862, at the age of 46, Wallace enlisted in Company H, 49th North Carolina Infantry Regiment of the Confederate army. Sadly, he did not survive the war, dying of disease in a Richmond, Virginia, hospital two months after writing this letter.

David Smith Wallace, son of David Henry Wallace and Nancy R. Williams, was married to Margaret Smith, daughter of John Beaty Smith and Mary Lineberger. As did his father, he served in the Confederate army, enlisting on September 21, 1864. His right arm was amputated due to a wound received at Hatcher's Run, Virginia.

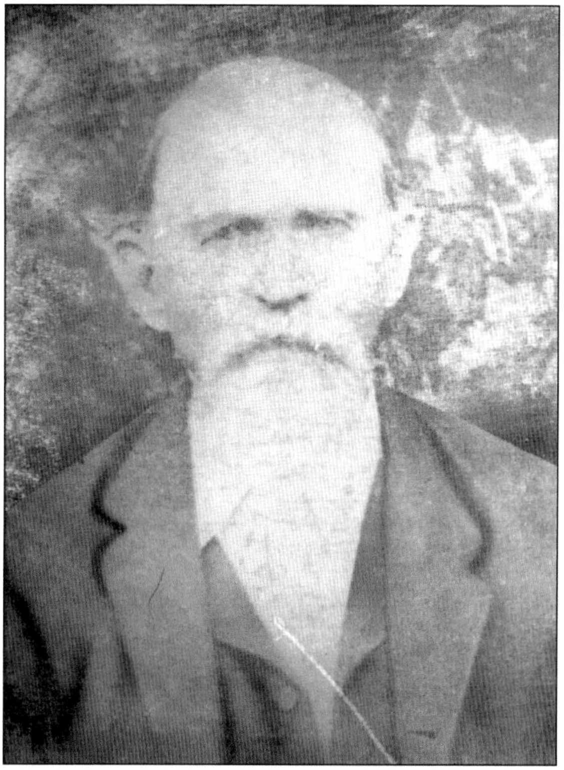

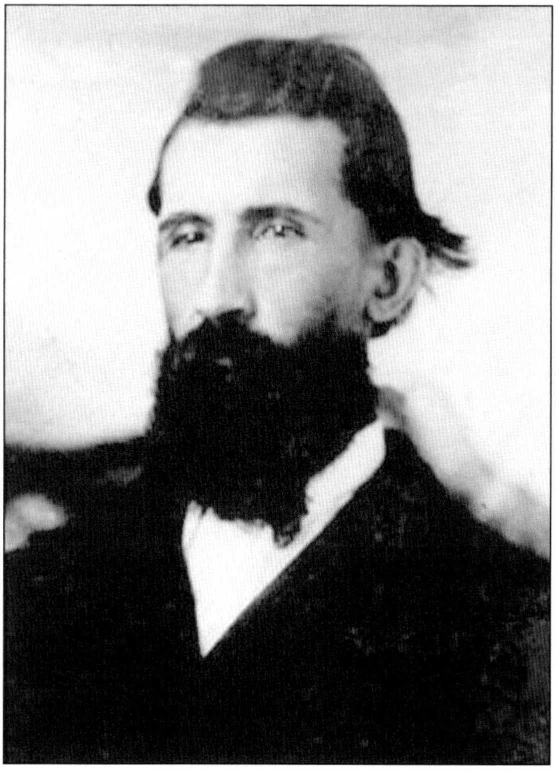

Gideon Abernethy enlisted in Company C, 28th North Carolina Regiment in 1861. This company fought in numerous battles, including Gettysburg, and was involved in the stacking of arms at the surrender at Appomattox. Abernethy became a farmer and a traveling schoolteacher after the war. While teaching in Brevard Station, he married Julia Ann Abernethy in 1871. They had two children, Ella and Robert Laban. Abernethy contracted meningitis during the war and he became blind and died in 1875.

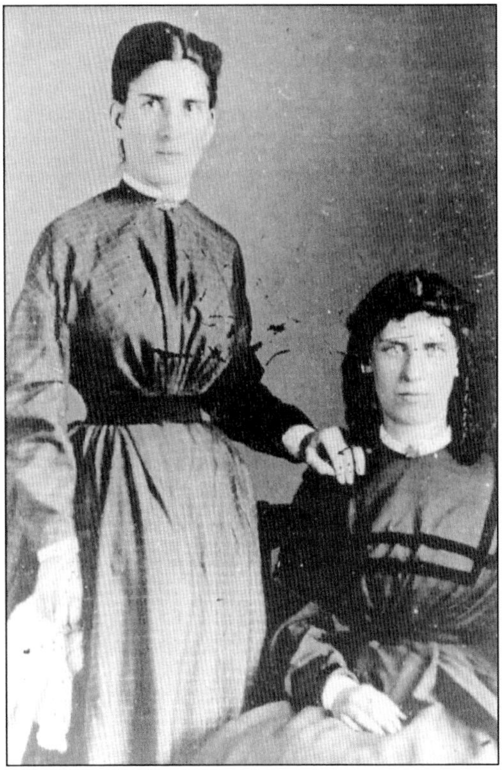

Pictured during the Civil War years are Philecta "Leckie" and Annadis "Addie" Smith, daughters of Hettie Rudisill and James Madison Smith. Philecta married John Rheinhardt and lived on Mariposa Road near Plank Road. She managed a post office in her home. Annadis married Albertus Rhyne, son of Louisa McGee and Daniel Rhyne, and they made their home in the Rhyne 1799 house, built by his grandfather.

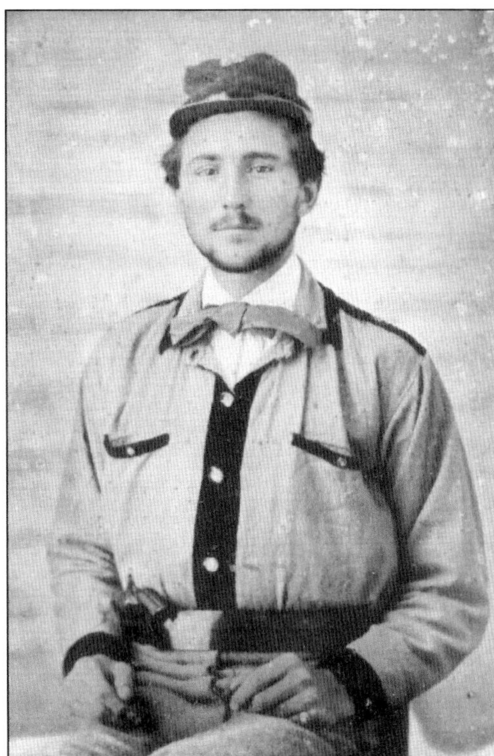

Albertus Rhyne moved by wagon to Clarksville, Texas, in Red River County and joined Company L, 29th Texas Cavalry of the Confederate army. After the war, he returned to Stanley. He first married Alice Yount, and their children were Bertie and Robert Rhyne. After the death of Alice he married Annadis Smith, and their children were Wixie Rhyne, who married Ben Hoover; Fred Rhyne, who married Alice Pegram Mason; Beulah Rhyne; and Richard "Dick" Rhyne, who first married Edith Abernethy and then Bess Peterson Wycoff.

Robert M. McGinnis was married to Elizabeth Wolfe. He enlisted in Company H, North Carolina 37th Infantry Regiment during the Civil War and was wounded at the battle of Manassas. McGinnis was the son of Amy Rutledge and John Al McGinnis, who was a deputy sheriff and one of the justices chosen to swear in the first justices for the new county of Gaston.

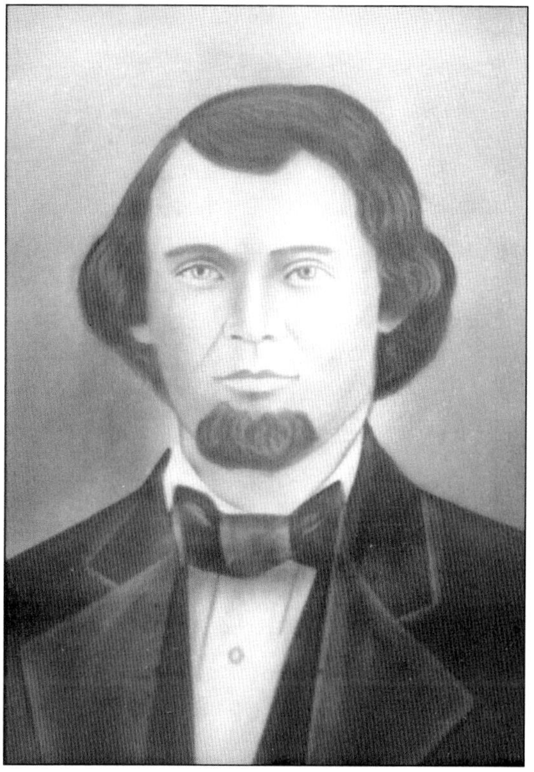

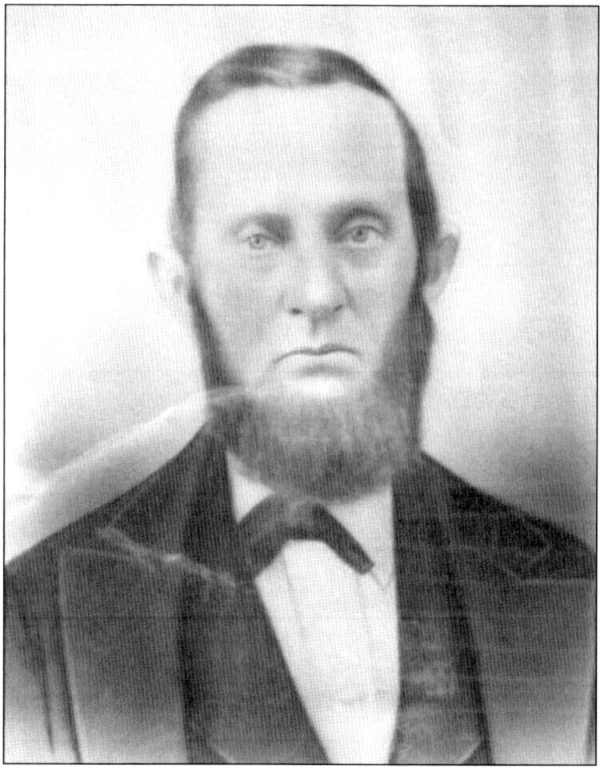

Jesse R. Peterson was a Lutheran minister who served many of the Lutheran churches in the Catawba River Valley, including Christ's Lutheran Church in Brevard Station. His name is on many marriage certificates of people who were wed in the middle to late 1800s. Peterson was an outspoken Democrat and during the lawless and violent Reconstruction period, his home, located just outside Brevard Station, was burned.

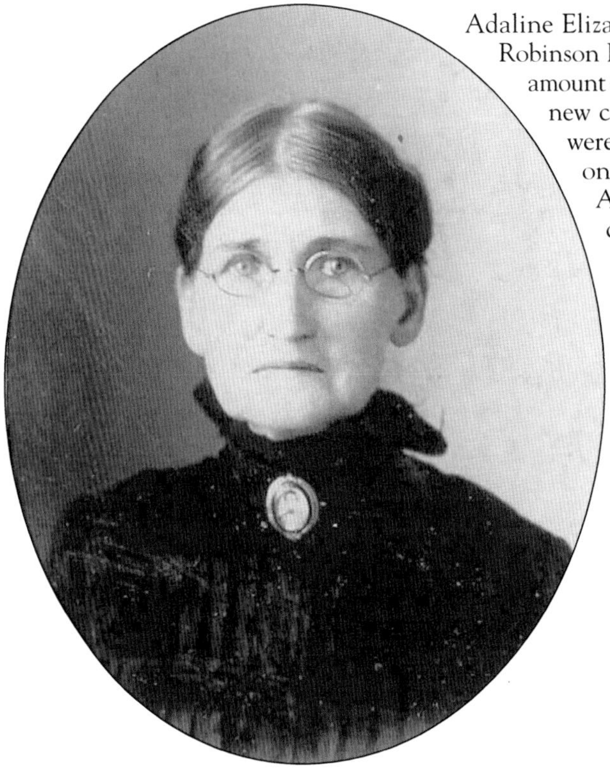

Adaline Elizabeth Summerow and her husband, Robinson Lee McLurd, acquired a considerable amount of land after making their home in the new community of Brevard Station. They were prominent citizens, and he served as one of the town's first commissioners. After her husband's death, Adaline continued to work in their mercantile store, which also functioned as the post office. She served two terms as postmaster for the town.

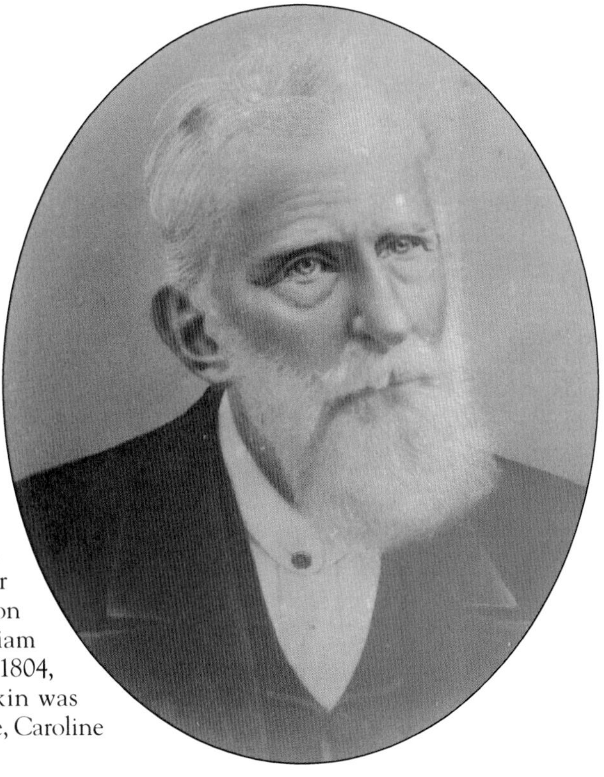

Richard Rankin was elected the first Gaston County trustee and a member of the House of Commons of North Carolina. His home, Willowside, is near Stanley on Willlowside Road. The son of Mary Moore Campbell and William Rankin, he was born September 24, 1804, and died September 14, 1899. Rankin was married three times: to Ann Hartgrove, Caroline Beatty, and Delia Bisaner.

Anna Sophia Smith, born in 1811, was the daughter of David Smith and Anna Elizabeth Arndt of Magnolia Grove. She married Andrew Carpenter, and they lived near her brother Milton Smith. Three of their sons were Confederate soldiers, and two were killed in the war. It is remembered that Sophia smoked a clay pipe, always wore a big bonnet, and almost always carried a whip.

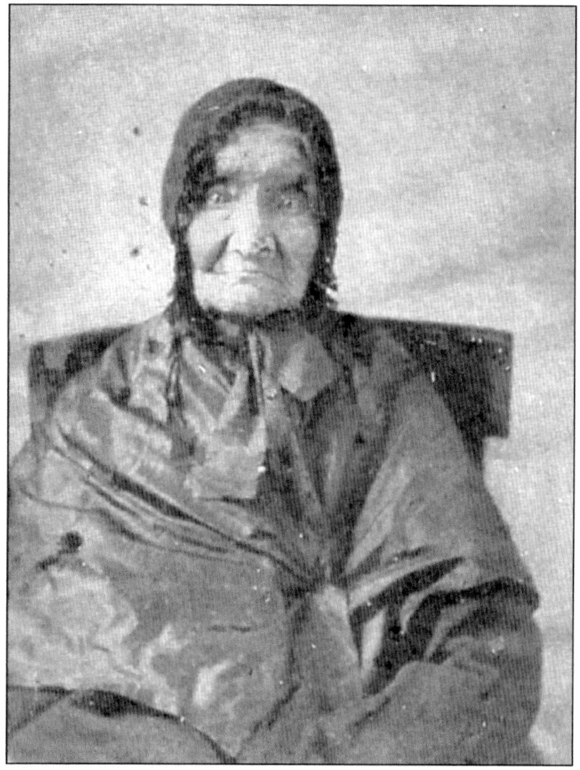

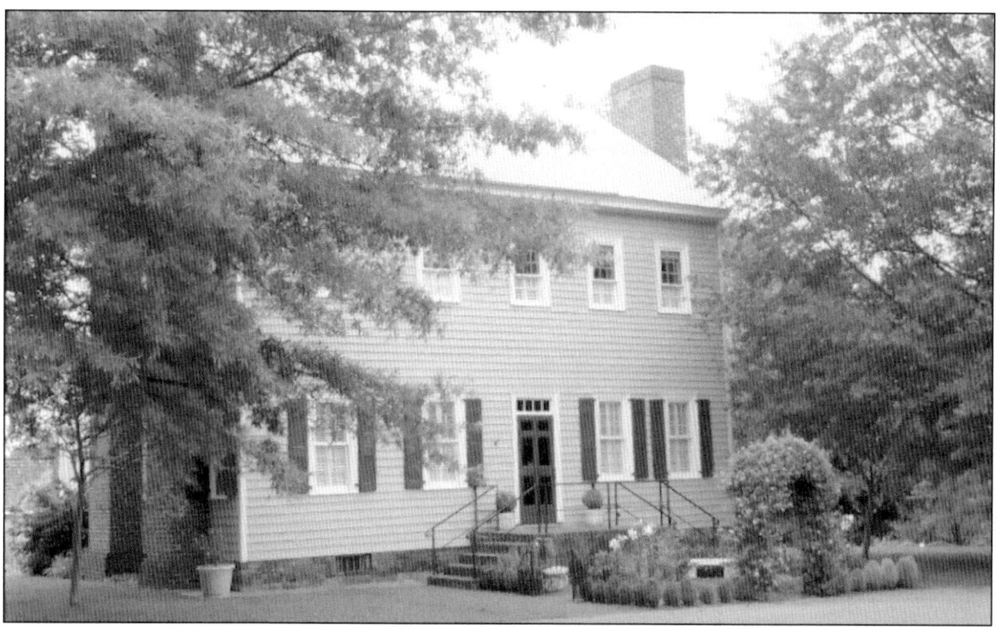

Sophia Smith and Andrew Carpenter lived in this house, called Happy Home, located on the stagecoach road, now Alexis Lucia Road, near Stanley Creek. They welcomed weary travelers into their home on the much-traveled route to the Catawba Springs Resort or on to Salisbury. The Federal-style home exists today after being restored by Suzanne and Gerald Deal. (Courtesy of Gerald Deal.)

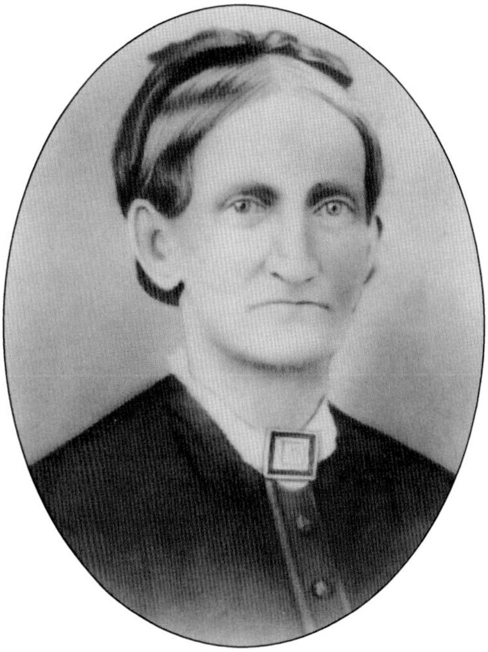

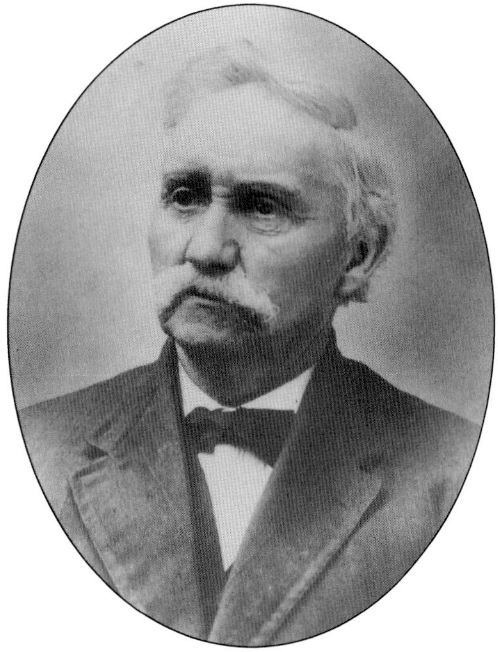

Pictured here are Frances Mason and Benjamin Franklin Carpenter. Benjamin Carpenter was the son of Anna Sophia Smith and Andrew Carpenter. In 1862, Benjamin enlisted in the Confederate army. After surviving the war, he and Frances married and became two of the first citizens in the newly incorporated community of Brevard Station.

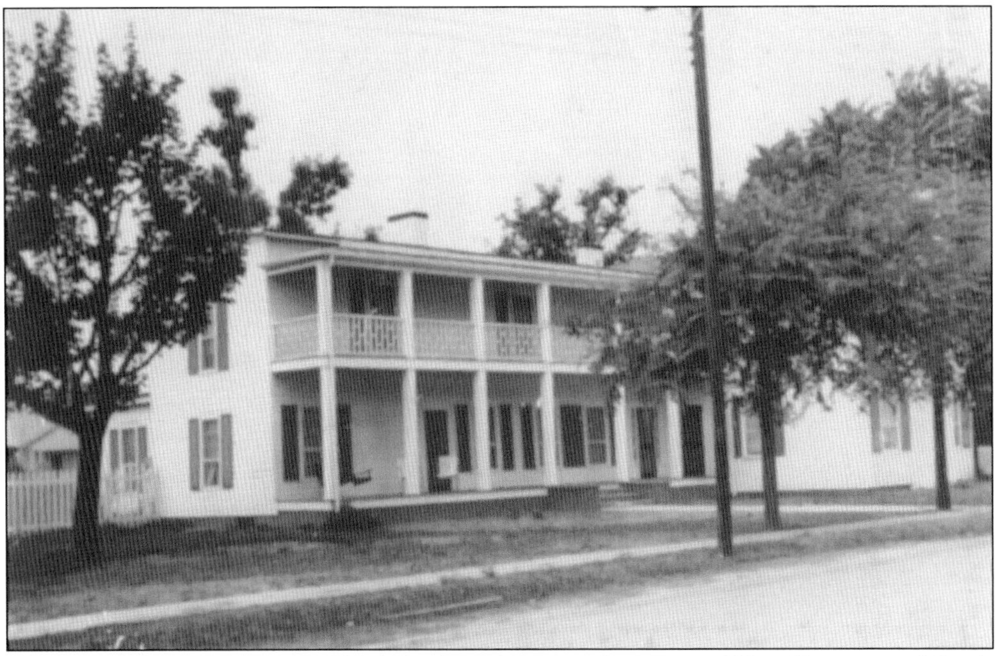

Benjamin and Frances Carpenter built this large house on the corner of West Chestnut and South Main Streets. They welcomed boarders into their home. One year, when the old school had been demolished and the new one was not yet finished, they allowed part of their home to be used as a school. Additionally, they sold groceries and clothing in a store attached to their home.

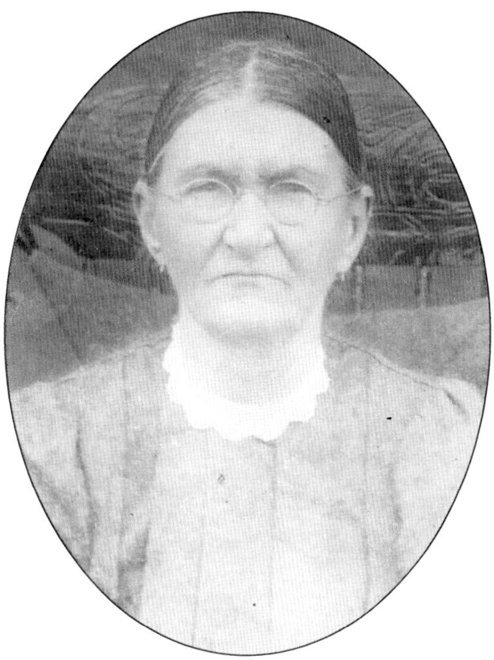

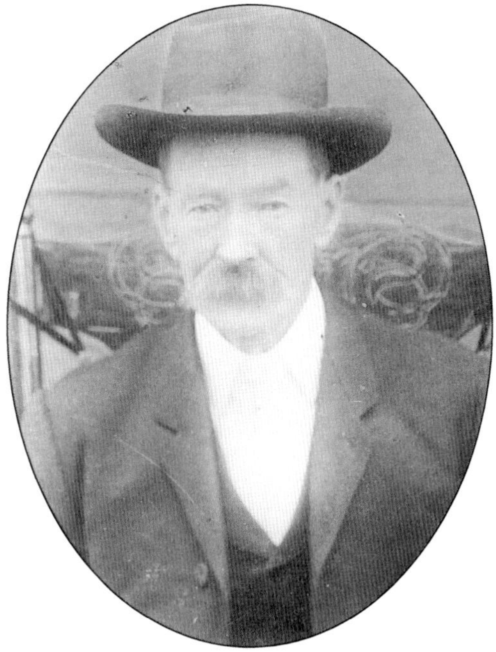

Pictured are Elizabeth Ann Bynum and Thomas Gregory. A story passed down in the family is that Thomas's father, Sanford Gregory, was killed in Dallas, North Carolina, in 1869 because he had refused to fight in the Civil War. Later, Thomas's mother, Emily, left Brevard Station with her younger children and moved to Colorado. Elizabeth and Thomas had seven children: William, Mary, Alice, Lula, Joseph, Janie, and Vertie.

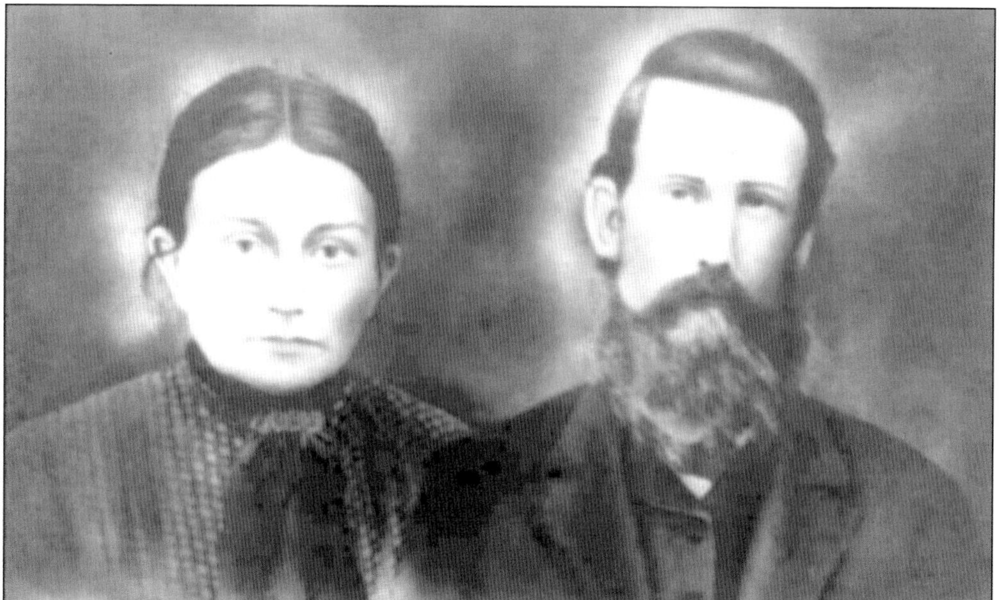

In this image are Rev. John Franklin Morris and his wife, Frances Catherine "Fannie" Stroupe. He was pastor of Bruington and Hickory Grove Baptist Churches simultaneously in 1883 and 1884. Church minutes stated that member Rufus Lay was paid to nurse seven members of the Morris family, when Morris, age 47, and three members of his family died of typhoid fever in 1899.

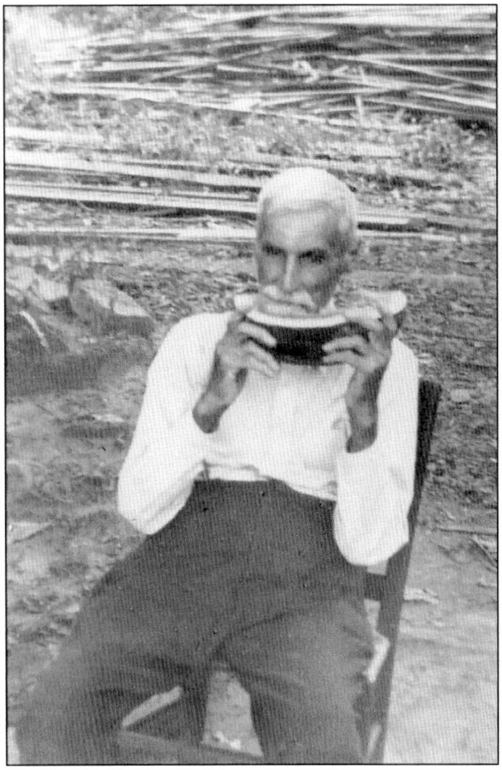

Everyone eagerly awaited the first watermelons to come from the fields. Pictured is Edgar Durant Thompson (1853–1945), son of Hannah Rhodes and Frances Thompson. He married Mary Jane Plonk in 1873. Edgar was one of the first investors in Stanley Creek Cotton Mill in 1891. Some other investors were Jacob Jenkins, Joseph Turner Abernathy, Augustus Farley, N.M. Rutledge, and Henry Michael Summerow. This eventually became Lola Gingham Mill.

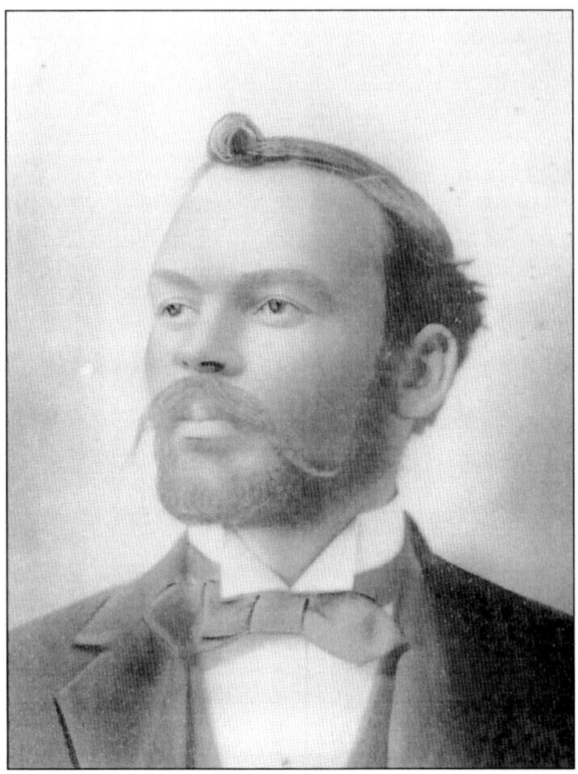

Augustus Farley and his wife, Jeannette Nantz, lived near the Tuckaseegee Road close to the Brevard Station depot. Farley was a large landowner and was successful in a sawmill business. He owned stock in the Dallas Cotton Mill and was one of the originators of the Stanley Creek Cotton Mills in 1891.

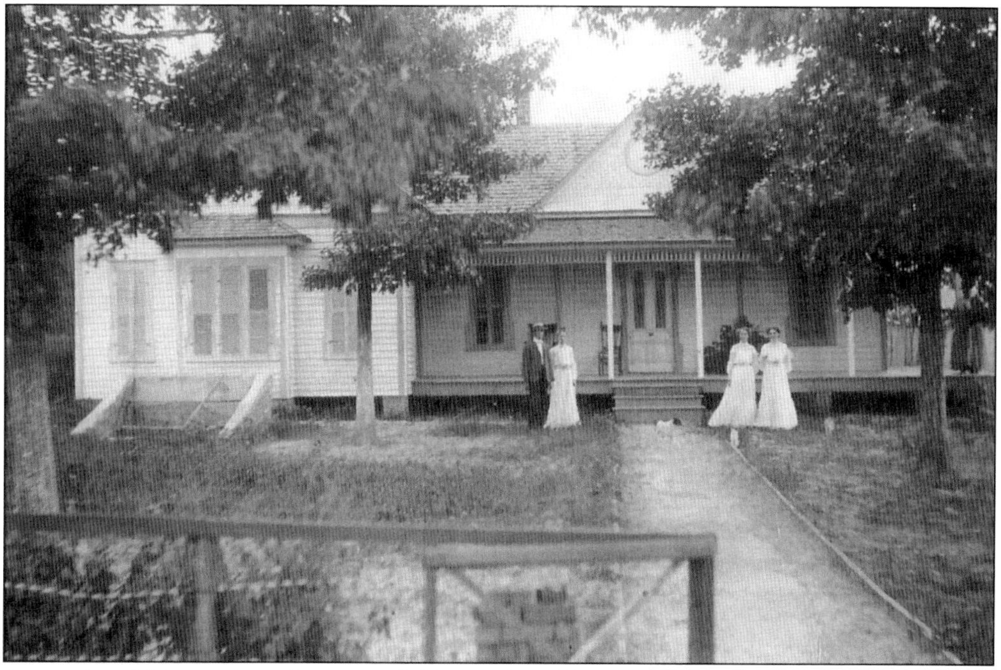

Pictured are Miles Andrew Carpenter (1872–1960) and his wife, Jennie Smith, along with Jennie's two sisters from Trenton, South Carolina. This photograph of their first home was taken in 1893. The lovely home exists today on South Main Street.

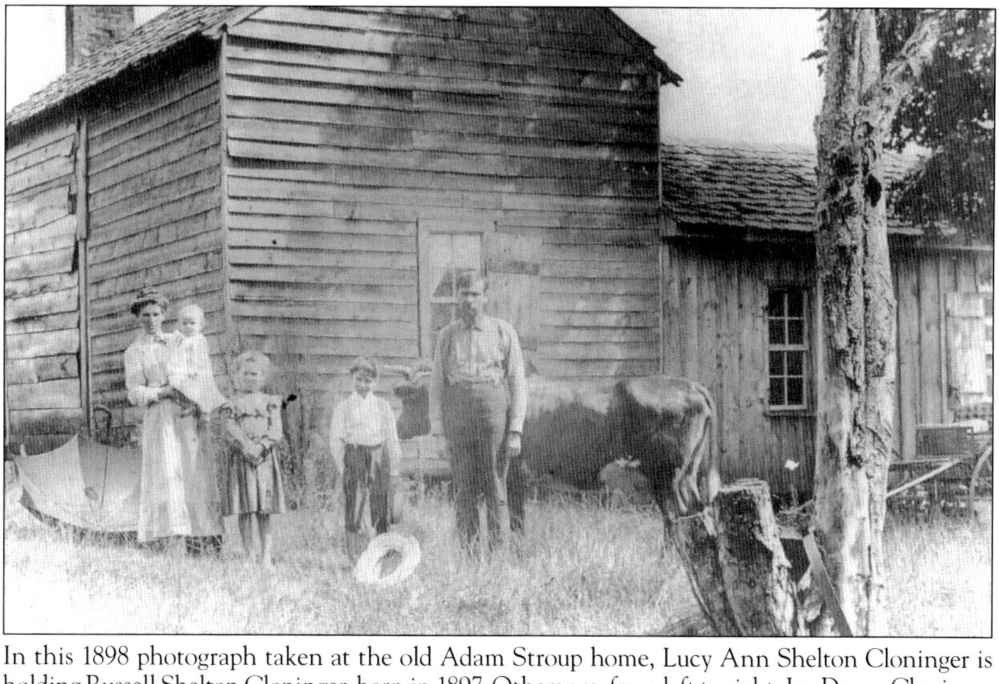

In this 1898 photograph taken at the old Adam Stroup home, Lucy Ann Shelton Cloninger is holding Russell Shelton Cloninger, born in 1897. Others are, from left to right, Iva Deane Cloninger Abernathy, Fred Meynardie Cloninger, and Arthur Frank McKenzie, with the family's cow and their fine buggy. Later, the house, occupied by the Hubert Cunningham family, burned to the ground. The parents escaped, but sadly, the eight Cunningham children perished.

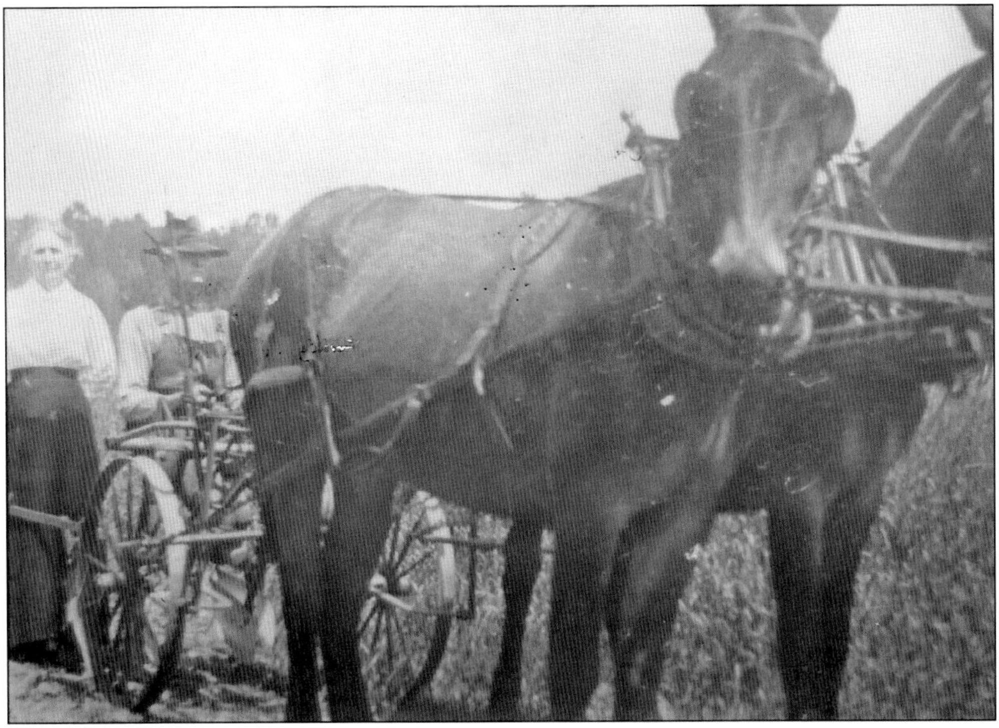

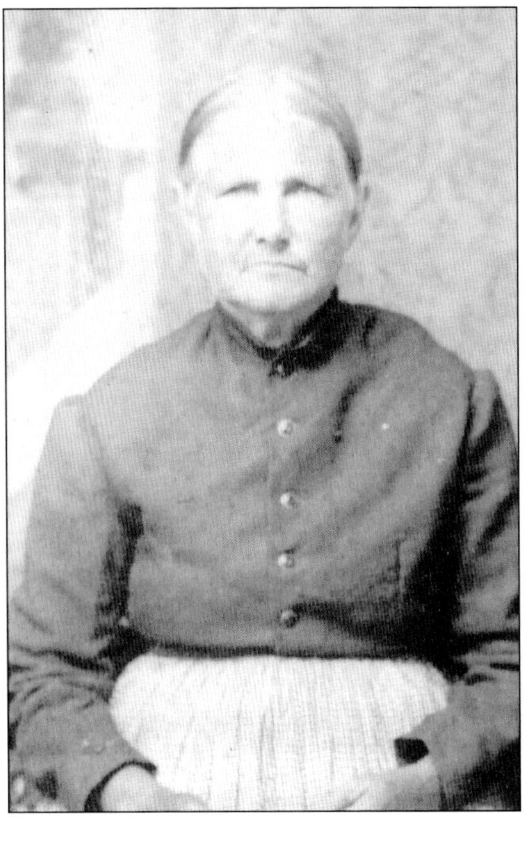

John Franklin Smith is pictured on his cultivator drawn by two mules. His wife, Carrie Mauney, stands beside him. Smith also owned a roller mill where he processed grain. Wheat and corn remained the staple crops in the Stanley area, with tobacco, cotton, and livestock also important farm products.

Sarah Brotherton was born in the Stanley area in 1825 and her family migrated to Missouri soon after. There, she married William Henry Shetley, born in 1809 in the Stanley area, whose family also migrated to Missouri. William was the grandson of the Stanley area pioneer Jacob Shetley.

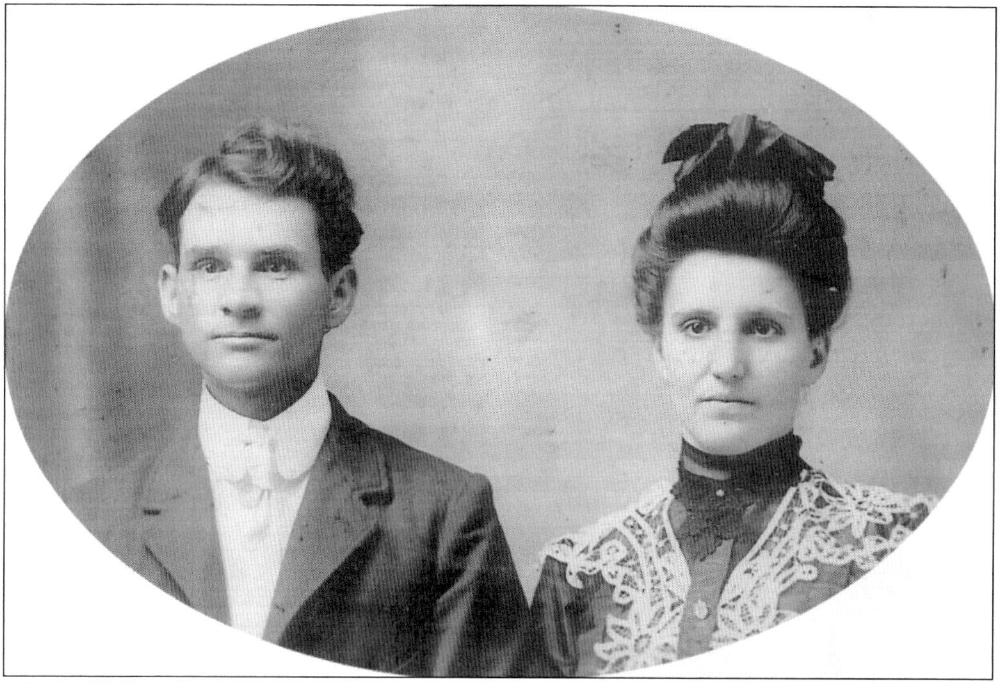

John L. Shelton served in the Army during the Spanish American War and later was deployed to the Philippines. After returning to Stanley Creek, he married Vera Thompson in 1904, and they lived near the railroad in a two-story house and operated a store next door. He was appointed postmaster in Stanley Creek in 1905 and was elected as alderman from the First Ward in 1915.

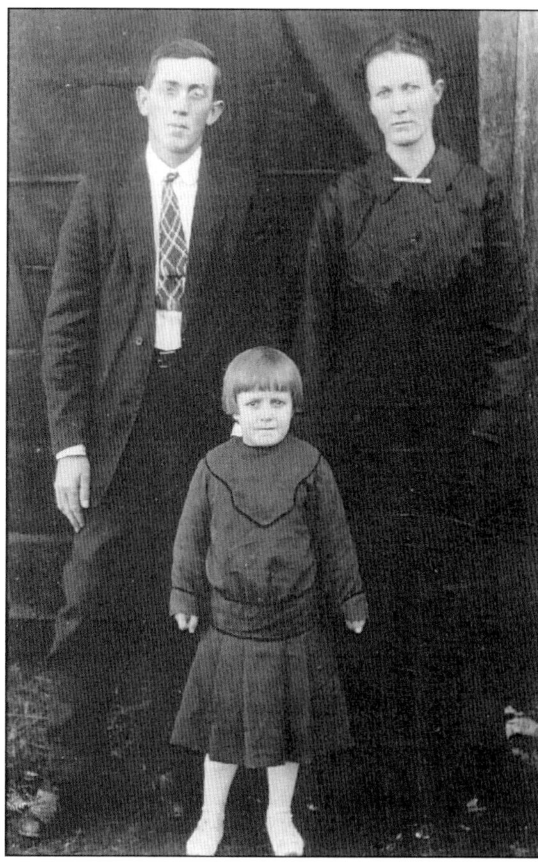

Giles Augustus Rhyne, born in 1887, was the son of Edgar and Maggie Rhyne. Pictured are Giles, his wife, Hattie Stroup, and their daughter Eva. Later, daughter Pauline was born. Hattie was the daughter of Anderson Stroup and Rebecca Morris. Giles and Hattie's daughter Eva married Robert L. Payne, and Pauline married Lloyd "Fuzzy" Brown. The family lived near the intersection of Rhyne and Alexis–High Shoals Roads.

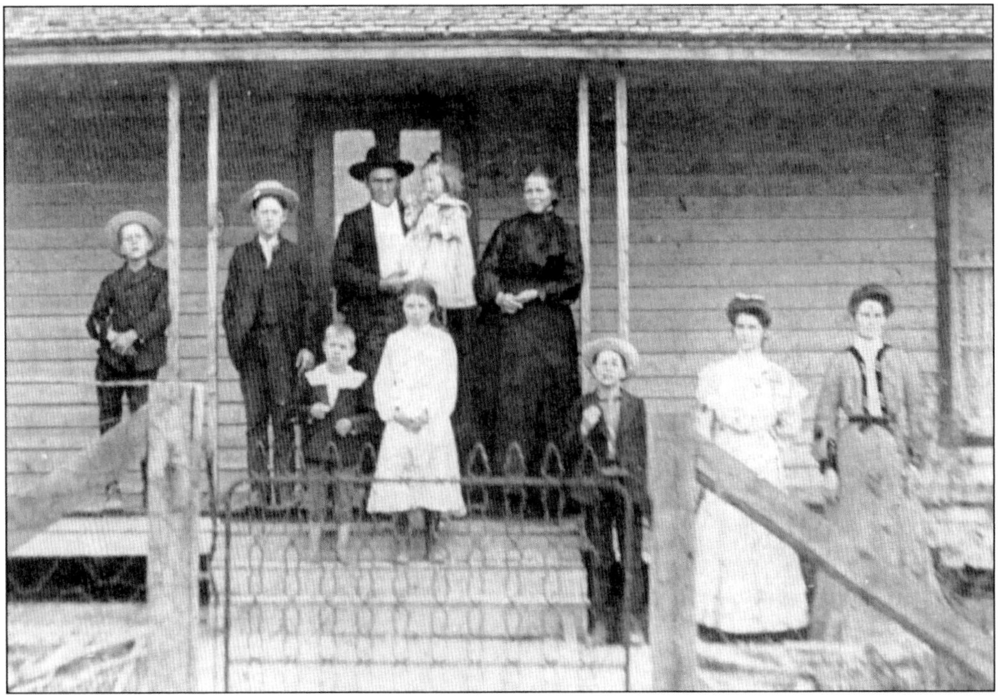

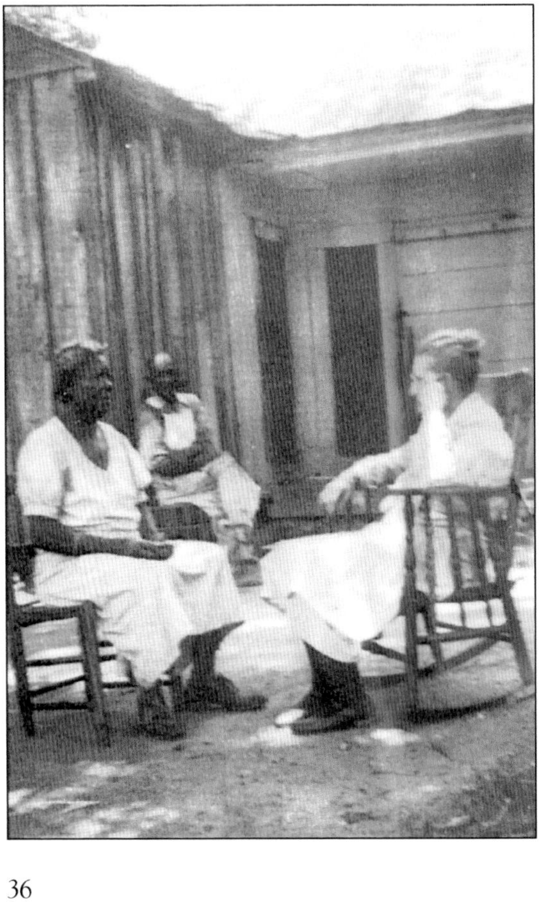

William Richard Cannon (1851–1931) was the son of John Franklin Cannon and Margaret Costner, who lived on the road to Lucia. William's property joined that of Thomas Rhyne of the 1799 house and the Derr and Rutledge properties. He married Emma Carpenter on November 3, 1879. Pictured from left to right are (first row) Fred, Eula Pauline, Wade, Bessie, and Lou Cannon; (second row) Walter, Claude, William Richard (holding Ruby), and Emma Cannon.

Addie Smith Rhyne (right) is enjoying a visit, sitting in the shade with Liza and William Beaty, descendants of former slaves of the Rhyne family. The families kept in contact over the years. (Courtesy of Alfred Rhyne, grandson of Addie Smith Rhyne.)

# *Three*

# Industries and Businesses

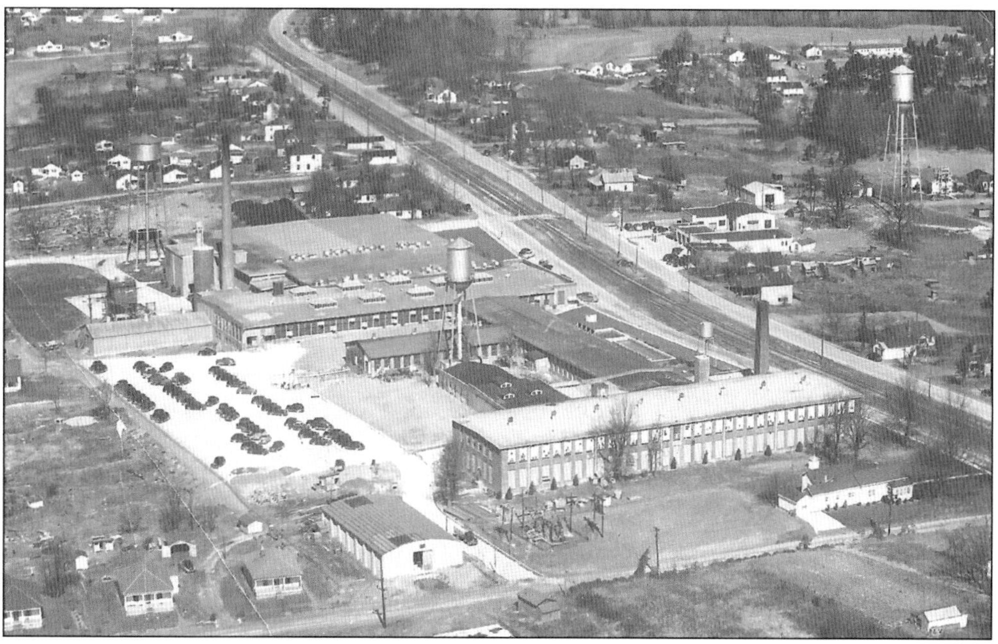

Decades after the Civil War, cotton mills began to appear throughout the South. Gaston County became the center of an industrial transfiguration due to abundant waterpower to run the mills. Cotton was grown locally and some was shipped by rail to the mills. The Stanley Creek Cotton Mill was built in 1891. In 1918, it became the Lola Manufacturing Company under the proprietorship of John C. Rankin, S.W. Robinson, and Robert Fulton Craig. This aerial photograph was taken around 1949.

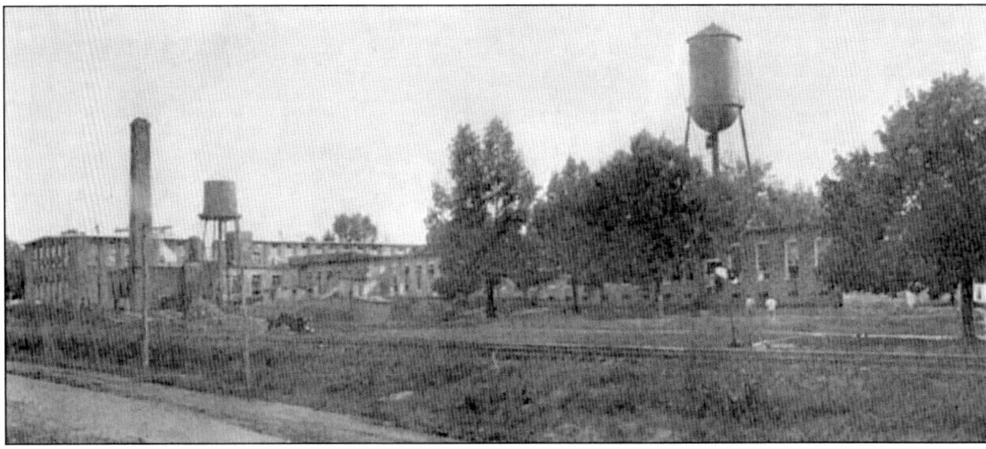

In 1919, John C. Rankin, S.M. Robinson, and Robert Fulton Craig acquired the Stanley Manufacturing Company and increased its size from 4,000 to 10,000 spindles, expanding it into Lola Mills. Craig served as the treasurer and superintendent. An advertisement in the *Southern Textile Bulletin* read, "Stanley is on the Seaboard Railroad Line in Gaston County, NC, a busy little city. The Lola Mills buildings are modern in construction with plenty of windows, well ventilated, heated and lighted. Their capital stock is $300,000 with 200 persons employed." The population of Stanley doubled from 1900 to 1930, as many people moved from farms and mountains to the mills for employment. Most workers lived in houses built and owned by the mills. These new families became part of the community, with their children attending school and worshipping in the local churches.

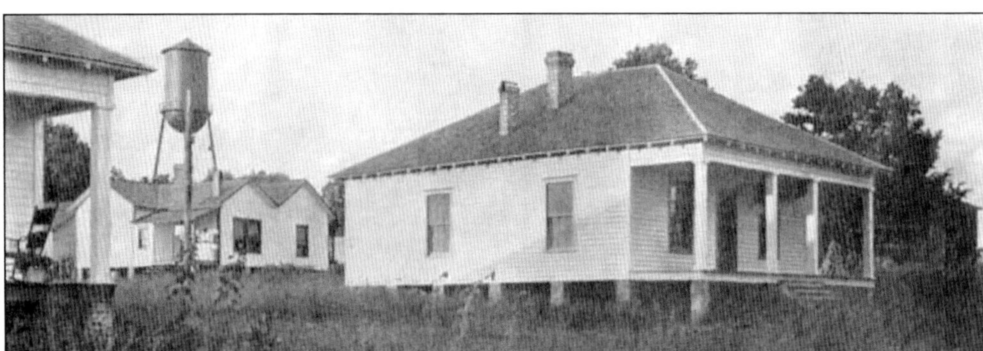

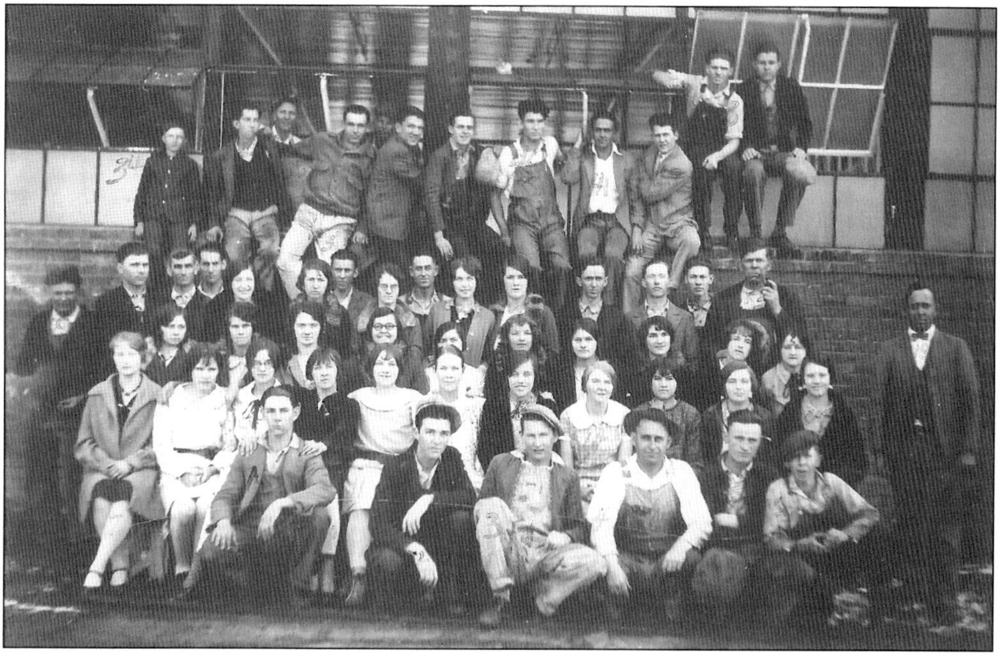

Katterman and Mitchell Silk Mill employees are pictured in the early 1930s. During the Depression years, these laborers worked extremely hard, long hours for little pay. Women and children worked alongside the men to feed their families. Brevard Station Museum has hundreds of such photographs, many with the employees' names, that have been donated by local residents.

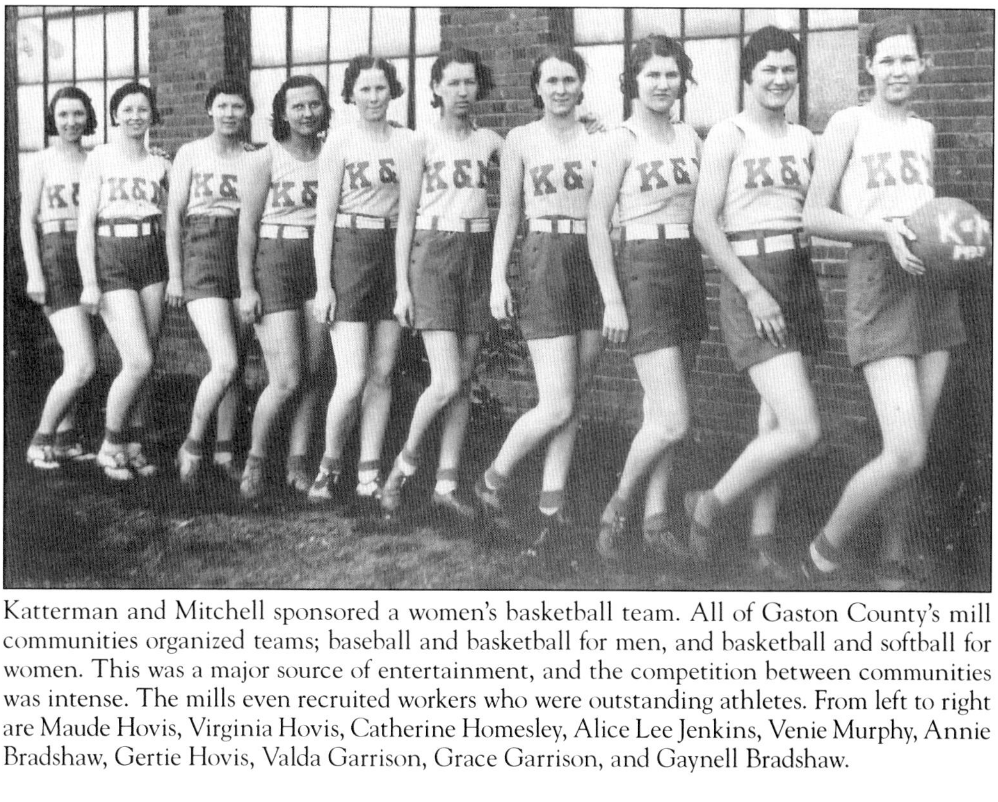

Katterman and Mitchell sponsored a women's basketball team. All of Gaston County's mill communities organized teams; baseball and basketball for men, and basketball and softball for women. This was a major source of entertainment, and the competition between communities was intense. The mills even recruited workers who were outstanding athletes. From left to right are Maude Hovis, Virginia Hovis, Catherine Homesley, Alice Lee Jenkins, Venie Murphy, Annie Bradshaw, Gertie Hovis, Valda Garrison, Grace Garrison, and Gaynell Bradshaw.

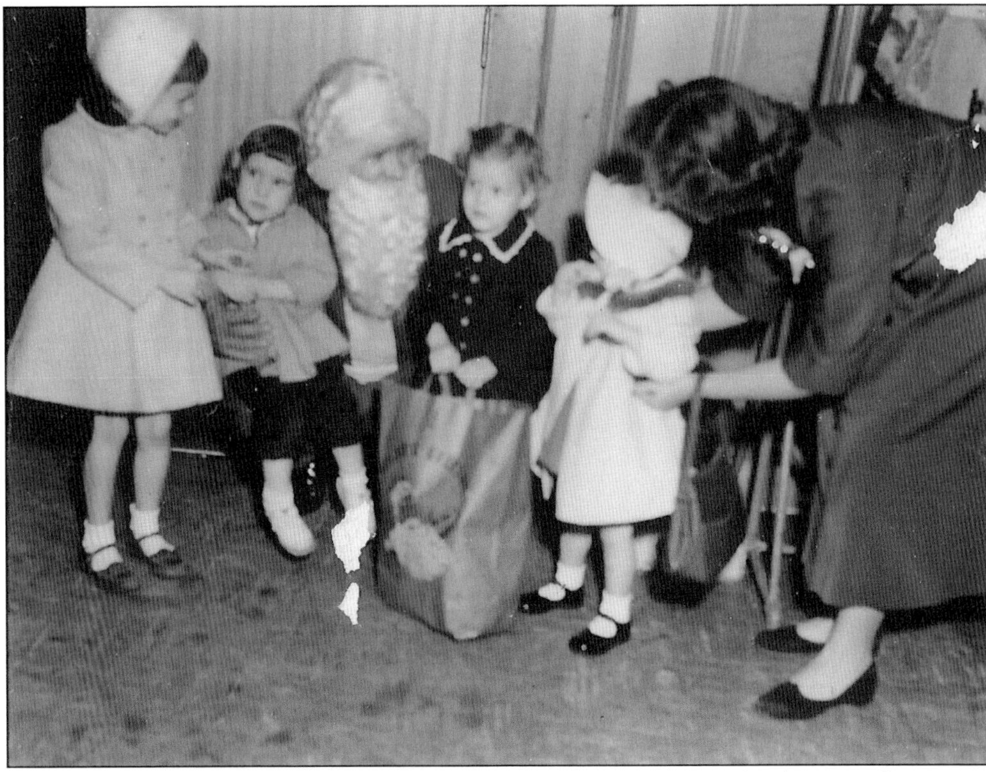

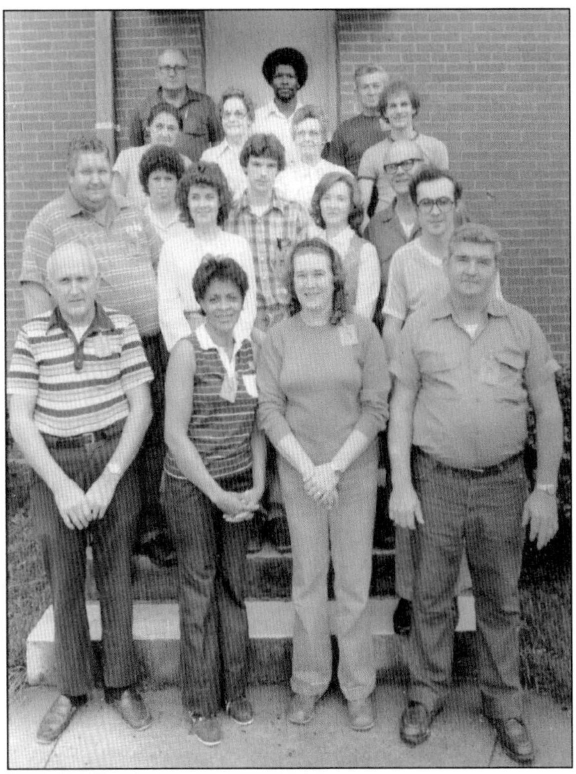

There was a family atmosphere among the J.P. Stevens mill employees. At Christmastime, Santa Clause gave out shopping bags filled with toys and candy to the children of employees, as seen in this photograph taken sometime in the early 1950s. Until his retirement, James Cannon seemed to be delighted to portray Santa for the children.

These J.P. Stevens employees, representing different departments, were photographed in the 1970s. They are, from left to right (first row) Neal Rhyne, Barbara McCorkle, Bobbie Fletcher, and Roger Lowe; (second row) John Gilbert, Dianne Caudle, Kathey Brown, and James Carpenter; (third row) Diane Summey, Gene Leagon, and Casper Spargo; (fourth row) Mozelle Watts, Florence Derr, Isabell Hovis, and James Summey; (fifth row) Paul Conner, Ronnie Floyd, and unidentified.

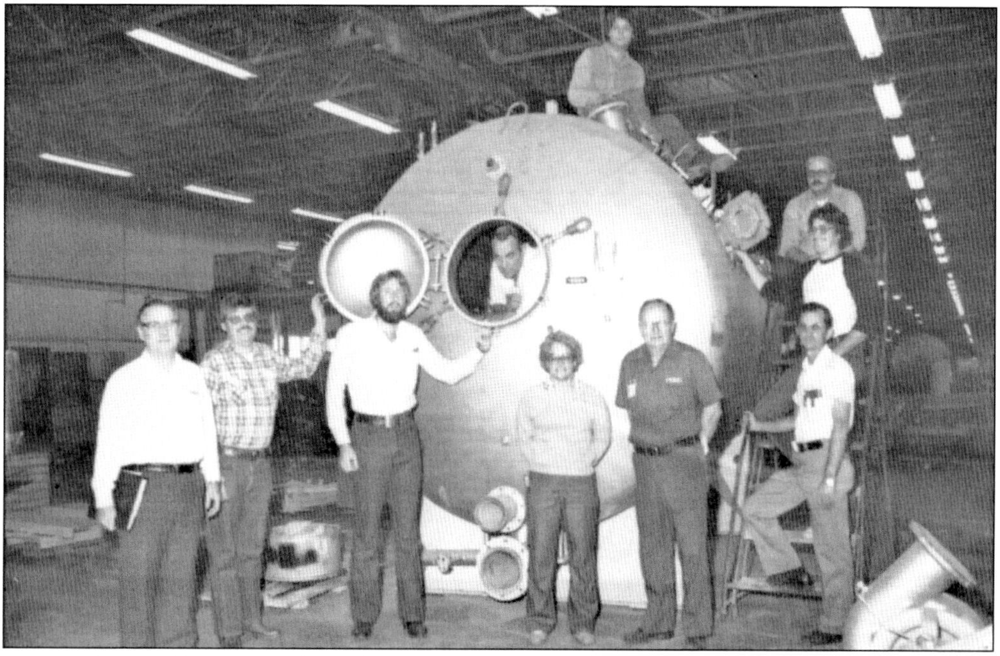

Gaston County Dyeing Machine Company began in 1921 as a result of resolving some textile dyeing machine problems. A patent was issued to William P. Hornbuckle and Robert Fulton Craig in the early 1920s. Their invention, the first American-made beam dyer, caught the attention of mills in the area, which began placing orders for the new machines. The company became one of the world's leaders in wet processing machines and control systems. Pictured above is the company's quality control staff. Below are employees of the company in 1939. From left to right are (seated) Amon Bumgarner, Joe Bumgarner, Jarrett Bumgarner, Gordon Hacker, John Cannon, Ott Bentley, Forrest Ballard, and George Hacker; (standing) Ed Gollner, Bob Wycoff, Bill Hornbuckle, Ralph Handsel, Ed Bentley, Jess Sherrill, Bill Edwards, Clarence Hoyle, Casper Brown, Walter "Iron Jaw" Bailey, and Sam Lineberger.

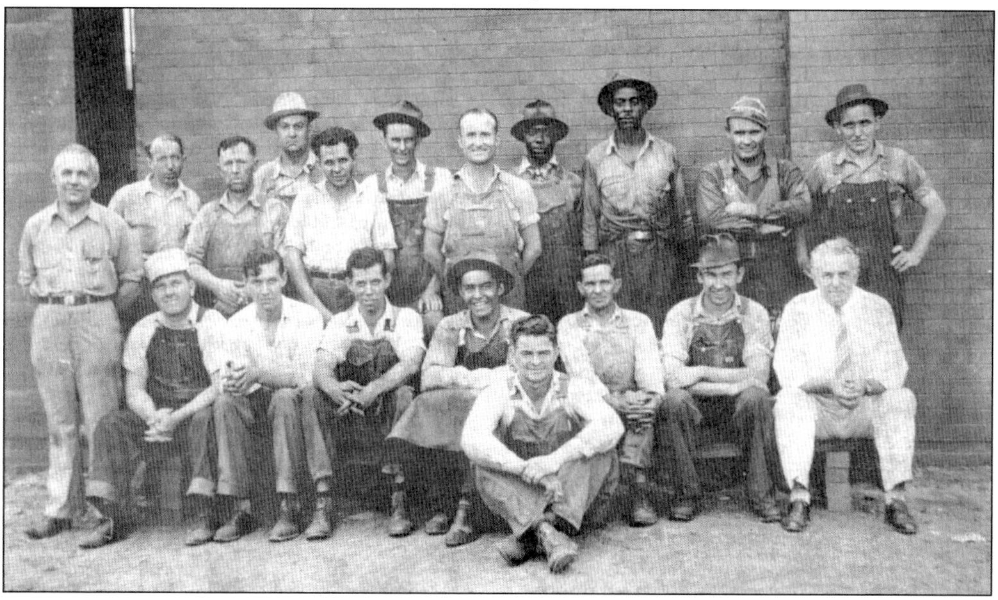

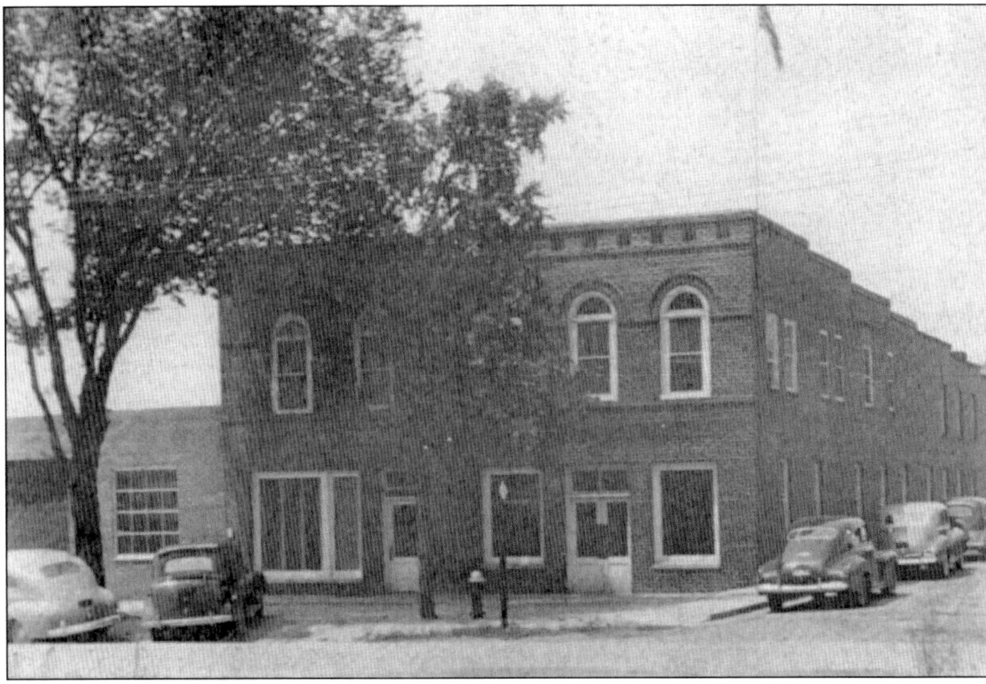

The stock market crash of 1929 failed to shut down the business of Gaston County Dyeing Machine Company. The headquarters moved into the former bank and store building in Stanley (pictured above). Hubert Craig, son of founder Robert Fulton Craig, entered the business. George H. Hacker, a German immigrant, joined the company in 1936, and his son Gordon later became a vice president of the company. Pictured below are company officers, from left to right, (first row) Walter Newcomb (sales manager), William H. Eikoetter (technical service), Hubert Craig (president), Max Craig (vice president), and Gordon Hacker (vice president and general manager); (second row) Ray Craig (vice president), Alfred Rhyne (chief engineer), John Luker (plant manager), Bill Carpenter (research engineering manager), Yates Craig (sales engineer), Harry Davis (outside fabrication manager), Calvin Donnan (controller), Bob Angle (southeastern sales representative), and Al Bagian (northeast sales representative).

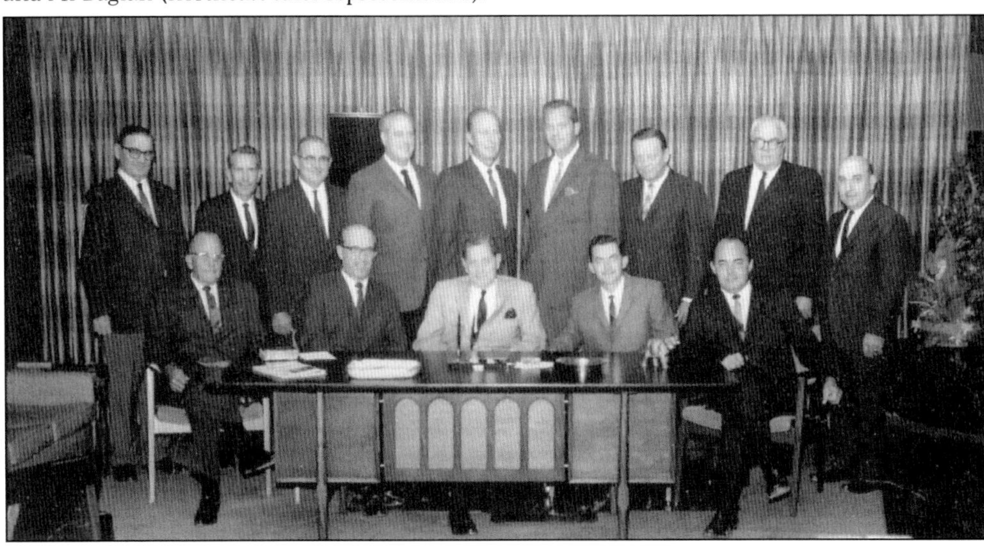

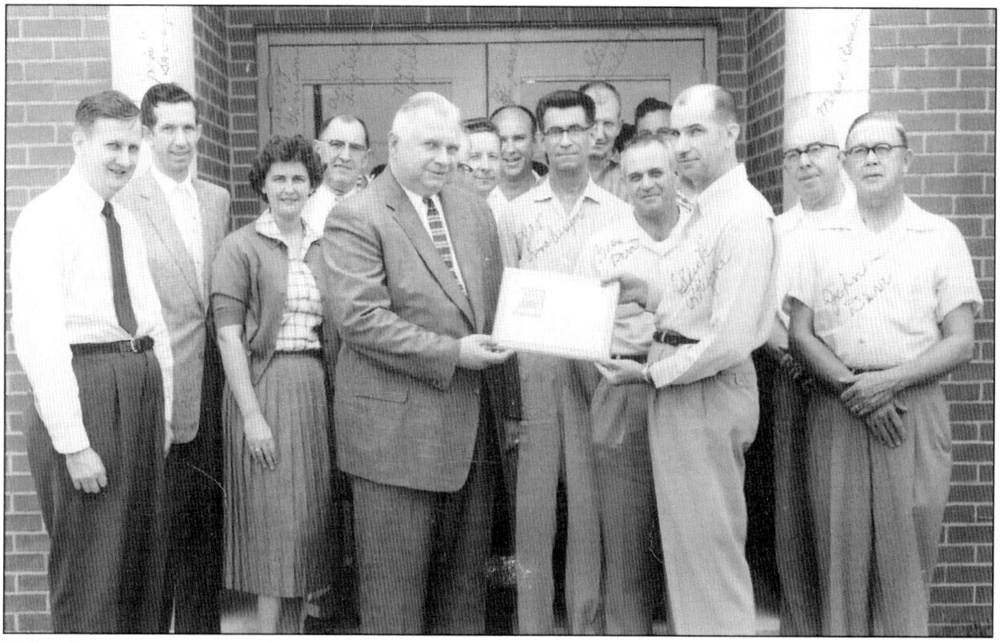

Talon Inc., a zipper manufacturer, chose Stanley for its new plant, and in late 1953, construction was completed on a $1 million factory that would employ 200 locals. A few years later, an addition was built doubling the size and employing many more. The company initiated and participated in many improvements to the town, including building sidewalks from the Talon plant all the way to Springfield School on the other end of town. Pictured above receiving an award from town officials are, from left to right, Fred Keefer, James Stroupe, Peggy Garrison, Arnold C. Taylor, James Hendley, Fred Phil, Dr. Joseph C. Fesperman, Judson Vipperman Lineberger, Stewart Dellinger, George Derr, unidentified, Mayor Glenn Rhyne, Marsh Cavin, and John Derr. The image below shows workers in the inspection department checking for defects in the zipper tape.

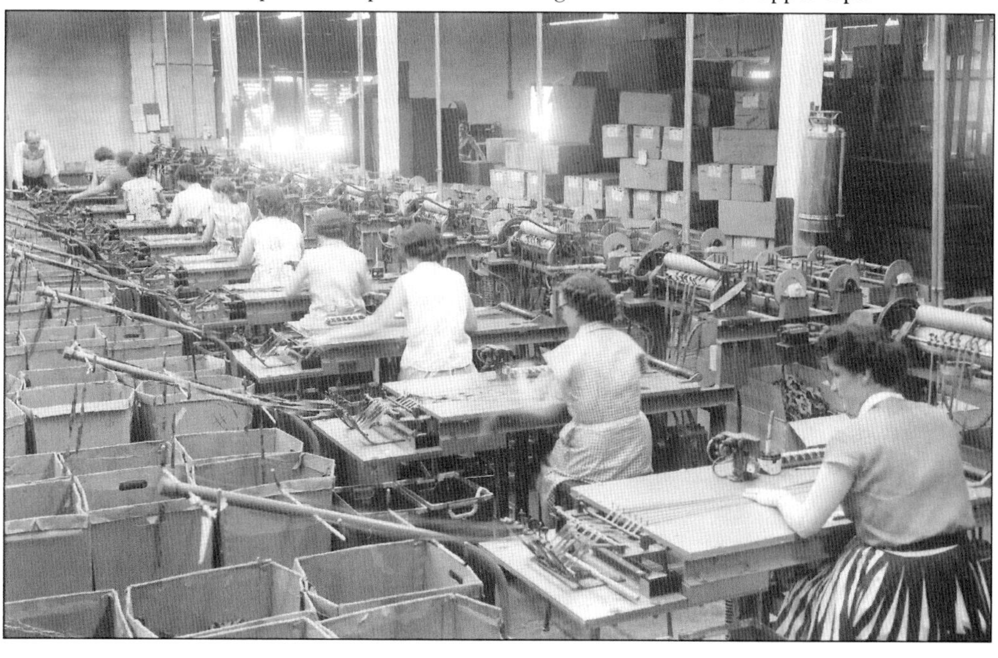

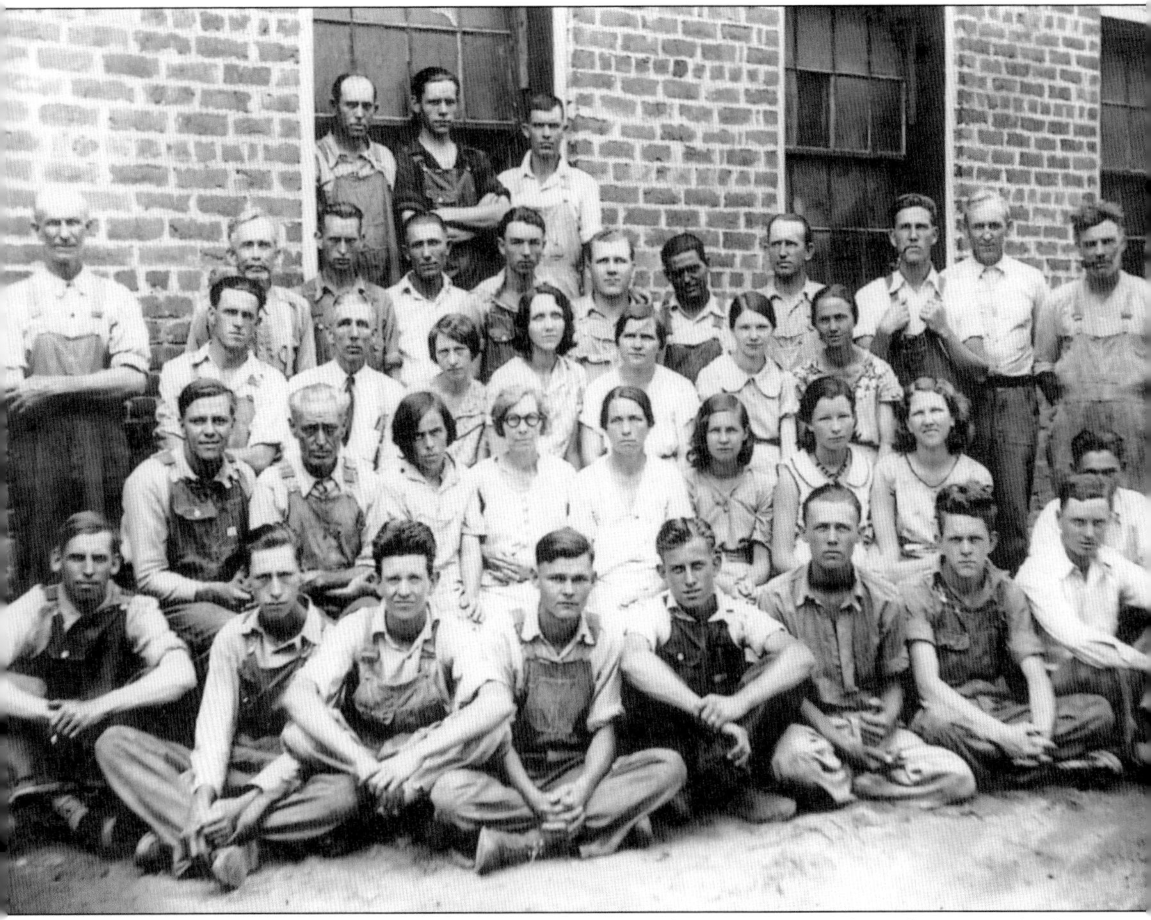

The Mariposa Mill was started in 1902 by Joseph Graham Morrison of Stanley. It was built on the site of the former Mount Welcome Forge on Leepers Creek. The management was passed to Morrison's son, Lt. Colonel Robert Hall Morrison. The mill was incorporated in 1911 to manufacture yarns and fabrics from cotton, wool, silk, flax, hemp, and other fibers. Later, it was called the Alba Twine Mill. Part of the building now stands in picturesque ruins. Employees of the Mariposa Mill pictured here are, from left to right, (first row) Bill Franklin, Dwight Lawing, Jack Fisher, Clyde Gardner, Henry Black, Will Kennedy, Ralph Fisher, and Bunk Jones; (second row) Fred Riddle, Dave Lawing, Cora Franklin, Alice Lawing, Maybell Riddle, Pauline Parnell, Faye Stone, and Mary Bumgarner; (third row) Ernest Williams, Jay Bumgarner, Edith Barber, Bonnie Fisher, Hassie Nantz, Martha Green, and Jane McGinnis; (fourth row) James Abernathy, Autry Barnet, Elton Lawing, John Bumgarner, Fred Stone, Amon Bumgarner, Ernest Barber, Emanuel Black, Rob Bumgarner, Tom Handsel (store manager), and Jim Connard; (fifth row) Charlie Jenkins, Marvin McGinnis, and Jim Jones.

Originally from the Pisgah Forest mountain area, William Garfield Hawley worked in 1919 at Carr Lumber Company as a lumber grader before starting his own business. He moved his family to Stanley in 1925 and operated his own sawmill. The enterprise prospered, and in the mid-1950s, Hawley retailed building supplies for several decades. After his death, the family sold the business to a company from Belmont, North Carolina.

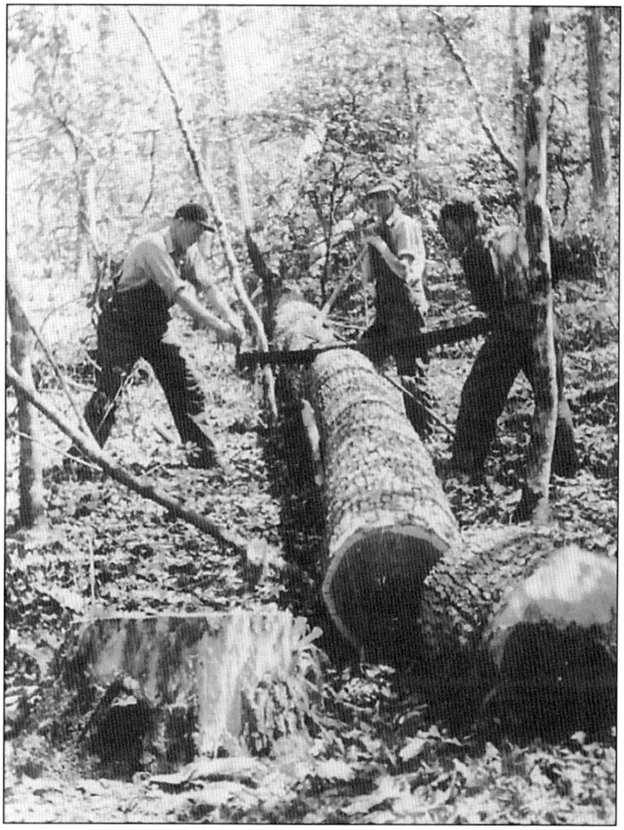

Russell Handsel was born in 1899 and grew up on the family farm on Mariposa Road. After Army service, Handsel married Lila Gertrude Huggins. He owned and operated a small country grocery store, and in the late 1940s, built Stanley's first self-service grocery, operating it until his retirement. Handsel is pictured inside his Handsel's Self Service Grocery store.

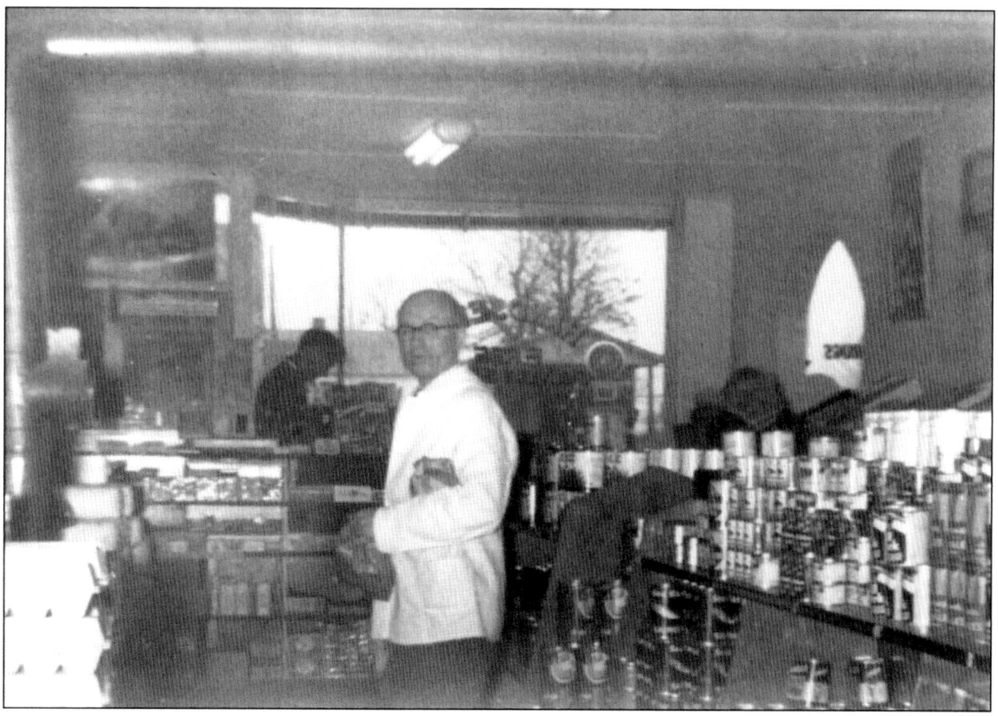

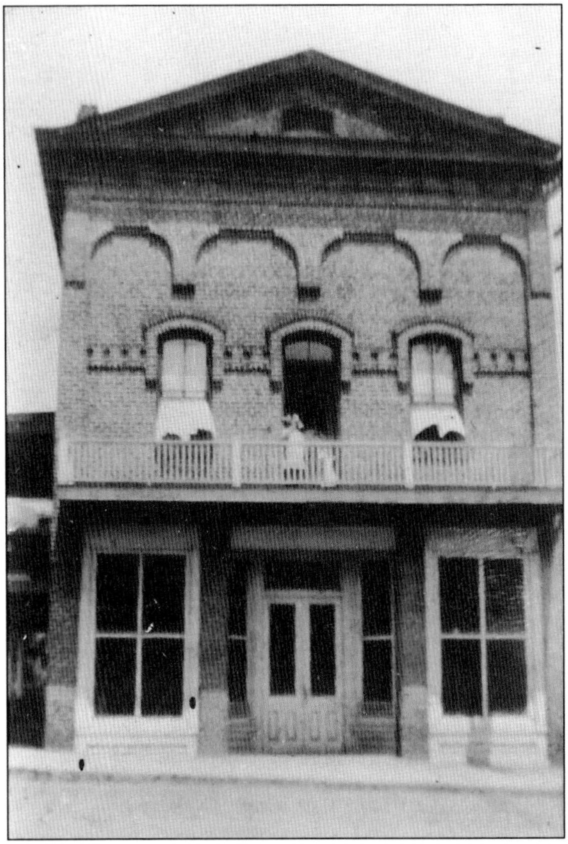

In April 1925, Wirt Hovis became owner of Carpenter Mercantile, pictured here, said to carry a full line of general merchandise. Hovis later operated Wirt Hovis Grocery and Dry Goods and W.W. Hovis Clothing Store. Unfortunately, this picturesque building was later torn down. Hovis was married to Jessie Harwell and served as Stanley alderman in 1921–1923, 1931–1933, and 1937–1939.

No town is complete without at least one grocery store/gas station, and Stanley was no exception. Here, Preston C. Fox proudly stands beside the Sinclair Gasoline sign outside his store, which was located on Old Mount Holly Road. Notice the bench behind him, which would have been reserved for gathering and passing the time of day. Also, take note of the old style gasoline pumps.

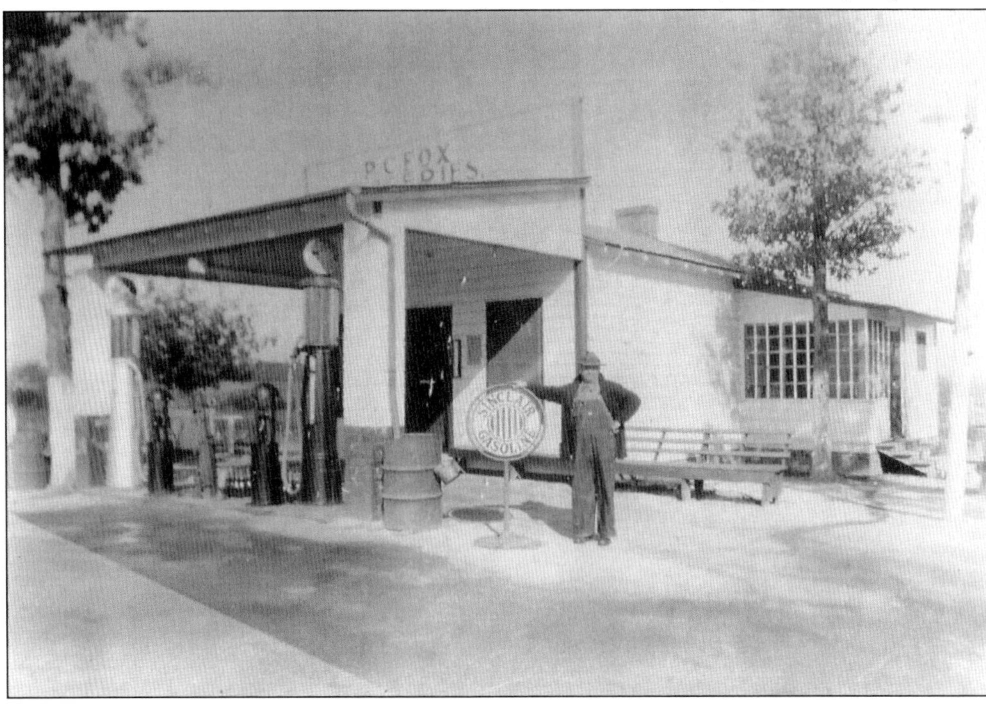

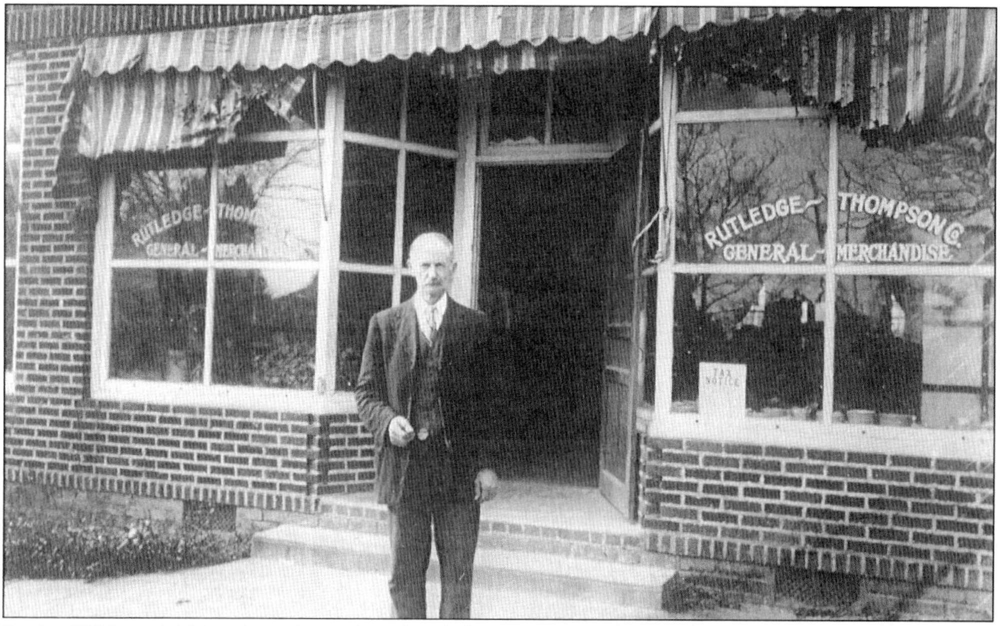


In the 1930s and 1940s, Joseph Graham Rutledge, in partnership with Wilburn Conley Thompson, operated this general merchandise store on South Main Street. Here, Rutledge appears to be waiting to welcome customers into the store. There is a tax notice in the window, along with dishes for sale. This is an example of typical storefronts along Main Street at that time.

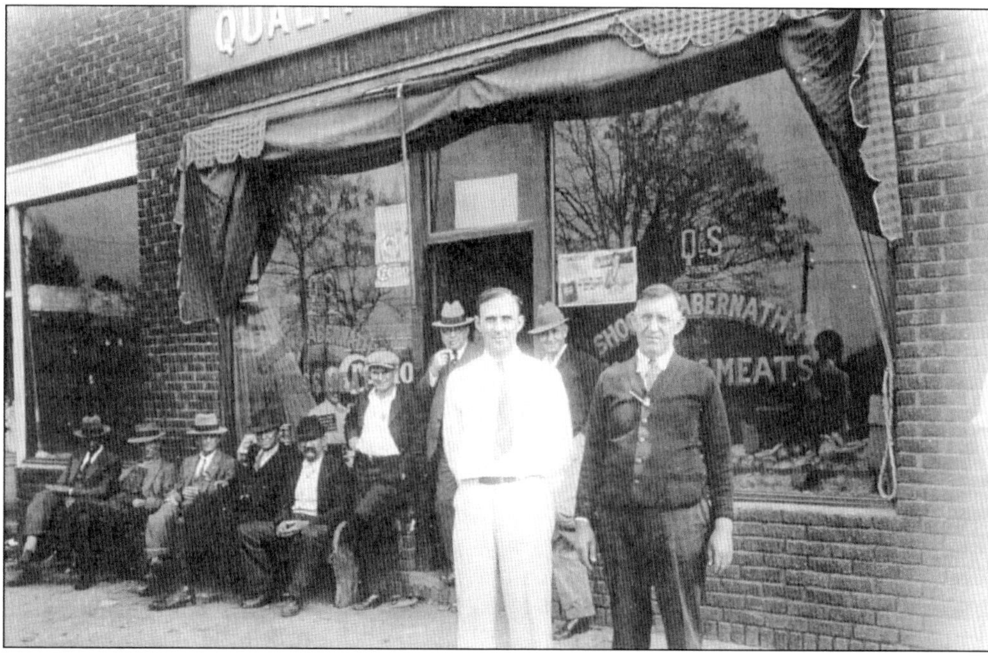


In the early 1930s, Warren Abernathy and Robert Shook partnered in operating one of the early grocery chains, the first to sell fresh meats along with produce and dry grocery items. It appears the male population of the town enjoyed gathering in front of the grocery store and relaxing. Abernathy died at an early age, while Shook lived to see his 100th birthday on September 5, 1975. The town of Stanley declared that day Mr. Bob Shook Day.

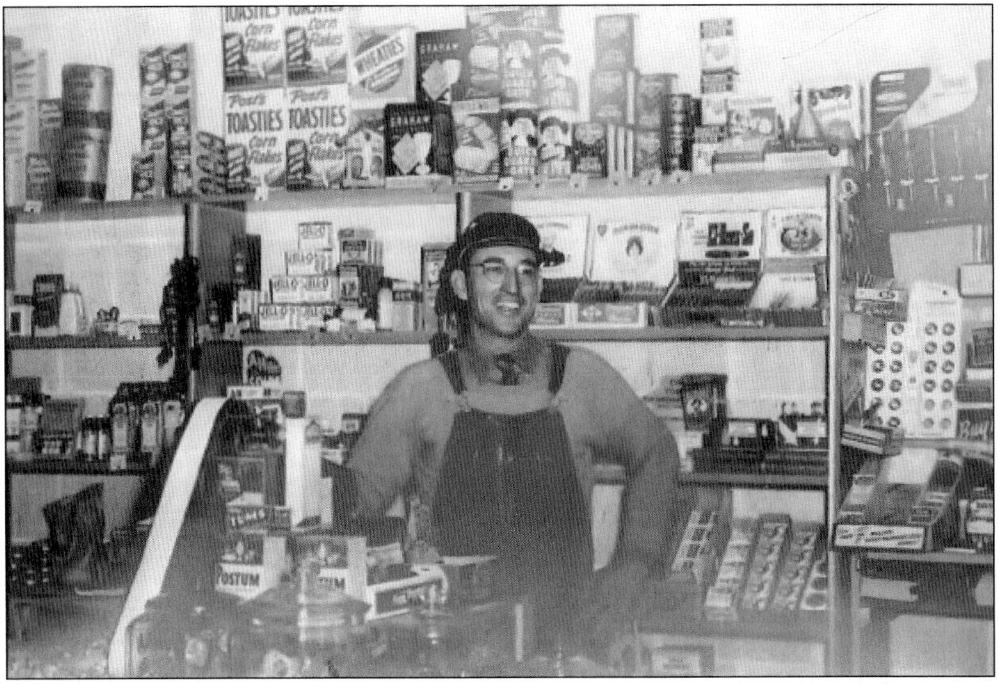

Pictured in the early 1950s with a happy smile and wearing his bib overalls and baseball cap is Jim Murphy behind the counter of his general store. The well-stocked shelves show many items still available today, which seem to prove that quality has staying power. This building still survives and currently houses a popular Papa John's pizza parlor.

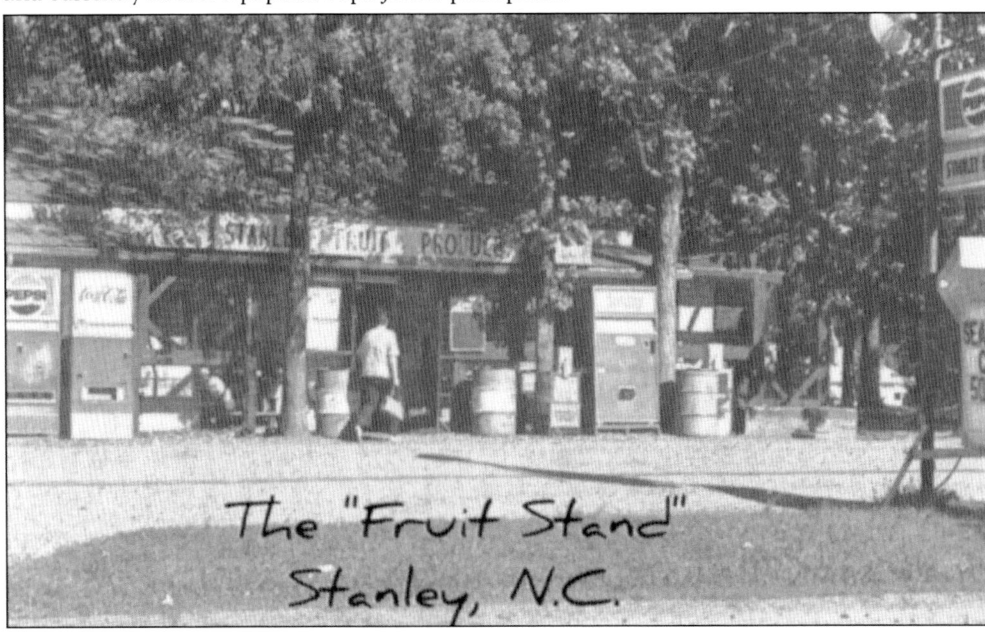

While the cities had their 7-Eleven convenience stores back in the 1950s and 1960s, Stanley had the "Fruit Stand," where everyone in the neighborhood went to pick up bread, milk, soft drinks, candy, and crackers. The place was not much to look at, with sawdust on the floors, but it gathered a lot of business. Arthur Barber started the business as a fruit stand beside highway 27.

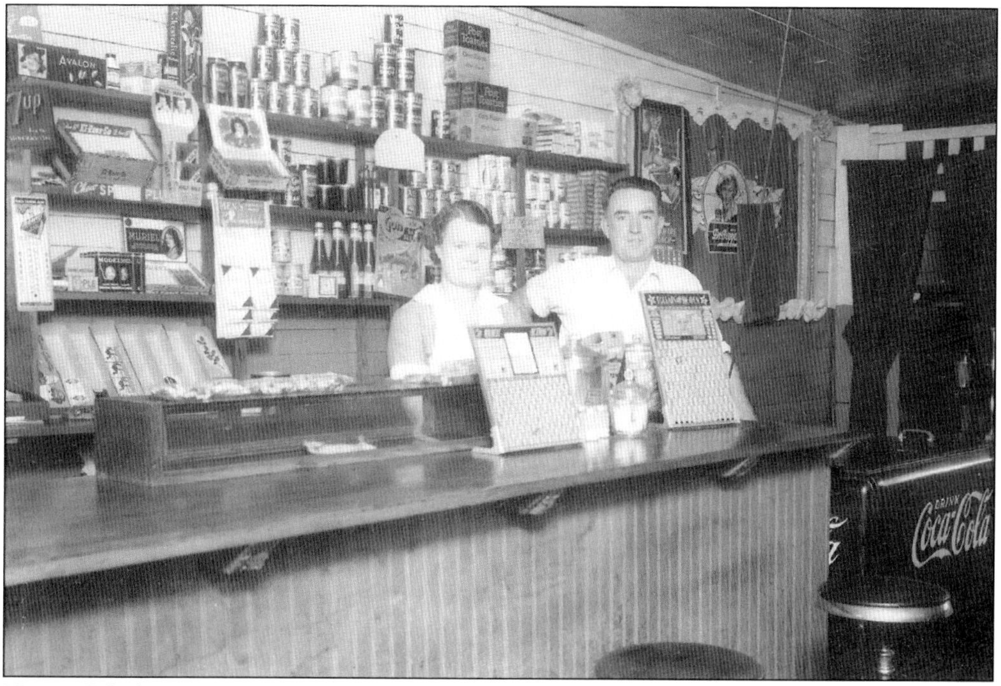


Horace Edgebert "Casey" Caldwell and his wife, Lilly Day, bought the North End Café around 1953 from Lonnie Bryson. It was located on Highway 27 North. A business card stated that beer, lunches, and sandwiches were served, and ladies were invited. Caldwell was a veteran of World War I, and he and Lilly lived on Plum Street.

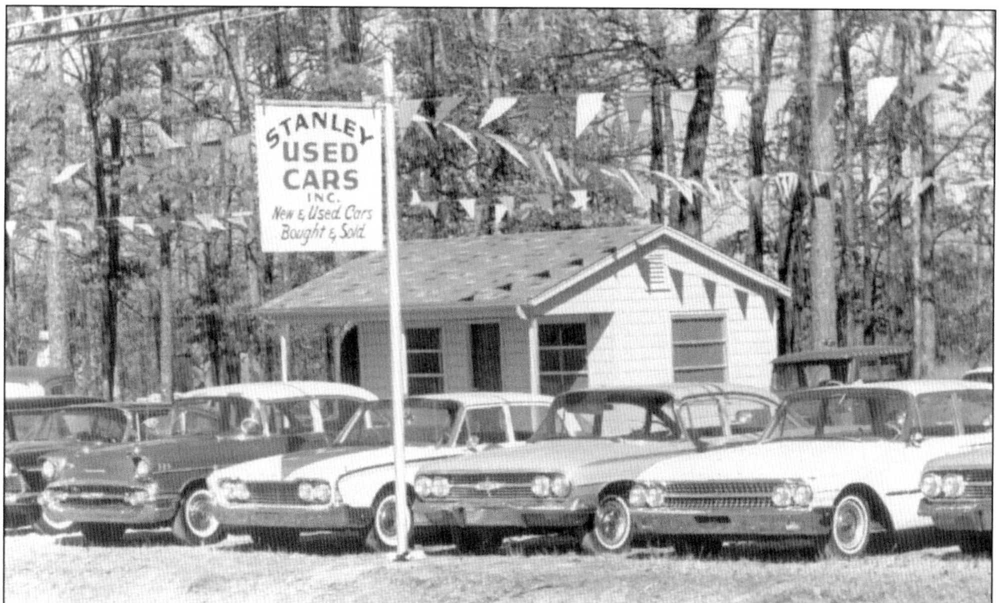


Stanley Used Cars, located on the corner of Blacksnake Road and Highway 27, was operated by David and Clayton Keever in the 1960s and 1970s. Fords and Chevrolets appear to have been very popular at the time, based on this photograph. Freida Long Robinson, Linda Ollis, Ronnie Lineberger, and Reggie Stone all recall buying a vehicle from the Keevers during that time.

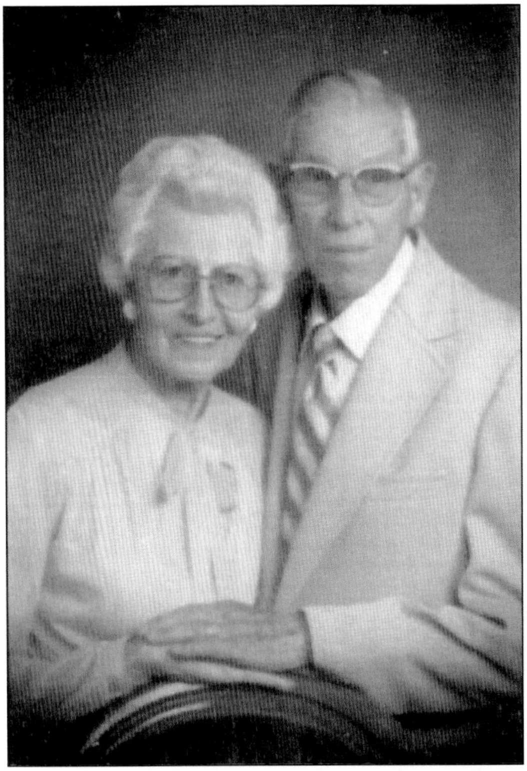

Paul and Edna Shook were grocers who, working together with other businesspeople in town, contributed to feed hungry families. Their generosity, according to the town barber, Robert Mauney, extended to the Stanley schools, the Salvation Army, and Christ's Lutheran Church.

Main Street in Stanley is home to the Stanley Florist Shop, operated previously by Cathy Ellis and currently by Robert Landers, a generous individual who cares for and supports the Stanley community. He keeps his eyes and ears tuned for any occasion in which his generosity might quietly be extended. Folks in Stanley have made the florist a popular business, proving that Landers's talent as a floral designer is recognized and appreciated.

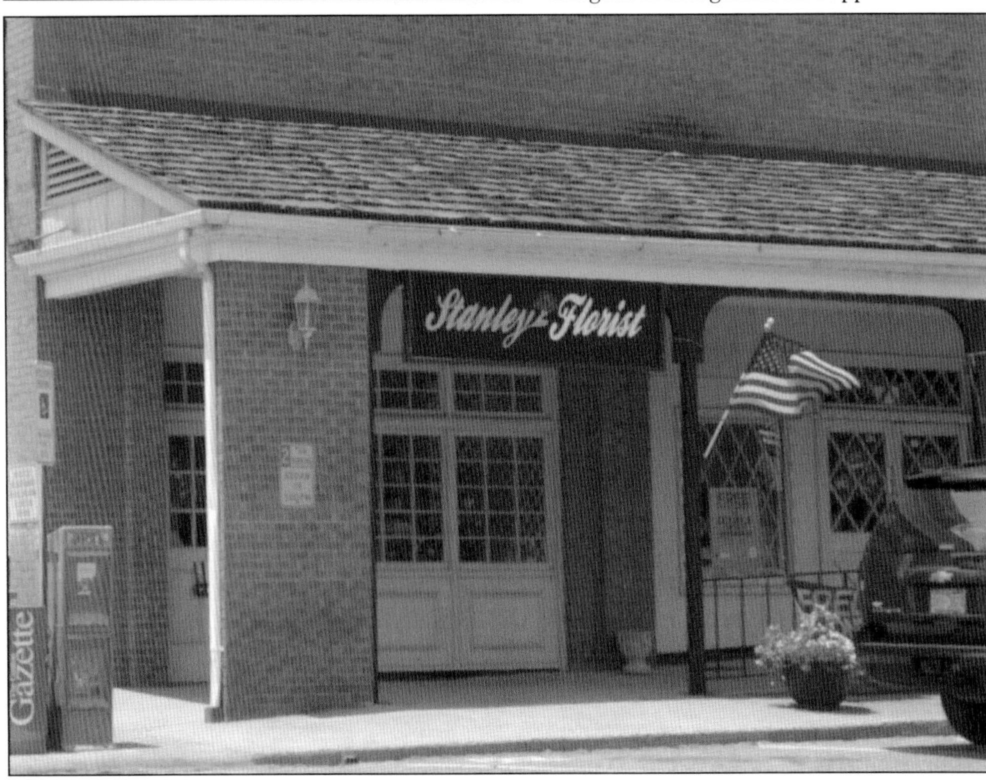

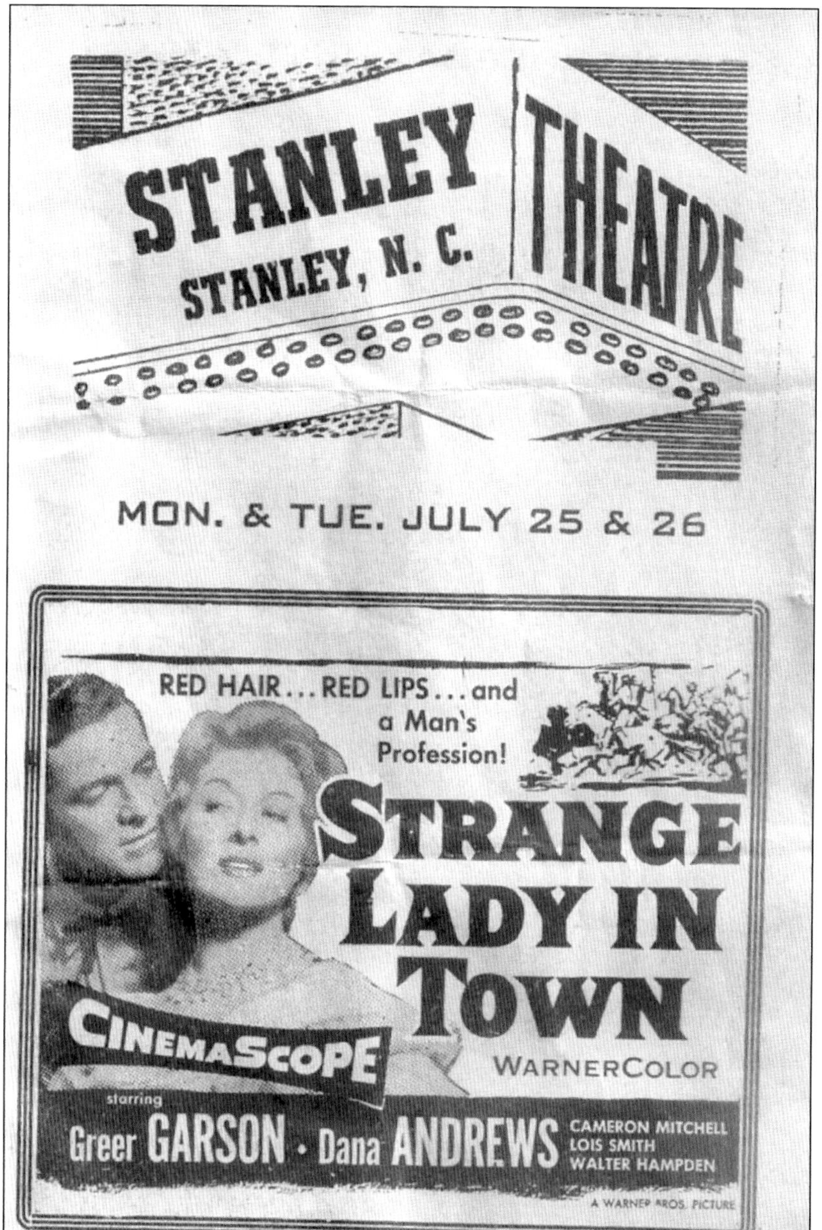


This is a Stanley Theatre movie playbill from the 1950s. The theater opened in 1948 on East College Street, and was managed first by Sue and Lewis Ballard and later by Betty and William B. "Bill" Smith. On Saturday mornings, most children in town went to "the show" to watch the Westerns and a short serial. The daily featured movie usually followed newsreels and a cartoon. On special occasions, stage shows were presented, sometimes with famous entertainers. In July 1948, there was an infantile paralysis (polio) epidemic in Gaston County, and children were not allowed to congregate at places such as movie theaters. So, that was the summer of no children at the Stanley Movie Theatre. Before integration, this was one of the few theaters in the area that allowed black citizens. The theater closed in the late 1960s.

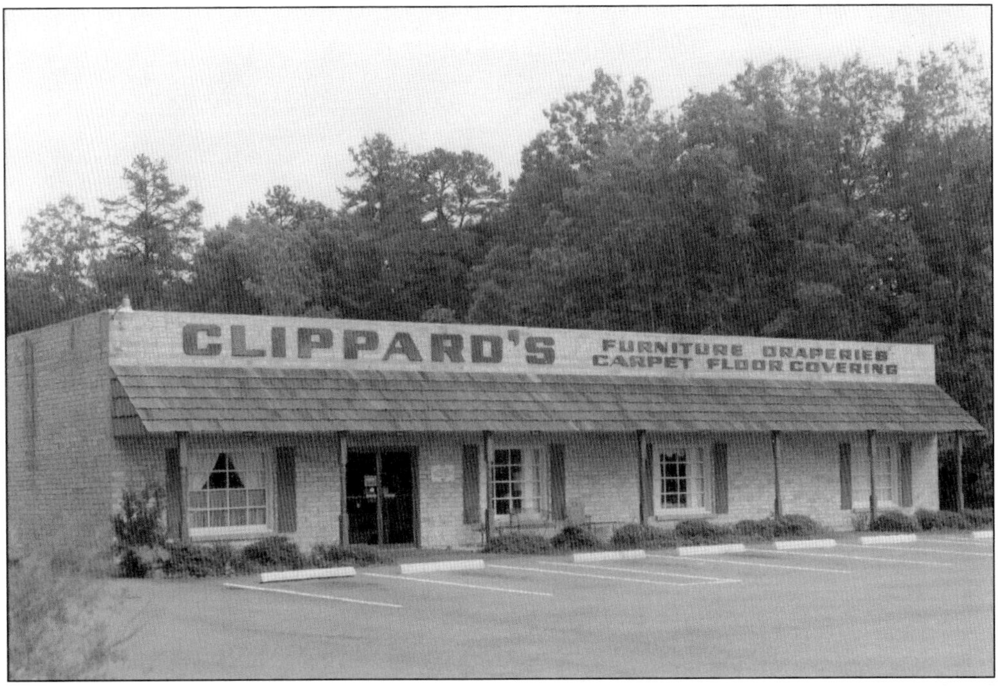


Kerry Clippard opened his first business in Stanley in 1970 selling paint, carpet, floor, and wall covering. In 1972, he built an 8,000-square-foot store and added furniture to his inventory. In 1982, he added a 10,000-square-foot warehouse. A 6,000-square-foot La-Z-Boy Gallery was added in 1992. Later, the front entry and the 14,000-square-foot floor space were renovated. Clippard sold the business to his son Steve in 1997 and retired.

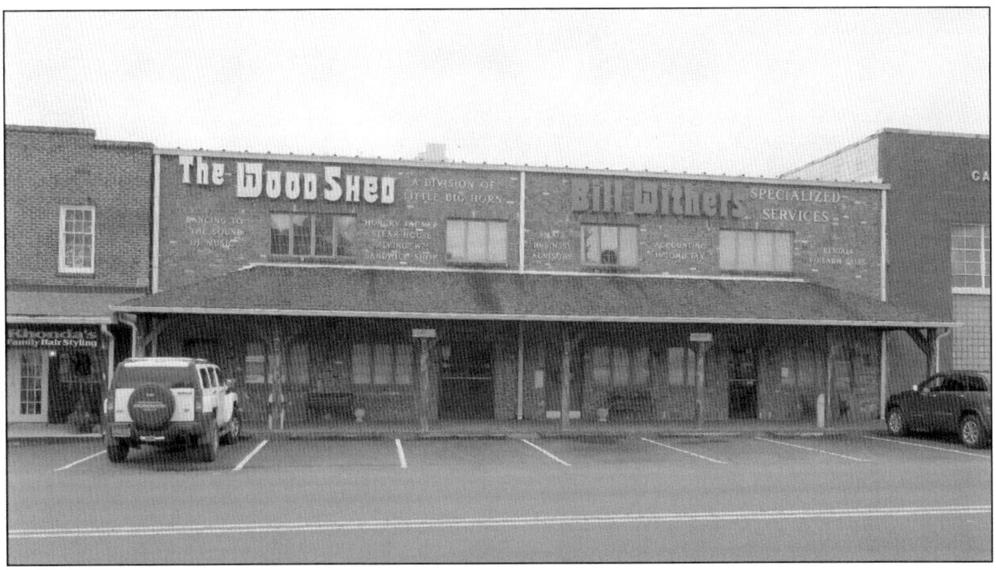


The Woodshed Steakhouse was opened in 1985 by William S. Withers in a new structure finished with carefully preserved bricks. The Withers family also runs a private party facility, the Little Big Horn, on the homestead of William's parents, John and Mary Smith Withers. William Withers served as the first chief of the Stanley Rescue Squad, as town clerk, and as mayor for two and a half terms. The Woodshed Steakhouse remains extremely popular in the Charlotte area.

# *Four*

# Service to the Country

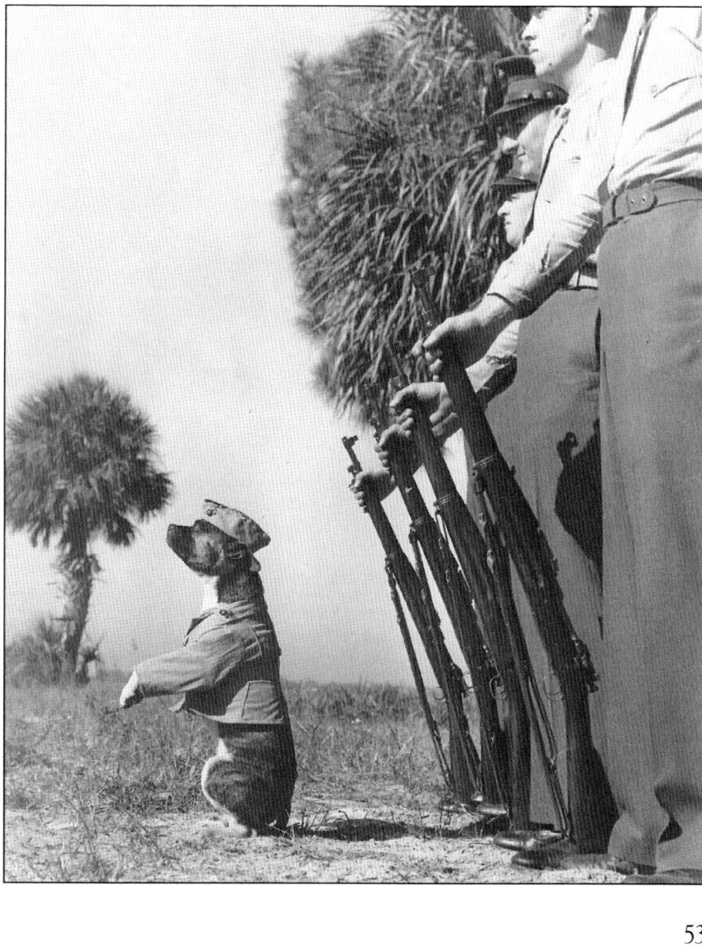

This uniformed dog is emblematic of service dogs in World War II, as they became a link for the brave soldiers to their far away homes and families. Found along with this unidentified photograph is a card belonging to US Marine private Thomas E. McSwain. Stanley men and women fought honorably in the all-too-frequent wars of the 20th century. This chapter aspires to honor a few of these veterans.

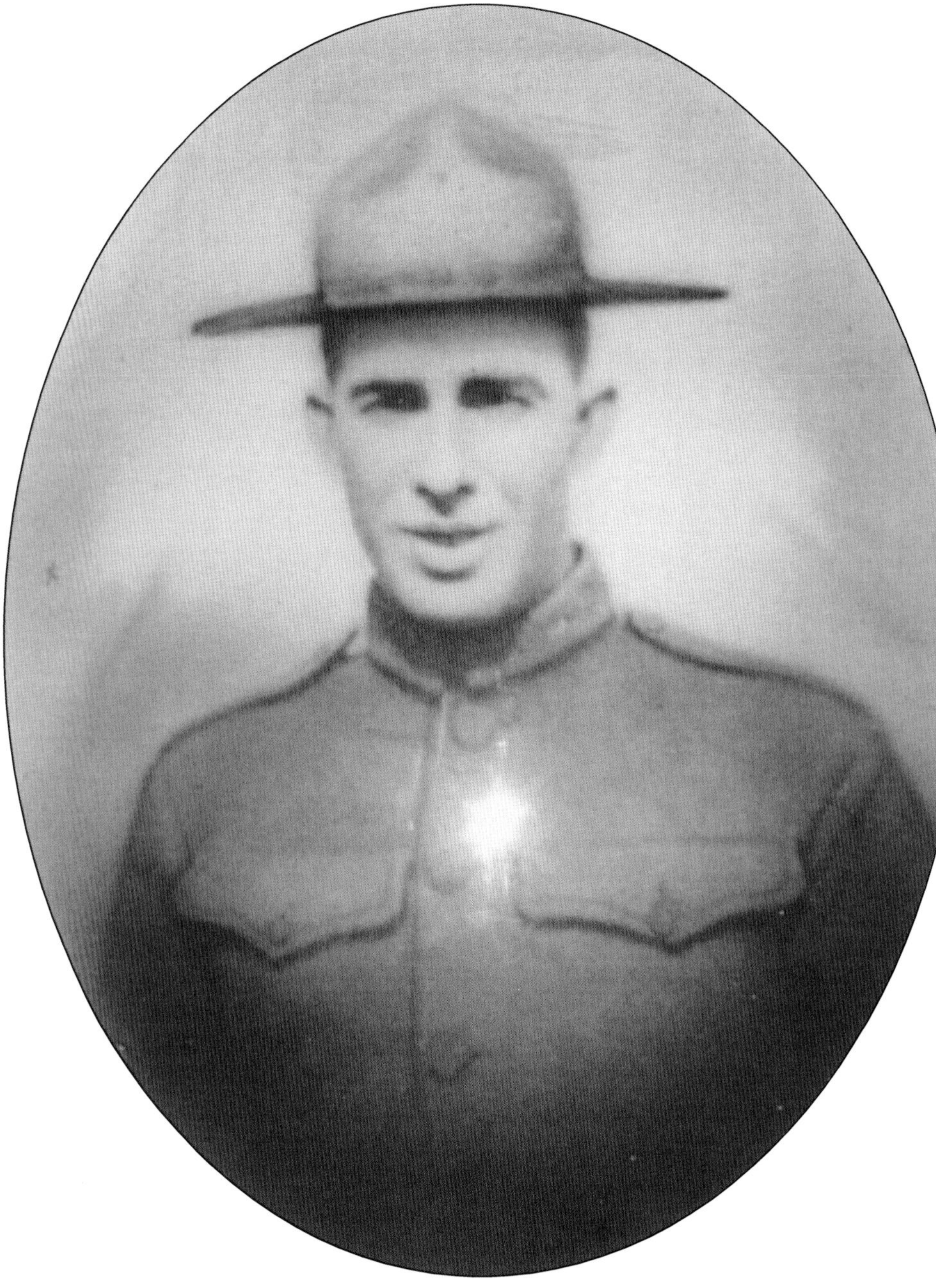

Born in 1895 in Mount Holly, Walter Marsh Cavin enlisted in the US Army in 1917. He served in the liberation of Belgium and France with the 105th Engineers. Returning to Mount Holly, he became a bank manager. In 1936, he moved to Stanley and was appointed postmaster. Cavin remained in the Army Reserves, so he was called to duty in 1941 as a finance officer and fought in the Battle of the Bulge. He retired as a lieutenant colonel and became the manager of Citizen's National Bank. Cavin was the first commander of the Rhyne-Cannon American Legion Post 266. He married Margaret Comer, and they had two children, Margaret and Walter Marsh Cavin Jr. He was part of the Gaston County Historical Society and worked to preserve the history of the county.

Jesse W. Joy served in the US Marine Corps from 1926 to 1936 and in the Naval Reserves until 1944. During his term of service, he was among 2,000 Marines sent by Pres. Calvin Coolidge to Central America in hopes of preventing the building of a canal across Nicaragua, and to restore order while protecting American lives and property in a conflict referred to as the Banana Wars.

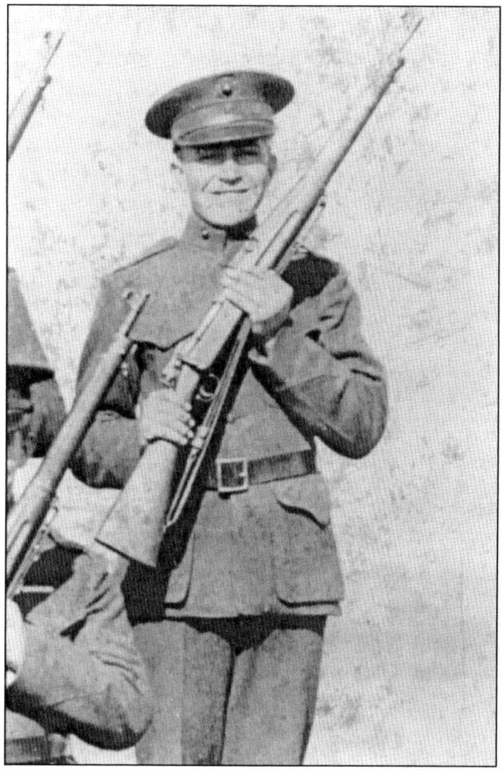

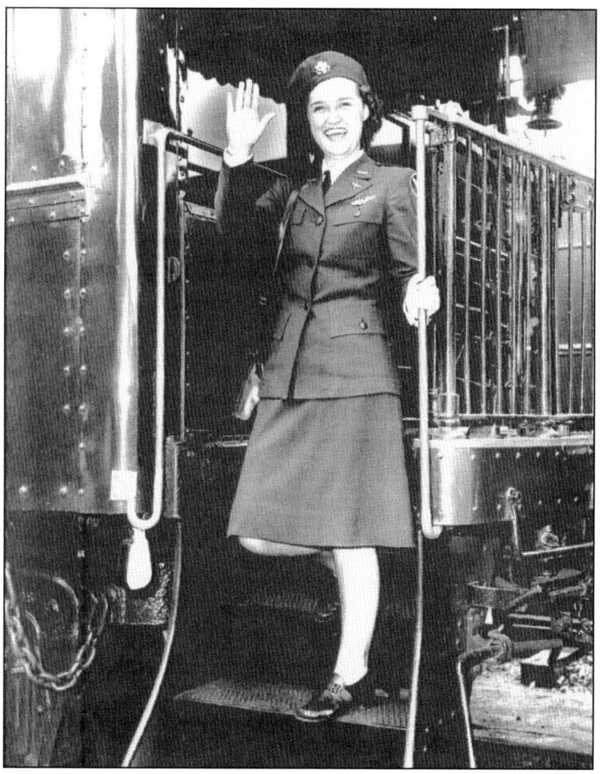

Mildred Taylor, daughter of Arnold C. and Ada Ensley Taylor of Stanley, graduated from Queens College in 1941 and quickly earned her pilot's license. She is pictured reporting for duty with the highly selective Ferry Command of the Women Airforce Service Pilots (WASP). Taylor flew cargo transport planes and helped train fighter pilots by towing targets for their practice shooting. In 2010, Congress recognized her and all the WASPs with the Congressional Medal of Honor. Taylor was married to Lt. General Winston Marshall.

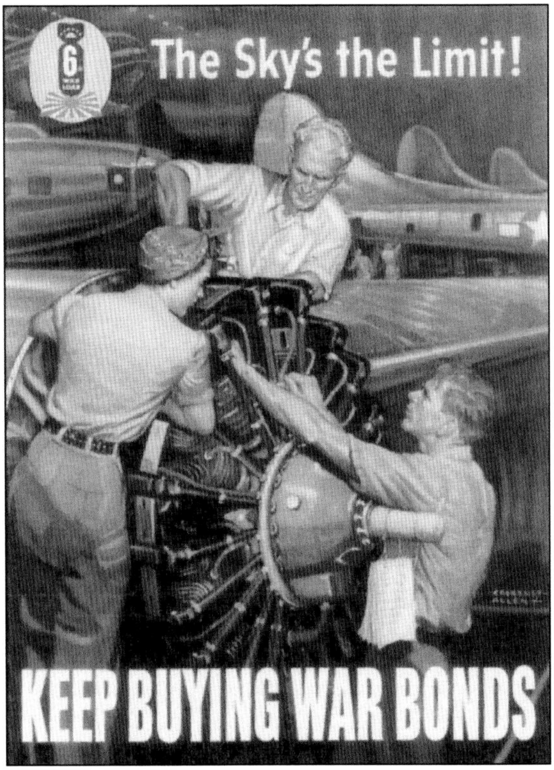


Stanley was the first community in Gaston County to exceed its E Bond quota of $13,000 during the sixth bond drive from November to December 1944. Posters produced by contemporary artists were distributed, urging citizens to buy defense bonds, which paid four percent interest to the buyer. More importantly, they financed the war efforts. Stanley was determined to do its share to speed the day of victorious homecoming for our boys.

During World War II, the nation was required to ration many things, such as food, clothes, and gasoline. Ration books with stamps that were removed when the named item was purchased were issued to each member of every family. There were different stamps for different items, such as sugar or gasoline. No new automobiles were built during the war years because all manufacturing was focused on production of weapons needed for the war effort.

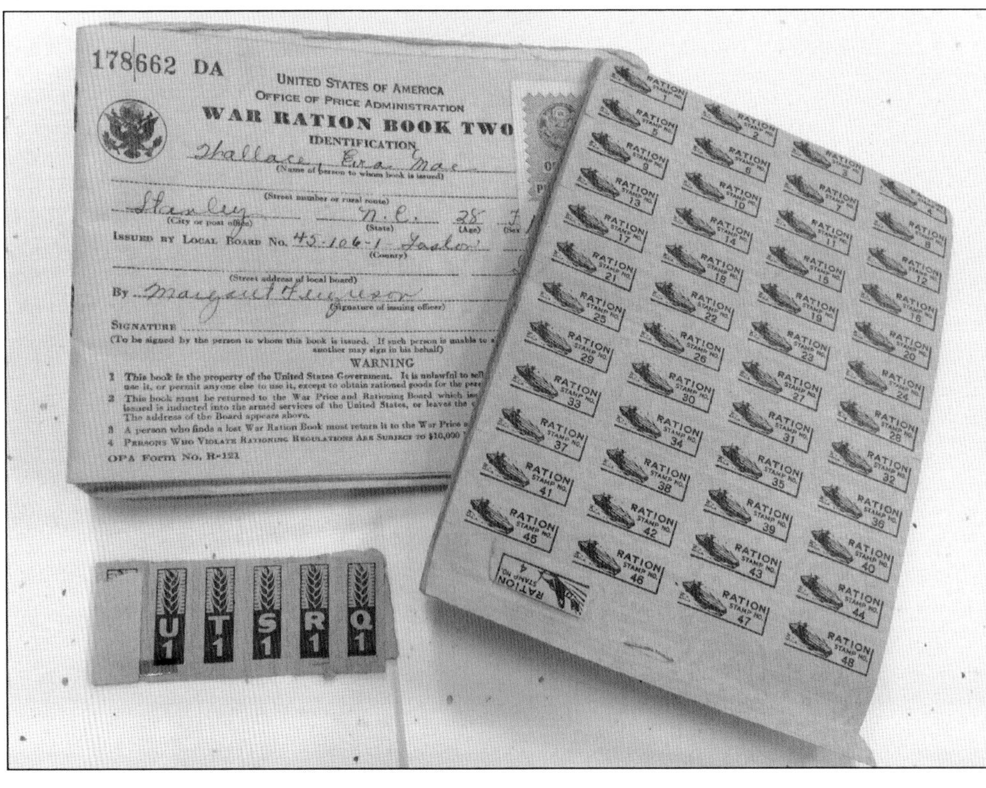

Robert Julius Mauney (right) is a World War II veteran who served with Patton's Third Army as well as with the Seventh, Ninth and Fifteenth Armies in four campaigns in Europe and Africa. Mauney was drafted in 1943 at age 18. He recalls being scared going into France three days after the D-Day invasion and said the company's humor helped minimize their fear. His opinion was that General Patton was the best general in the world. Mauney was never captured but had a number of narrow escapes, having been under fire for 248 days on the front. He learned to judge the distance of incoming artillery by its sound. After leaving the service, he returned home and became a barber (below), a profession he followed for more than 50 years. Over the years, becoming aware of veterans' struggles, Mauney has persisted in contacting any politician he believes could help veterans' rights.

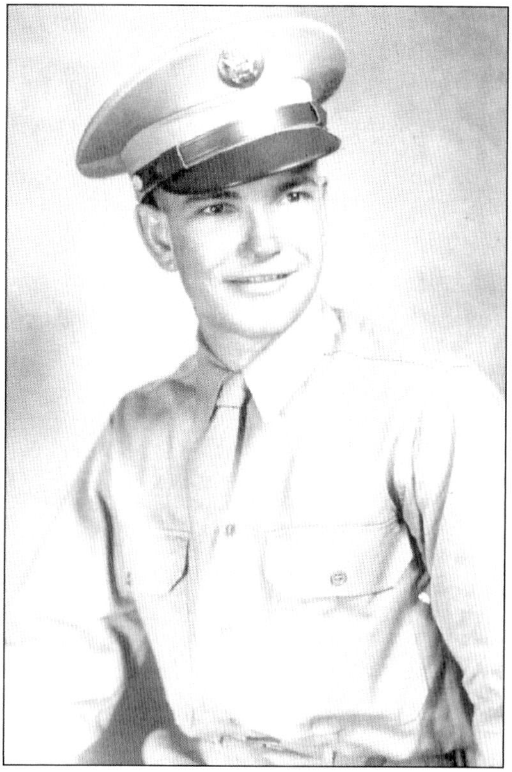

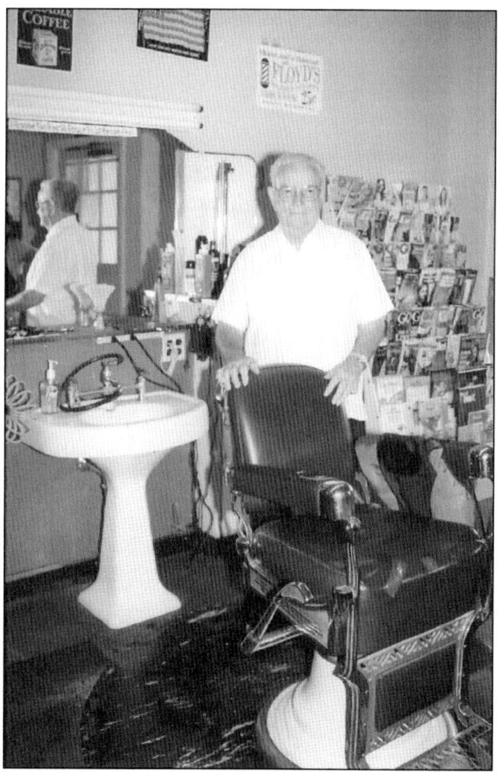

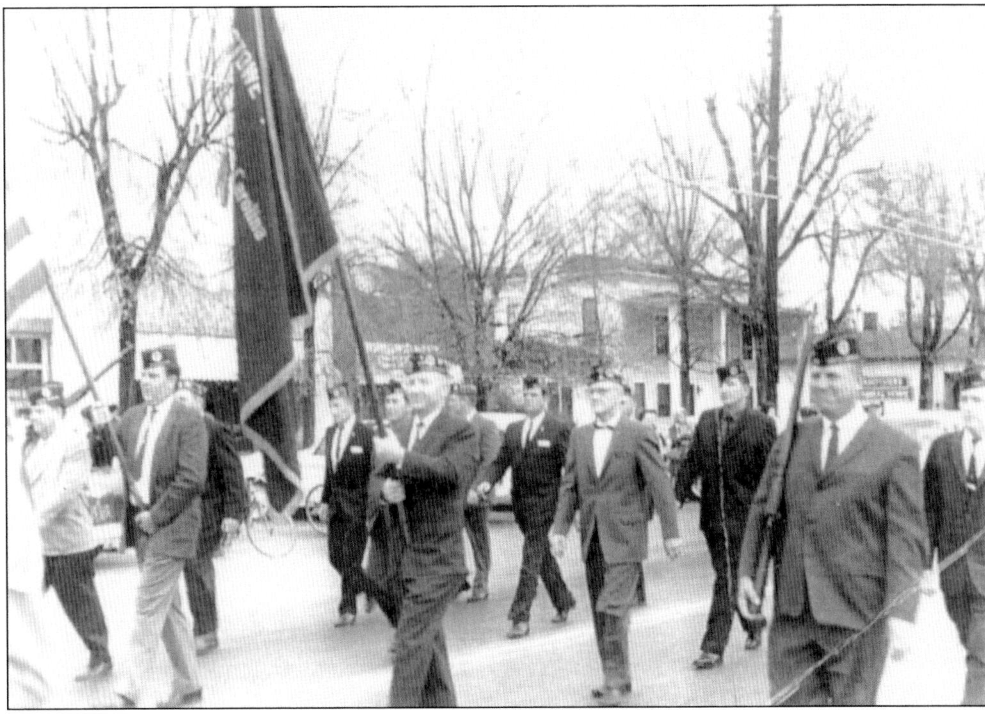

Shown above are members of the Rhyne-Cannon Post 266 American Legion marching in a parade down Main Street to celebrate Veterans Day. The American Legion in Stanley was named to honor two veterans killed in World War II. Shown below are Neil E. Cannon (left) and Jacob Walter Rhyne. Their names were chosen to represent the Legion because Sergeant Cannon was the first soldier from Stanley killed, and PFC Jacob Rhyne was the last. Cannon died on March 30, 1943, in Carthage, Tunisia, North Africa, and is buried there. Private First Class Rhyne was killed on the island of Iwo Jima on February 19, 1945, just before his 21st birthday, and is buried in Hawaii.

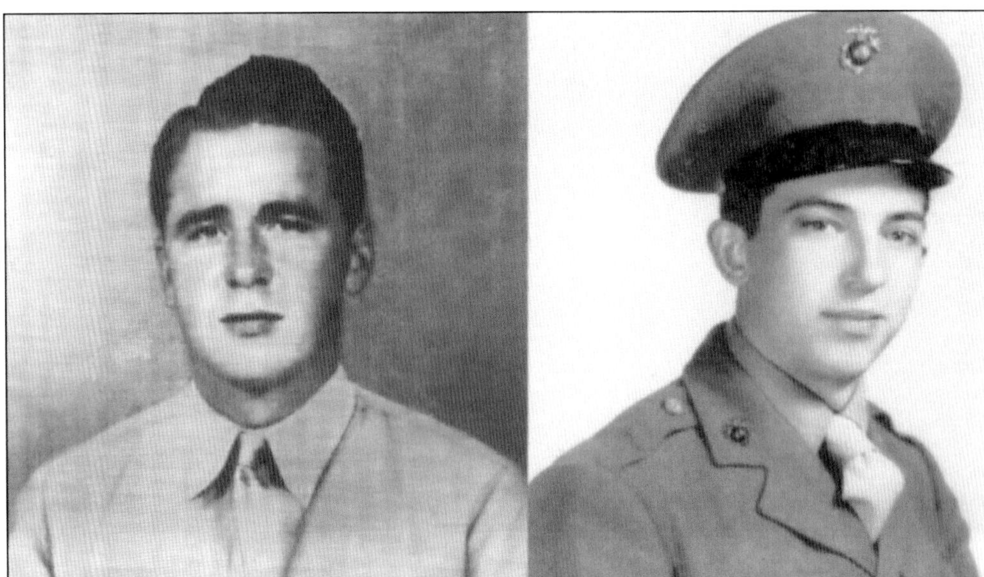

This charming picture shows Lathie Smith, wife of Vernon Homesley, with children Ralph and twins Johnnie and Eloise Homesley. During World War II, Homesley was one of the "War Mothers" who had a flag in her window to indicate the number of sons fighting in the war. Her flag had five stars for sons James, Mack, Johnnie, Jack, and Ralph, who all returned home safely.

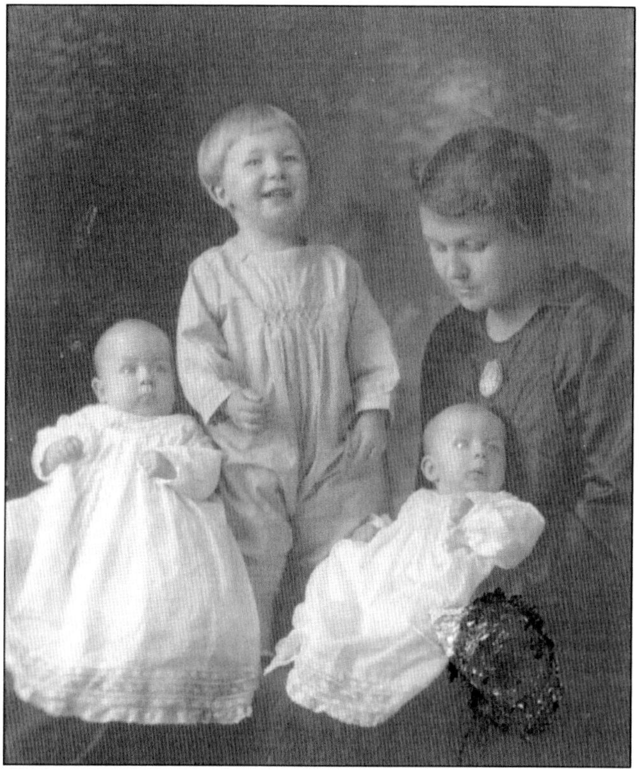

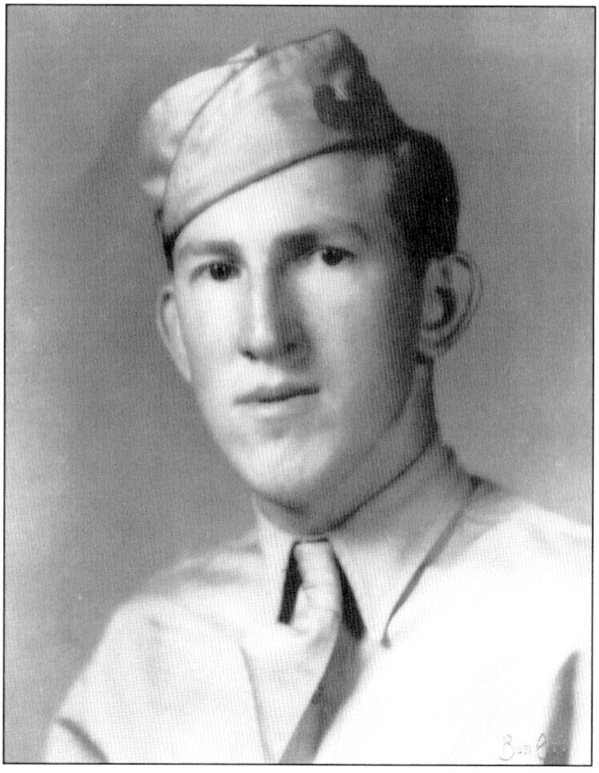

When Grover Farmer went into the Army during World War II, he took with him a daily devotional book given to him by Bruington Memorial Baptist Church. This was a gift to all the Stanley men leaving for war. Private Farmer was killed in action on July 30, 1943, and buried in Gela, Sicily, before his body was exhumed and buried in Long Creek Cemetery in Dallas, North Carolina.

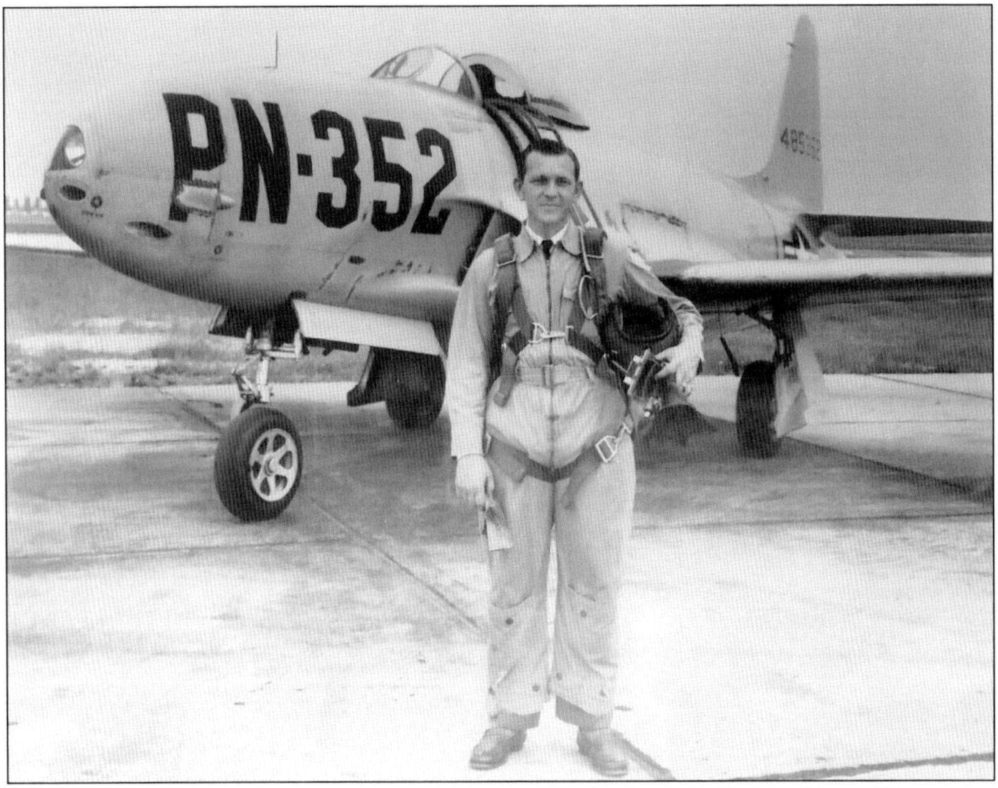


On March 10, 1948, Herbert Henry Hoover was the first civilian pilot to break the sound barrier. Chuck Yeager was the first military pilot to accomplish the feat. Hoover was the son of Benjamin R. Hoover and the stepson of Wixie Rhyne Hoover. He was married to Ruth Rhyne and was the father of Susan and Hank Hoover. Hoover lost his life on August 14, 1952, testing the B-45 bomber.

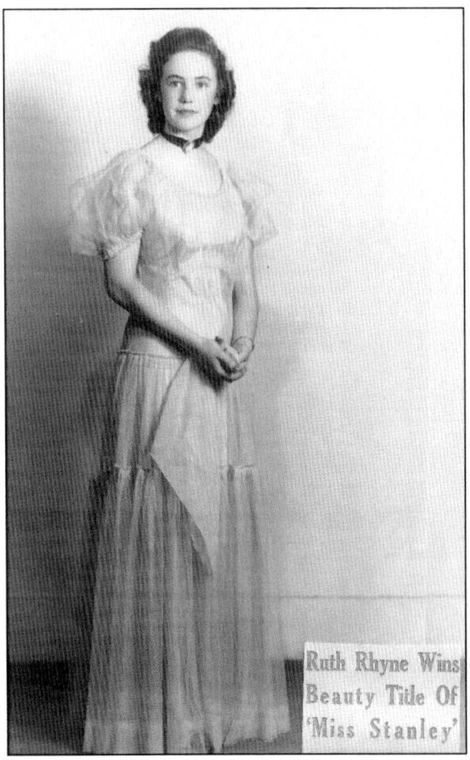


In this photograph from the 1940s, in the evening gown she was wearing when she won the title of Miss Stanley, is Ruth Rhyne, daughter of Richard M. and Edith Rhyne. The beauty pageant was well attended and much enjoyed by folks in the Stanley area. She later married Herbert Henry Hoover, the civilian test pilot.

William Rhyne Hawley enlisted in the US Navy in 1951 during the Korean War, one of the bloodiest wars in history. Hawley was assigned to the USS *Manatee*, a refueling ship. He remembers the ship riding out a major typhoon off the coast of Formosa. Hawley was discharged in 1955 and returned to Stanley and civilian life.

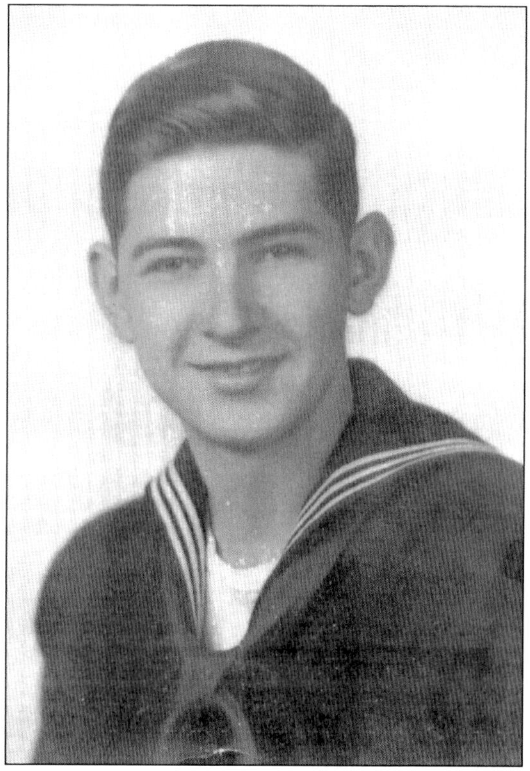

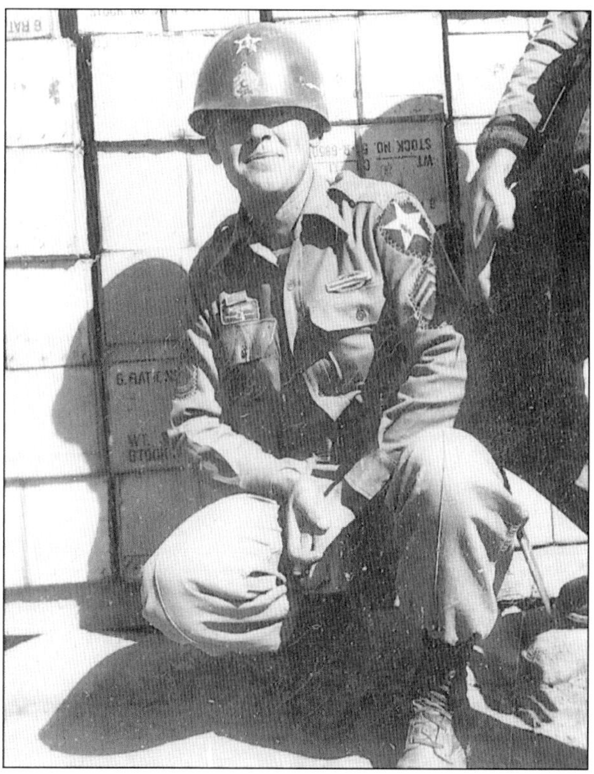

Marvin Jimmie McGinnis served during the Korean War. He was classified as a cook and baker. He earned the Korean Service Medal with three Bronze Service Stars, the United National Service Medal, and the Combat Infantry Badge. McGinnis was not wounded during this conflict and was honorably discharged February 2, 1953.

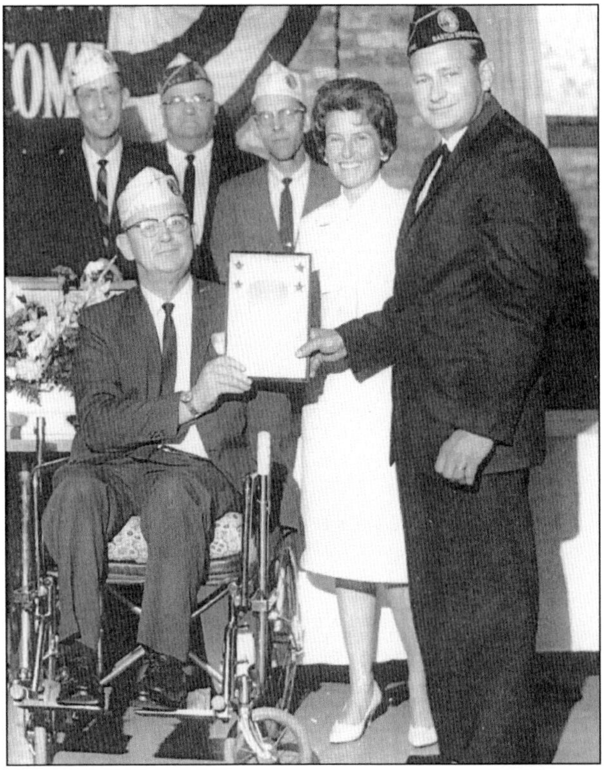

PFC Jack Sipe (right) was with Company A of the 378th Engineer Construction Corps in Korea when he was injured in combat and lost his right leg. He was awarded the Purple Heart. After discharge, he enrolled in the Veterans Vocational Rehab Program. In 1965, he was named Veteran of the Year in North Carolina. Sipe became a skilled electrician and held a top electrician position at Gaston County Dyeing Machine Company.

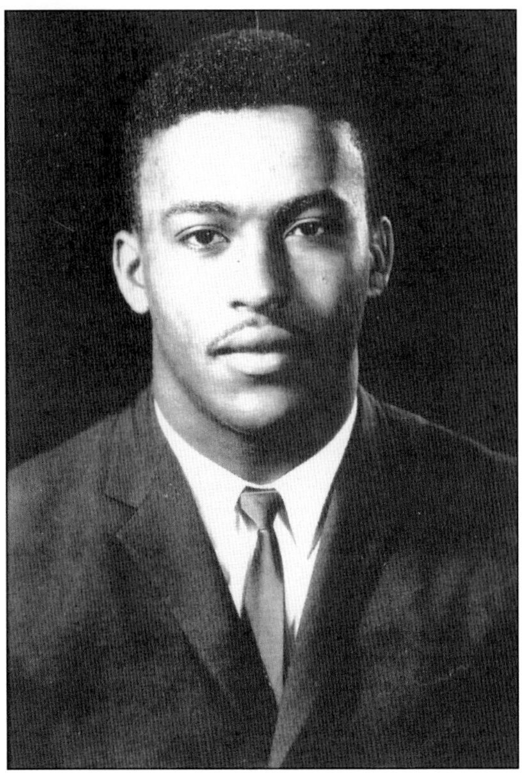

Capt. Earl Carlyle Brown started flying while in Air Force ROTC. After graduation, he joined the Air Force as a pilot during the Vietnam War. His plane was shot down over Laos in 1969, and he and his crew were missing for 26 years. A memorial service was held at Springfield Baptist Church with his wife, Shirley, daughter Olivia, and family. In 1995, the Pentagon confirmed his death, and he was buried at Arlington National Cemetery with full military honors.

Born in 1966, Phillip McCorkle, son of Thomas Barber McCorkle and Barbara Cassels McCorkle, served as a US Marine during Operation Desert Storm. He was married to Iris Froneberger, who passed away on January 20, 2014. They were the parents of daughters Jasmia and Jessica and son Nolan.

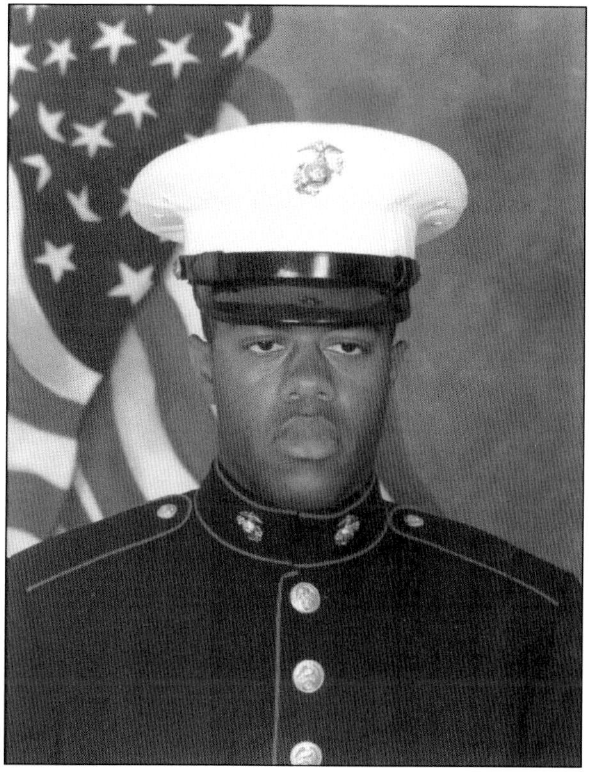

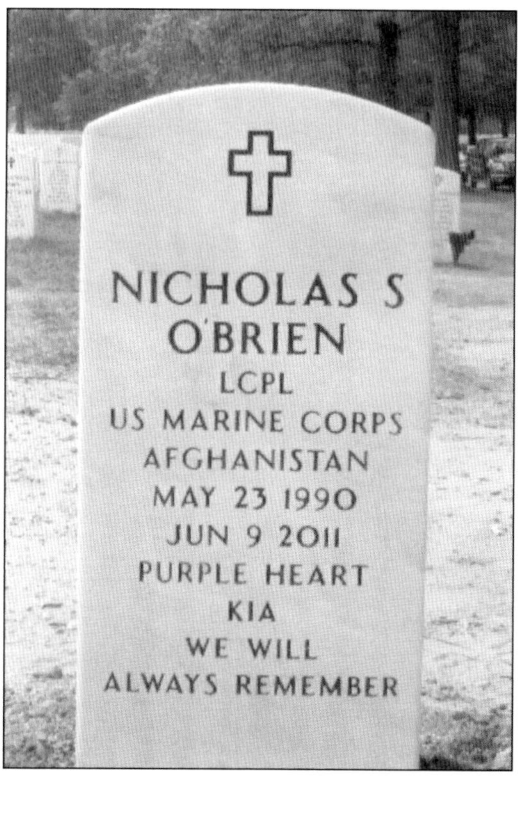


Lance Corporal Nicholas S. O'Brien was determined to follow in his father's footsteps to become a Marine. He refused to be deterred from joining the armed forces and became an honor graduate and a top shooter in his platoon. He was conducting combat operations when a roadside bomb exploded, taking his life in Helmand Province, Afghanistan, on June 9, 2011. O'Brien was buried in Arlington National Cemetery.

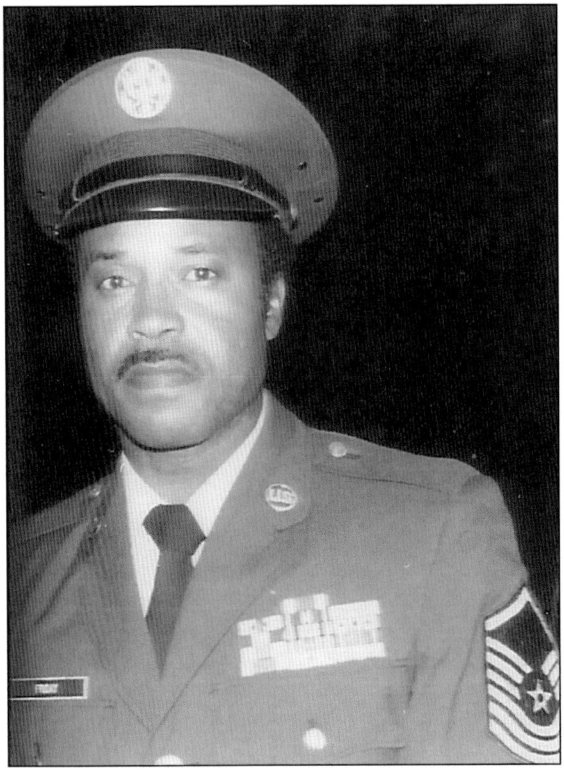

SMSgt. Gene A. Friday, son of William A. and Marjorie Friday of Stanley, served 28 years with the US Air Force as a communications–computer systems superintendent. Among his medals, he received a Republic of Vietnam Gallantry Cross and Republic of Vietnam Campaign Medal. He married Laverne Bannister and raised three sons and a daughter.

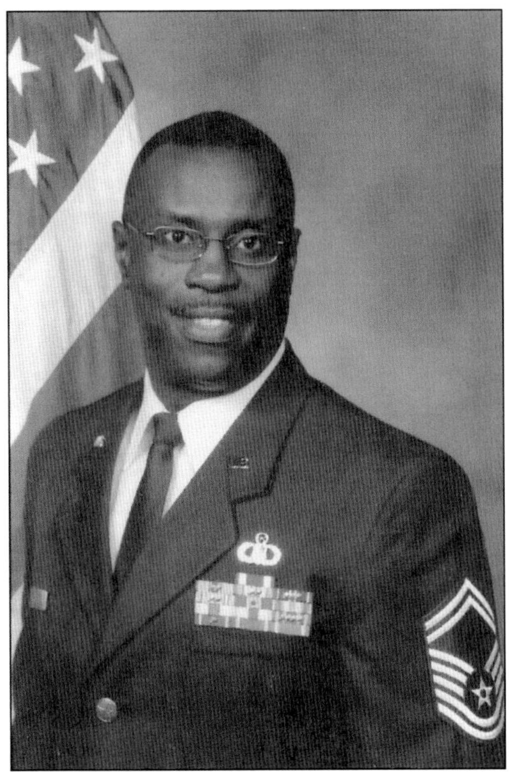

On March 31, 2006, a retirement ceremony was held at Elgin Air Force Base to honor the meritorious service of SMSgt. Jeffery E. Friday after 26 years of distinguished service in the armed forces.

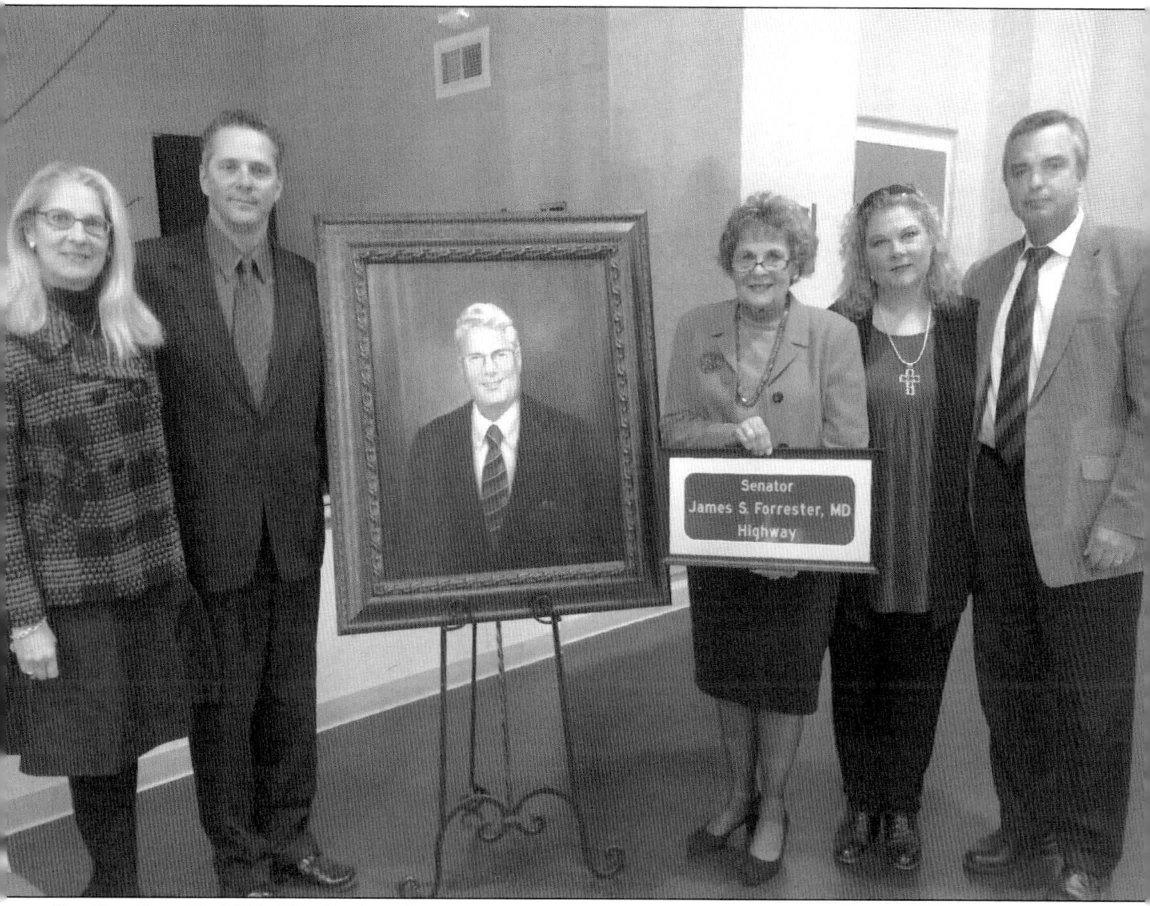


On October 30, 2015, North Carolina transportation secretary Nick Tennyson dedicated a five-mile span of North Carolina Highway 27 in honor of Sen. James Summers Forrester, MD. Pictured from left to right are Wynn Forrester Maxwell; James Summers Forrester Jr., MD; Mary Frances All Forrester; Mary Paige Forrester; and her husband, Tom Blalock. Forrester was born in Aberdeen, Scotland, educated in North Carolina, and practiced medicine from 1963 to 2010 in Stanley. He served as a deacon of the First Baptist Church. During the Vietnam War, Forrester was chief flight surgeon in the Air National Guard, participating in the air evacuation in Vietnam, and was a recipient of the Legion of Merit Award. At his retirement, he held the rank of brigadier general. Forrester reactivated in 1990 during the first Gulf War. He was a Gaston County commissioner from 1982 until 1990 and was serving his 11th term in the North Carolina Senate when he died in 2011. He was buried in Arlington National Cemetery. Among numerous other awards, he received the Order of the Long Leaf Pine.

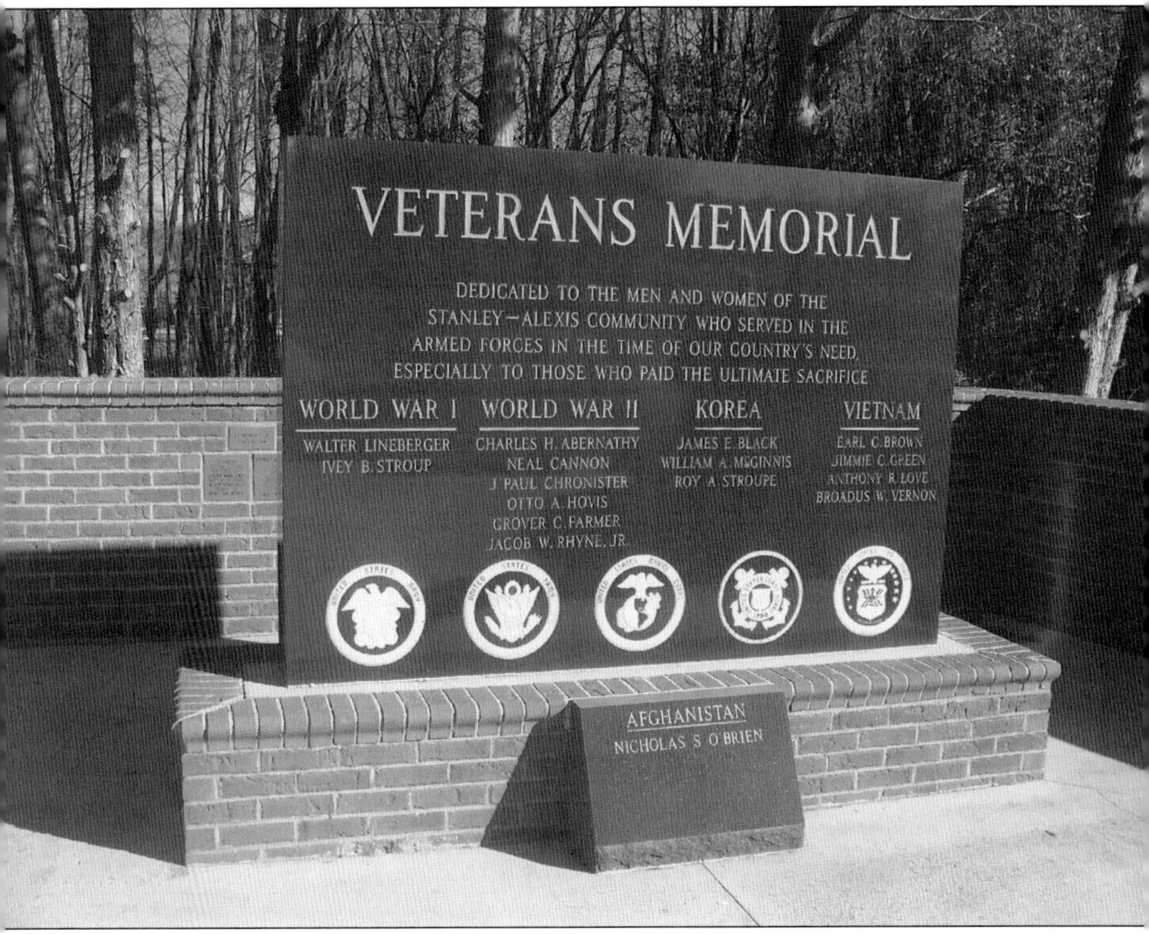


In recognition of Stanley's new veterans' monument, a dedication ceremony took place on May 23, 1998, (Memorial Day), with Congresswoman Sue Myrick, state senator James Forrester, Mayor Harold Jones, the Stanley Middle School Band, the First Baptist Church Senior Choir, the US Marine ROTC unit from East Gaston High School, the American Legion Sons of the Legion Unit 266 Honor Guard, and others. Also, three mothers of Vietnam War veterans placed flowers on the monument base.

*Five*

# SCHOOLS AND SPORTS

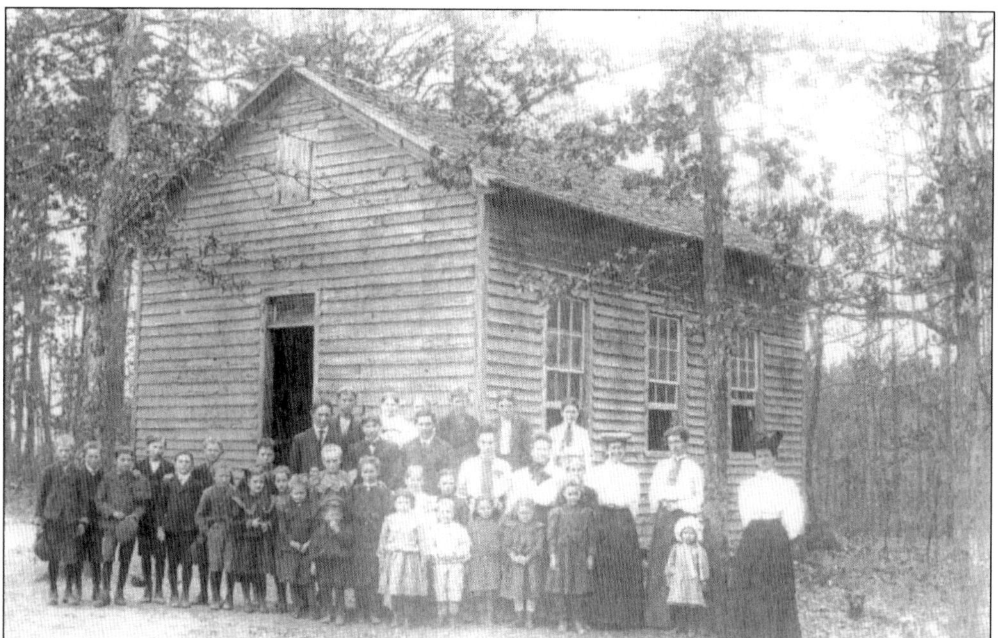

In years past, many school buildings served dual purposes. Classes were held there on weekdays, and church on Sundays, which may have been the case with this school building. These children of various ages are shown with their teacher, Katherine "Tat" Derr, who taught all grades in this one-room schoolhouse. This building is believed to have been located near the Derr home on East Chestnut Street.

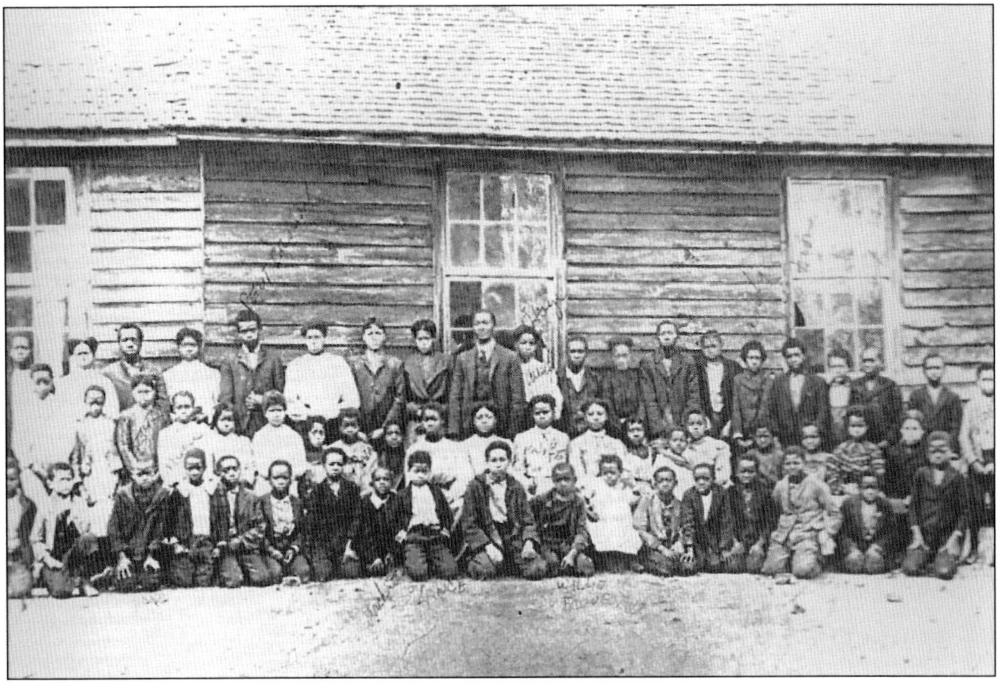

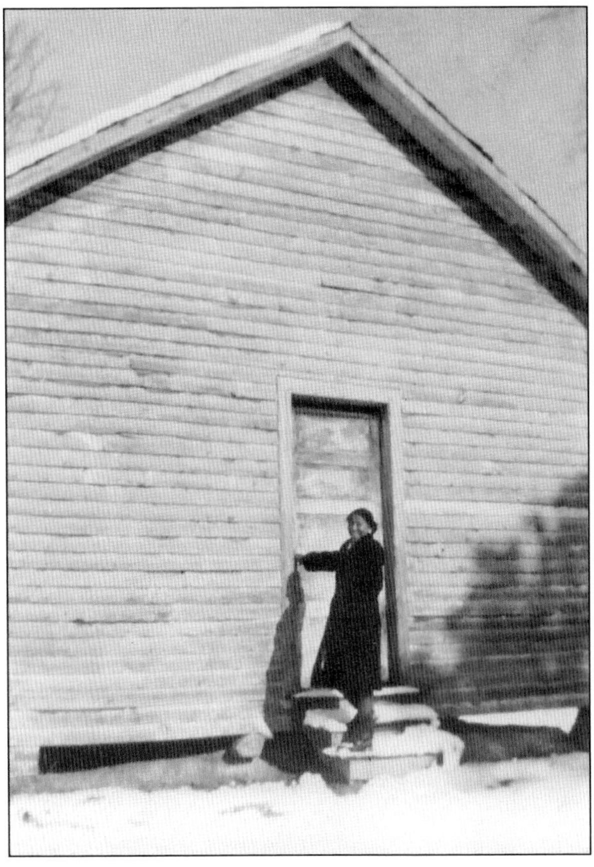

A recorded deed indicates Will Derr, Rufus Friday, and Abram McDowell purchased land in 1879 on which to build Springfield School. A building was constructed by the members of Springfield Baptist Church and the surrounding community. In 1881, numbers and boundaries were designated for all area schools, and Springfield School was given the no. 9. This photograph was taken around 1900. (Courtesy of Lois Brown Barnett.)

The Luckey School was built in 1907 on the property of Miles and Daisy Luckey on the Alexis-Lucia Road. One of their daughters is shown on the front steps. This school was for black children during segregation, and all ages were taught in one room. The Luckey School closed in 1940; after that, black children attended Springfield School in the town of Stanley until integration in the 1960s.

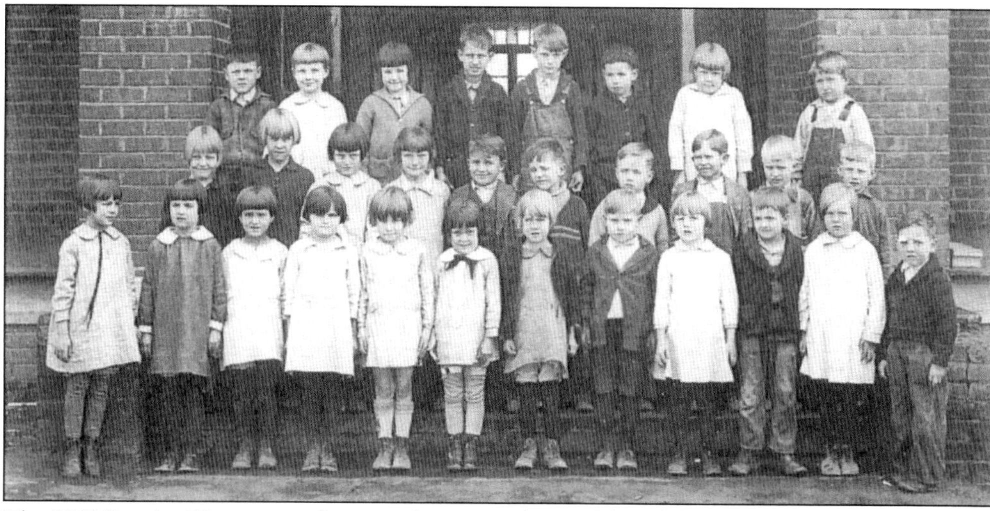

The 1926 Stanley Elementary class seen here is made up of, from left to right, (first row) Catherine Morris, Vlada Morris, Lucille Hawley, unidentified, Edith Whitley, Evelyn Hager, Bonnie Buchanan, Jake McGinnis, Althia Smith, Hall Morris, unidentified, and Jack Morris; (second row) Helen Lowe, Ruth Lewis, Laura Jane Cloninger, Catherine Spargo, J.T. Hovis, Earl Drew, Billie Moore, Floyd Medlin, Frank Hager, and Marvin Helms; (third row) Bill Grice, Sarah Taylor, Helen Rhyne, unidentified, George Summey, Sam Bentley, Alma Hester, and William McCorkle.

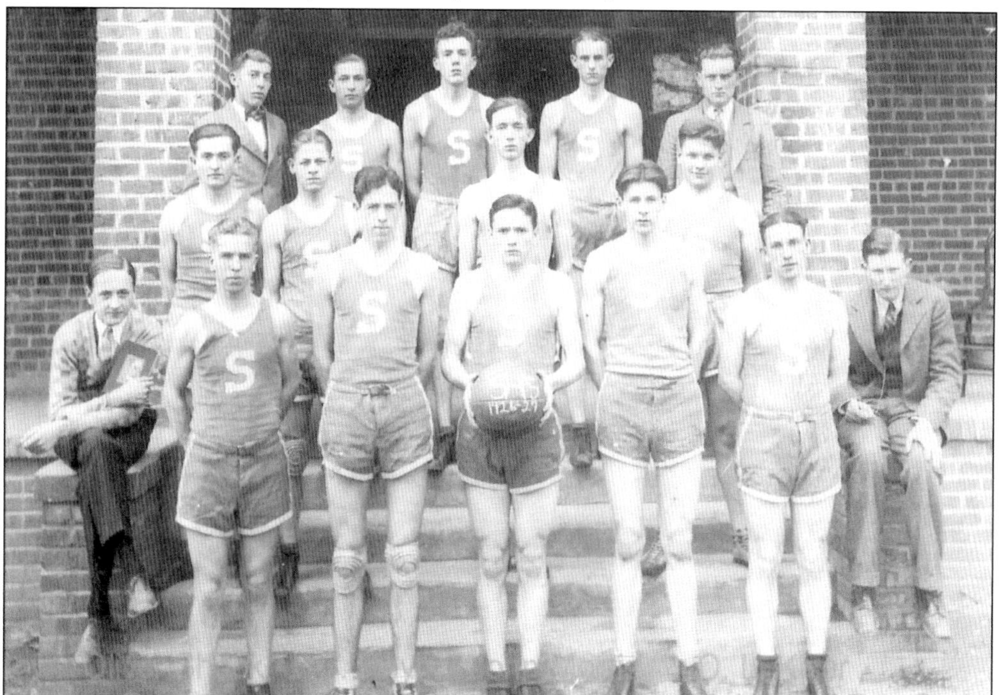

This photograph shows the 1926–1927 basketball team from Stanley High School; from left to right are (first row) Carlyle Rutledge (scorekeeper), Merton Robinson, Johnnie Dawkins, Gary Triplett (captain), Graham Abernathy, Boyce Groves, and Henry Mack Dellinger (timekeeper); (second row) Pugh Abernathy, Fred Clemmer, Edgar McKelvey, and Ray Craig, (third row), Oliver Shook, J.B. Rhyne, John Morris, unidentified, and Oscar L. Kiser.

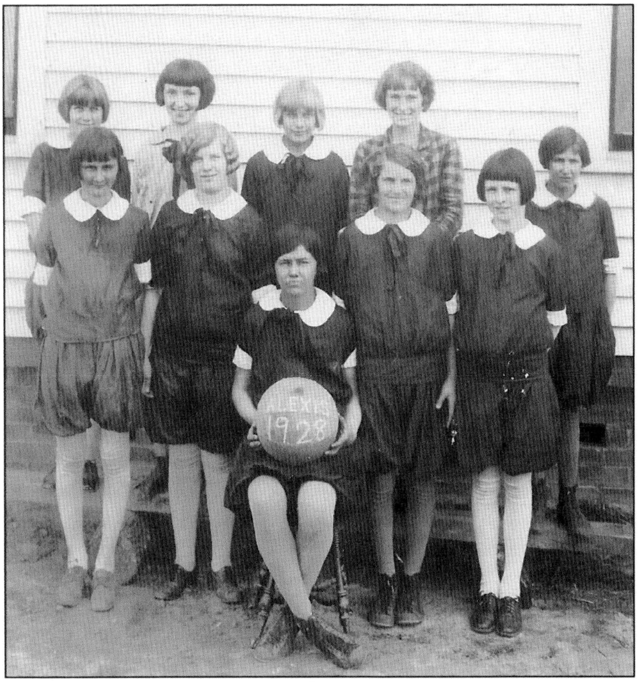


In this photograph is the 1928 girls' basketball team standing in front of the Alexis School. From left to right are (first row) Bessie Sherrill, Helen Abernathy, Grace Garrison (seated), Valda Garrison, and Ruth Abernathy; (second row) Edith Abernathy, Maude Hovis, Edith Sadler, Gertie Hovis, and Leona Hovis. These girls are fashionably dressed in their bloomer uniforms with the Peter Pan collars.

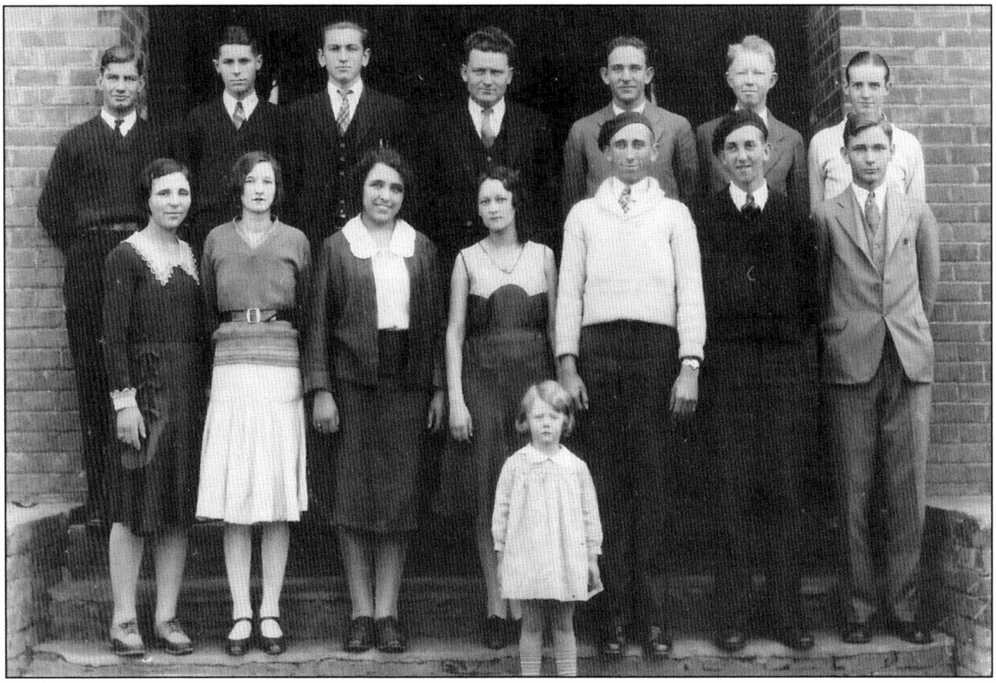

In this photograph of the Stanley High School graduating class of 1931, the child in front is unidentified, but the rest are, from left to right, (first row) Betty Abernethy Smith, Idell Spargo, Lucille Boyd, Margie Whisnant Clemmer, J.B. Rhyne, Augustus Black, and Oscar Moore; (second row) John Hall, David Hovis, T. Alfred Lineberger, Oscar L. Kiser (superintendent), Charles Parlier (principal), Henry Stroupe, and James McKeown. Kiser retired in 1967 after a long, distinguished career.

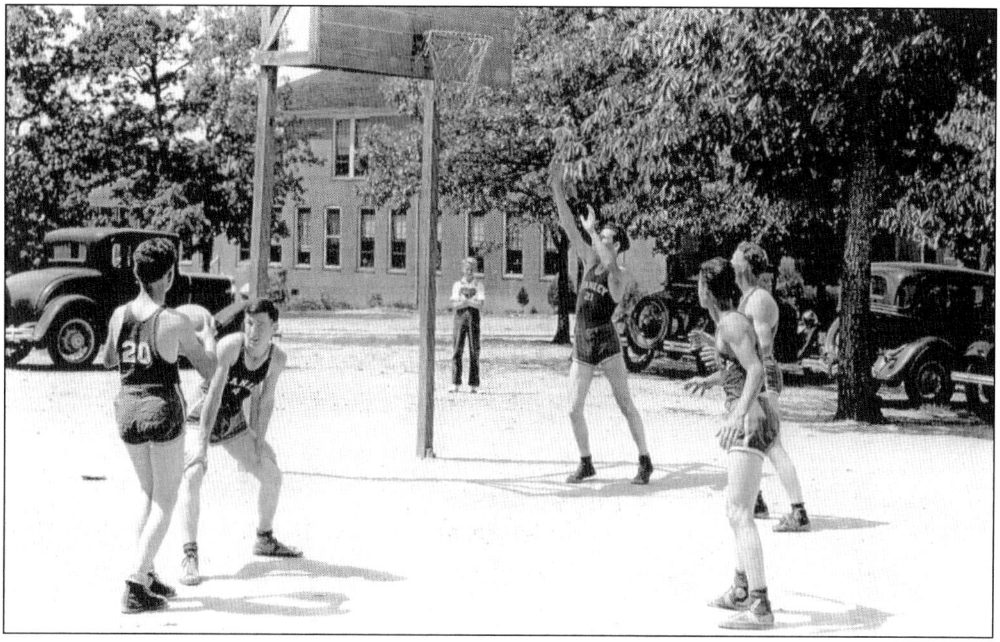

This group of basketball players appear not to mind the dirt court as they practice for an upcoming game around 1936. The automobile on the left is thought to have belonged to the basketball coach, Wales Sigmon. Interest in sports continues to be a tradition with the people of Stanley. Players are, from left to right, Jack Morris, Paul Hamilton, Lloyd Long, Winfred Webb, and Robert Craig. The child watching in the background is Ned Cannon.

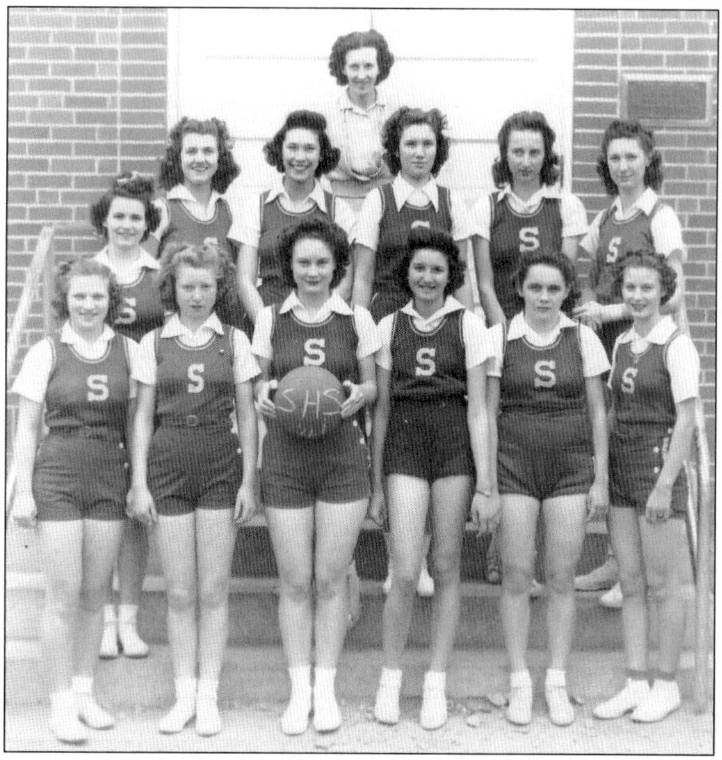



In this photograph of the 1941 Stanley High School girls' basketball team are, from left to right, (first row) Ellen Lineberger, Elsie Lutz, Margaret Cloninger, Betty Handsel, Merle Bentley, and Sarah Helms; (second row), Lucille Hovis, Martha Smith, Martha Dean Ballard, Ruth Hammack, Lois Stone, and Ada "Nez" Dellinger; (third row) Fannie Carpenter Kiser (coach). In the 1940s, the girls' basketball teams had six players and played half-court games. No one could cross the mid-court line, and players were limited to two dribbles.

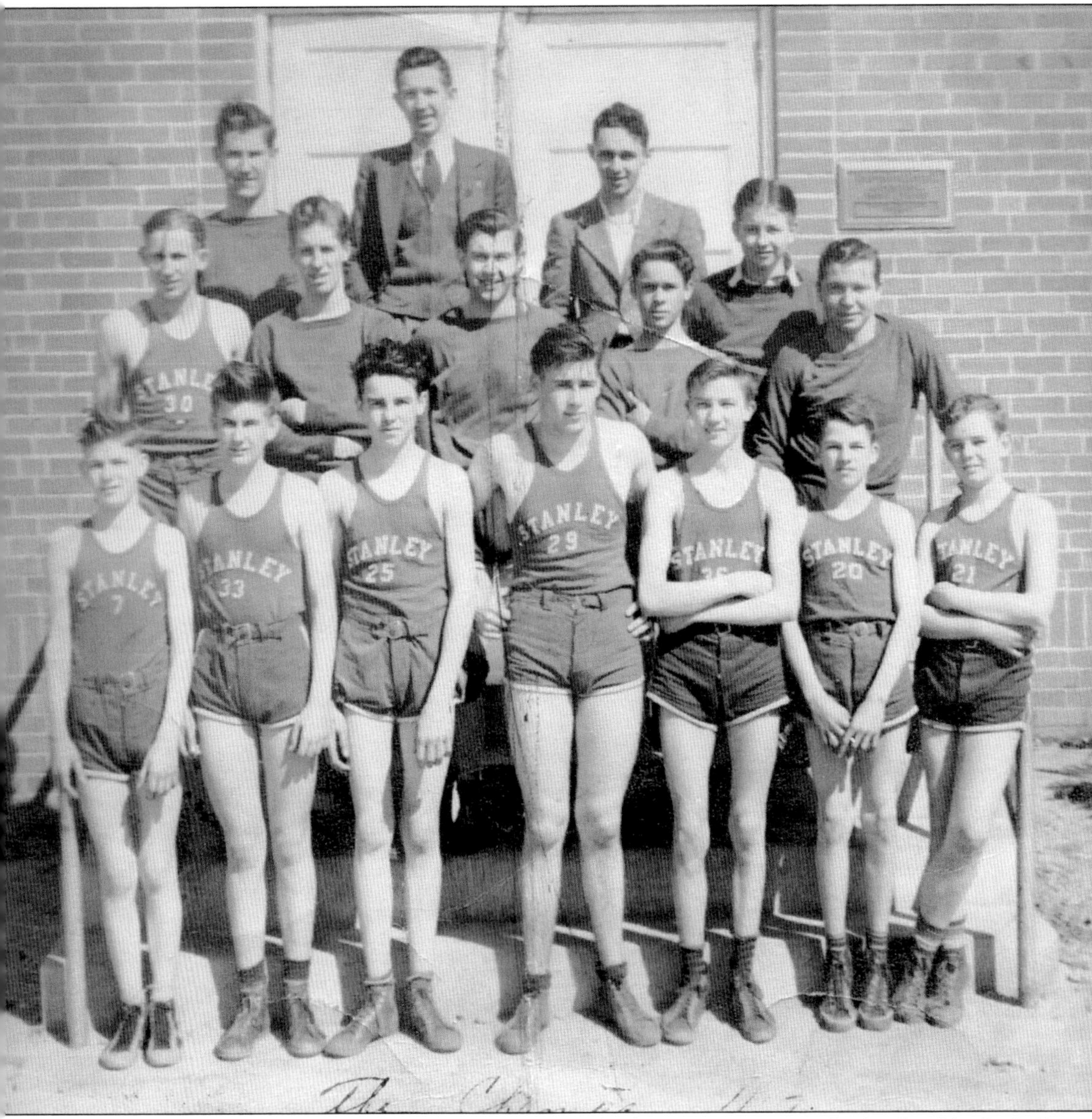

In 1942, the Stanley High School Blue Birds were the first Gaston County high school basketball team to win a state championship. The team had not lost since 1938 and won five straight Little Seven Conference titles. No player was over six feet tall. Coach Wales Sigmon built on speed and defense. From left to right are (first row) Mack Homesley, Spencer Shelton, Louie Abernathy, Bill Smith, Jack Homesley, Clarence Clemmer, and Bob Withers; (second row) Harry Sadler, Yates Craig, Jack Cannon, George Moore, and Lloyd "Fuzzy" Brown; (third row) David Long, James Stroupe (coach), Jack Bentley, and Herbert Cannon.

Remembered as being very kind to all the schoolchildren, Tom Rozzelle was the janitor at Stanley schools in the 1940s. Rozzelle has descendants living in the area. The school bus is from the early 1940s; in those days, buses were only for children who lived outside the city limits. Early buses were cold, and the country roads were muddy, making for some uncomfortable travel.

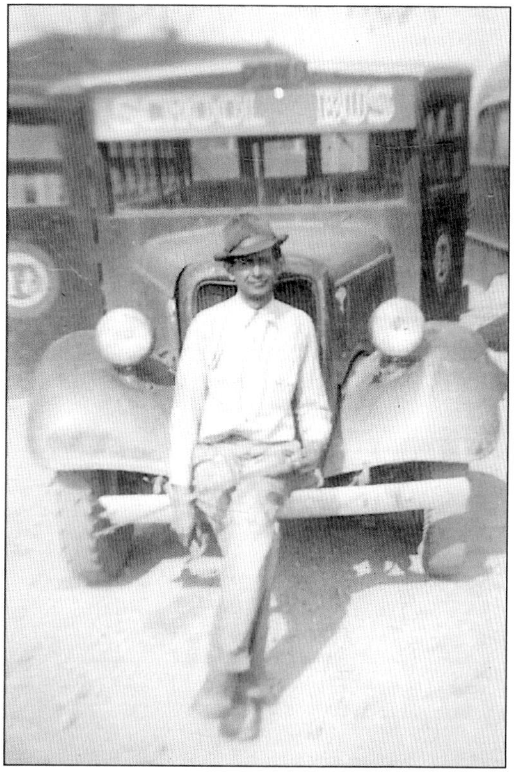


Ersie Stroupe's third- and fourth-grade (1943–1944) flute band includes, from left to right, (first row) Velva Dean Payne, Christine Whitley, Libby Stroupe, Celestine Helton, Lewis Armstrong, Daphne Stroupe, and Carolyn Moore; (second row) Doris Powell, LaVonne Stroupe, Joyce Armstrong, Don Bynum, Ovelia Armstrong, and Shirley Frasheur; (third row) Andy Murphy, Reuben Fisher, Bill Cope, Doris Hoover, Inez Kiser, Shirley Smith, and Joyce Helderman; (fourth row) Bobby Rudisill, Owen Chronister, Freeman Tate, Richard Wallace, Ralph Handsel Jr., Virgil Whitley, and Curtis Clippard.

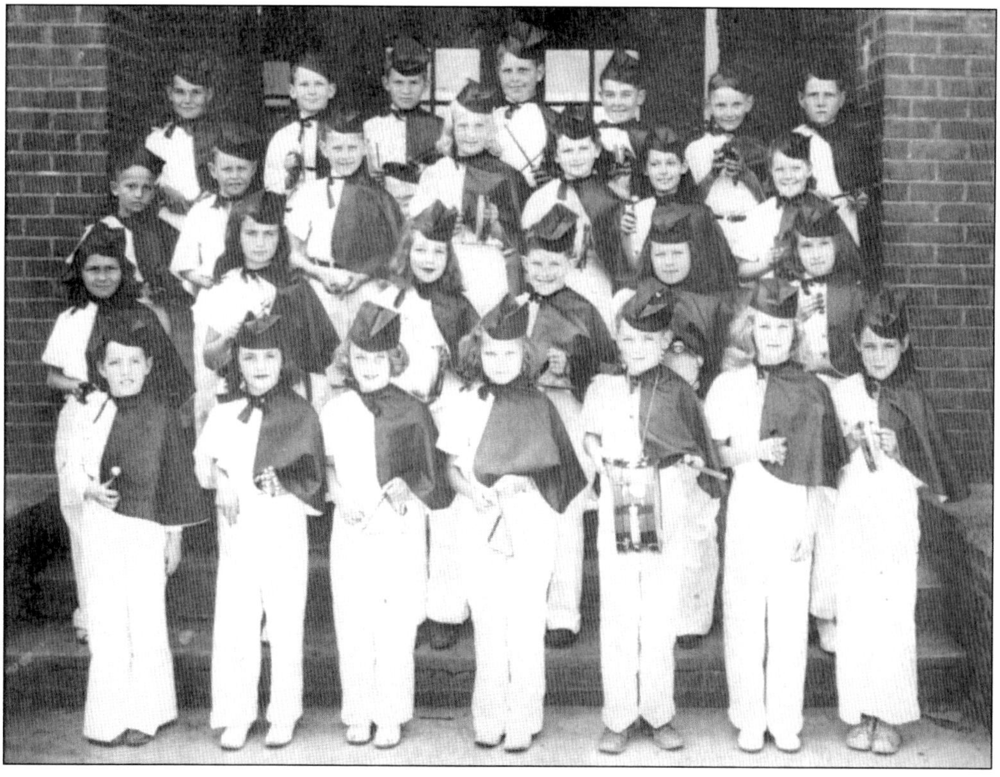

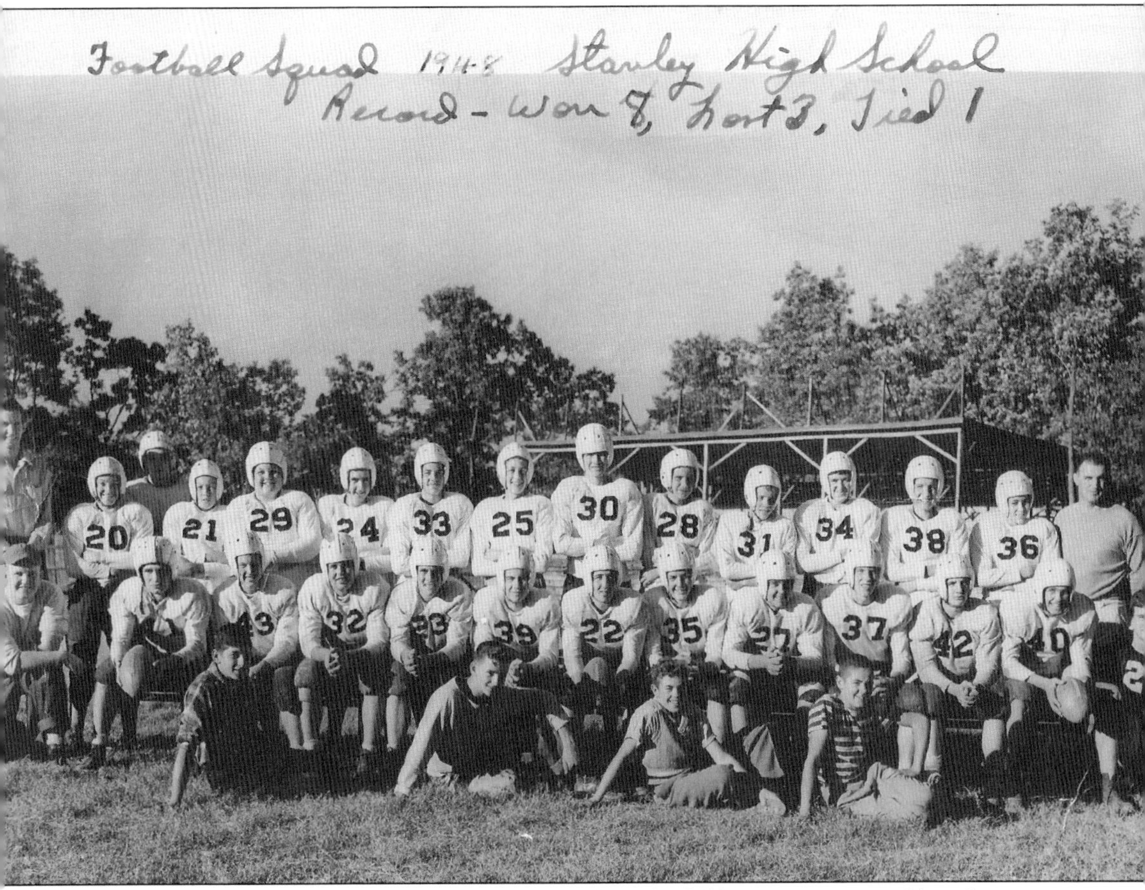


The first Stanley High School football team took to the field in 1948 in second-hand equipment, but with a first-rate coach and players. Assistants William B. Smith and James Caliendo named the team the Blue Devils. From left to right are (first row) managers Bill Hawley, Virgil Whitley, Lewis Armstrong, and Willie Handsel; (second row) Bob White (assistant), Bill Pucket, Wayne Wallace, Ray Connor, LaVon Abernathy, Jack Clippard, Archie Small, Riley Skidmore, Ralph Handsel, Joe Saunders, Ralph Smith, Jack Hinkle, and Neb Hollis (assistant); (third row) James V. "Poke" Stroupe, Dean Brooks, Alfred Homesley, Don Mauney, Franklin Laughter, Archie Huskins, Bob Smith, James Lingerfelt, Owen Chronister, Ralph Webb, Ray Freeman, Bill Rowland, Darrell Hoover, Buddy Moore, and Richard M. Thompson (coach).

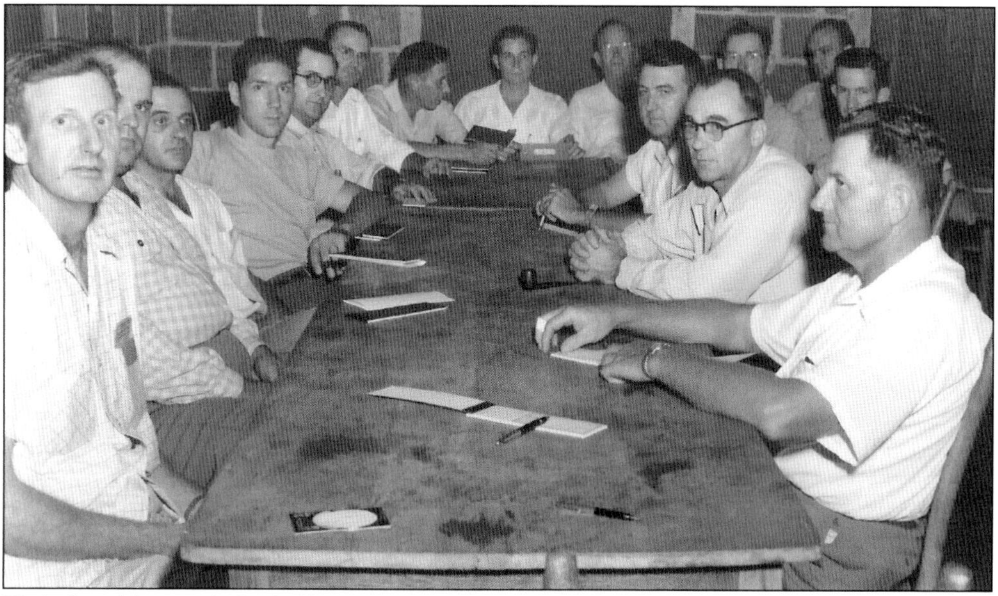

With the addition of a football team, it was determined that an upgrade was needed for the school sports program. The Stanley Athletic Committee was formed by local citizens to support the needs of the teams. From left to right are Stewart Dellinger, Lewis Ballard, George Derr, Don Markwalder, Berry J. Cauble, Jim Whitley, Harry Moore, Jacob McGinnis, Archie Saunders, William Hazel McGinnis, Taylor Moser, James V. "Poke" Stroupe, William B. Smith, John Fonville, and Oscar L. Kiser.

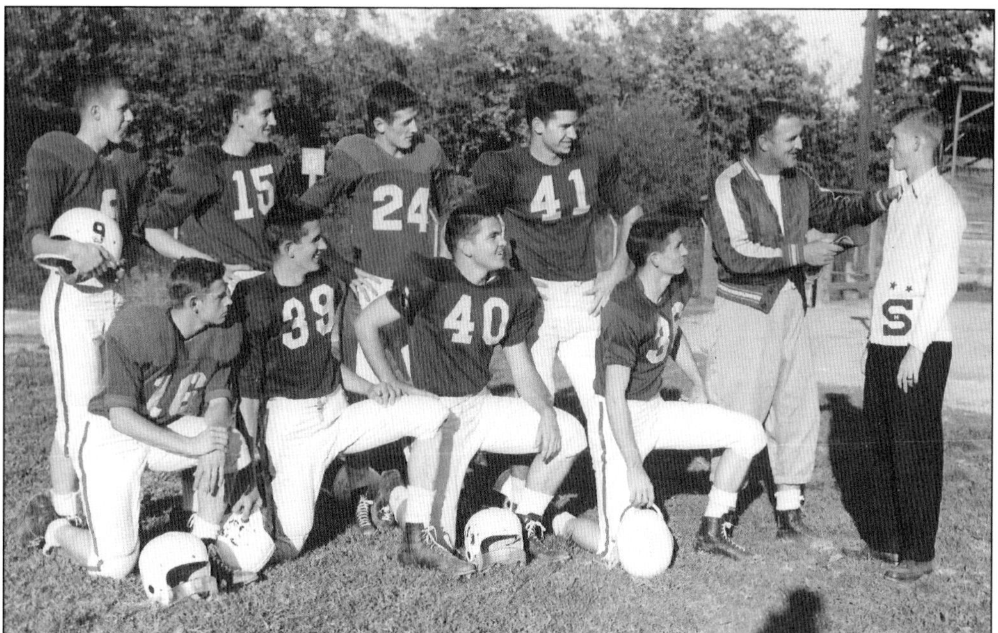

Richard M. Thompson, who grew up in Mount Holly, came to Stanley as the football coach in 1948. He coached football, baseball, and track at Stanley High School. Thompson was named Stanley's Man of the Year in 1967. Citizens presented him with a new car in appreciation of his efforts with the youth. In 1973, he was admitted to the Gaston County Sports Hall of Fame.

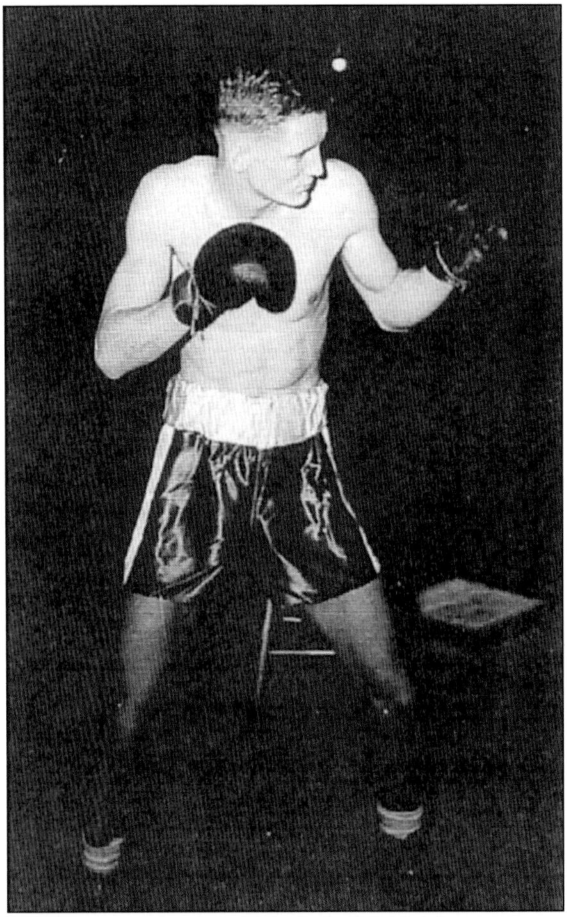

As early as the 1920s, young Stanley men such as Frederick Wellington Thompson (left) and Walter "Iron Jaw" Bailey were boxing contenders. Boxing matches were the highlight of entertainment all over the country during the 1950s, and local newspapers at the time reported on boxing bouts. Boxing was also a sport at Stanley schools during that period. Pictured below is the school boxing team of 1949–1950.

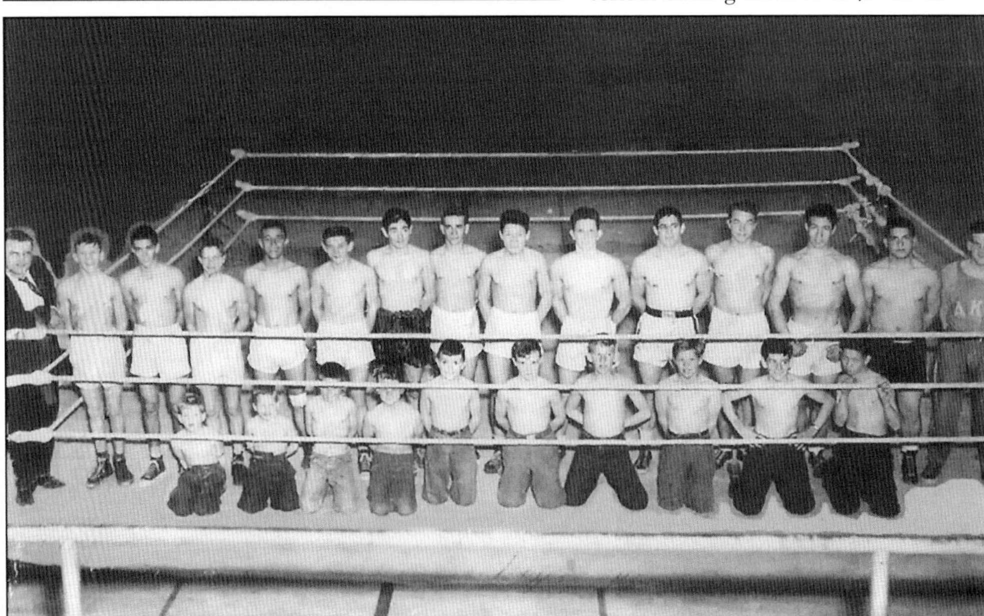

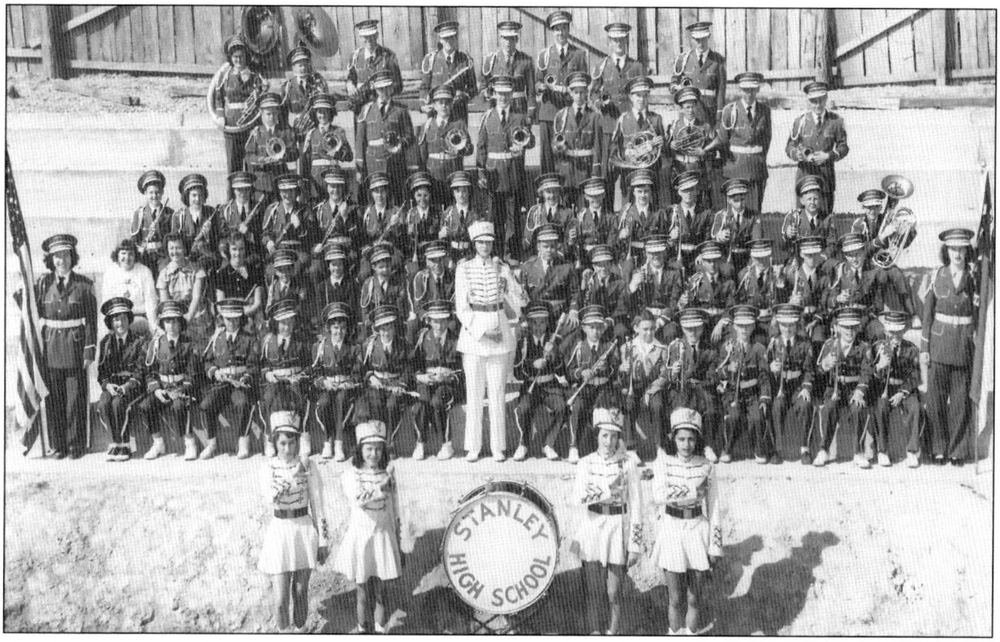


Stanley was justifiably very proud of its brand new 1952 high school marching band, which was sponsored by the Stanley PTA, with Stewart Dellinger as the band's chairman. This program gave all children an opportunity to have a music education. Michael Wise was the band director, and Betty Abernethy was the drum major. Majorettes were, from left to right, Shirley Payne, Marcia Martin, Marilyn Wallace, and Marles Shook.

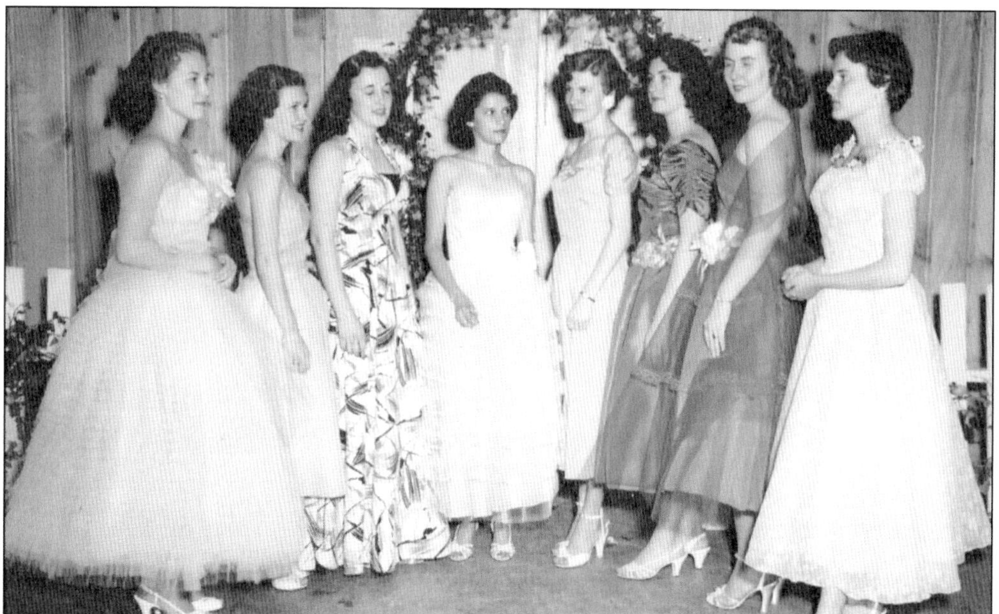

The junior-senior high school prom was anxiously awaited by teens each year. In 1955, these lovely young ladies dressed up for the banquet are, from left to right, Ann Reid, Libby Moore, Kay Fonville, Marilyn Wallace, Shirley Morris, Doris Ann Flowers, Carolyn Caldwell, and Moonyene Funderburk. (Courtesy of Bob Rowland.)

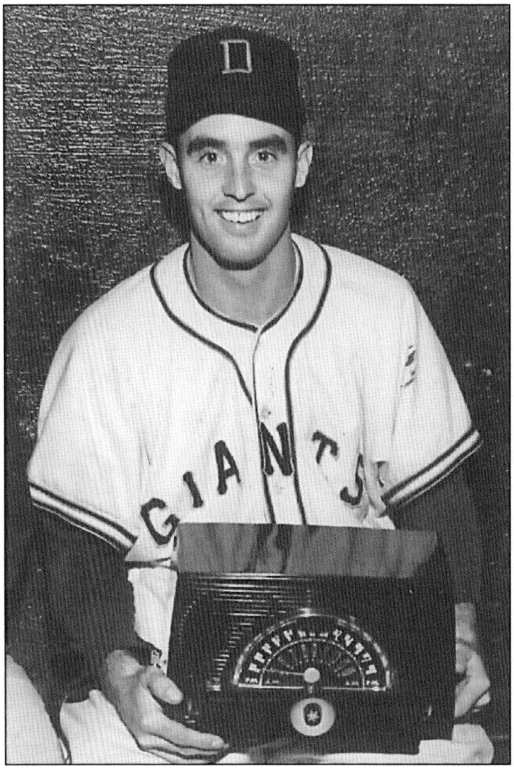


Bobby Elliott Caldwell played all sports at Stanley High School. After school, he signed with the Lincolnton Cardinals, a minor league affiliate of the New York Giants. His team, while at spring training, was chosen to be in the movie *Big Leaguer.* The main actors were Edward G. Robinson and Vera Ellen. Caldwell had a speaking part, exciting his friends back home in Stanley.

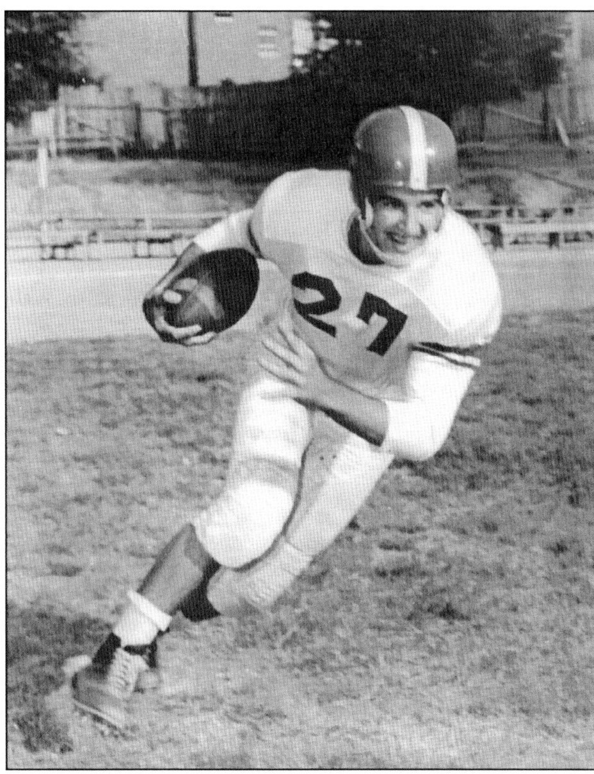


Ask any sports-minded person from Stanley, "Who is the best football player from your town?" and, without hesitation, the answer comes, "No question, Charlie Handsel!" Handsel was said to be the "stuff of which legends are made," and he performed up to that standard. Handsel made football history by completing the 100-yard dash within 10 seconds in full equipment and setting a number of other records. His team won the state championship in 1955. Today, he remains the only Stanley High School player to ever participate in a Shrine Bowl game.

Baseball was always a popular sport in Stanley. Ted Wade Abernathy (right) became a Major League relief pitcher, playing with the Washington Senators, Cleveland Indians, Chicago Cubs, Atlanta Braves, Cincinnati Reds, St. Louis Cardinals, and Kansas City Royals. He married Margie Clemmer and returned to Gaston County, where he was active in many organizations. The Stanley High School baseball team in the photograph below includes, from left to right, (first row) Bill Hawley, Lavon Abernathy, Jack Hinkle, Virgil Whitley, and Bill Rowland; (second row) Charlie Brooks, Billy Jack Groves, Boyce Hester, Charles Stephens, and Tommy Cannon; (third row) Ted Abernathy, Ted Garner, Joe Saunders, and Bill Puckett.

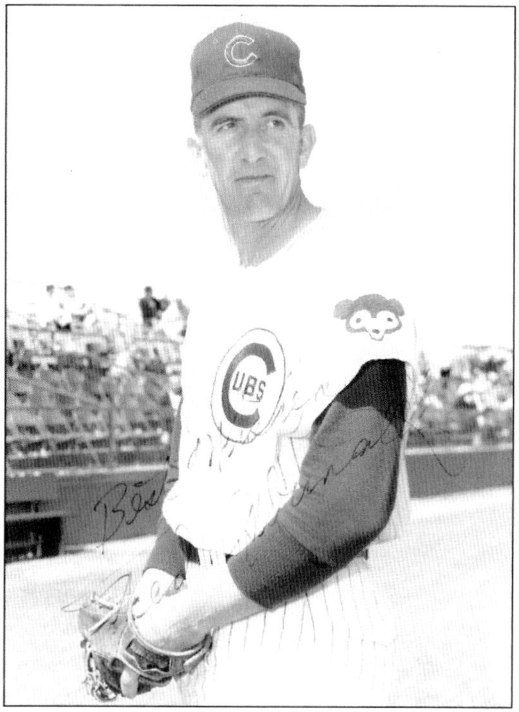


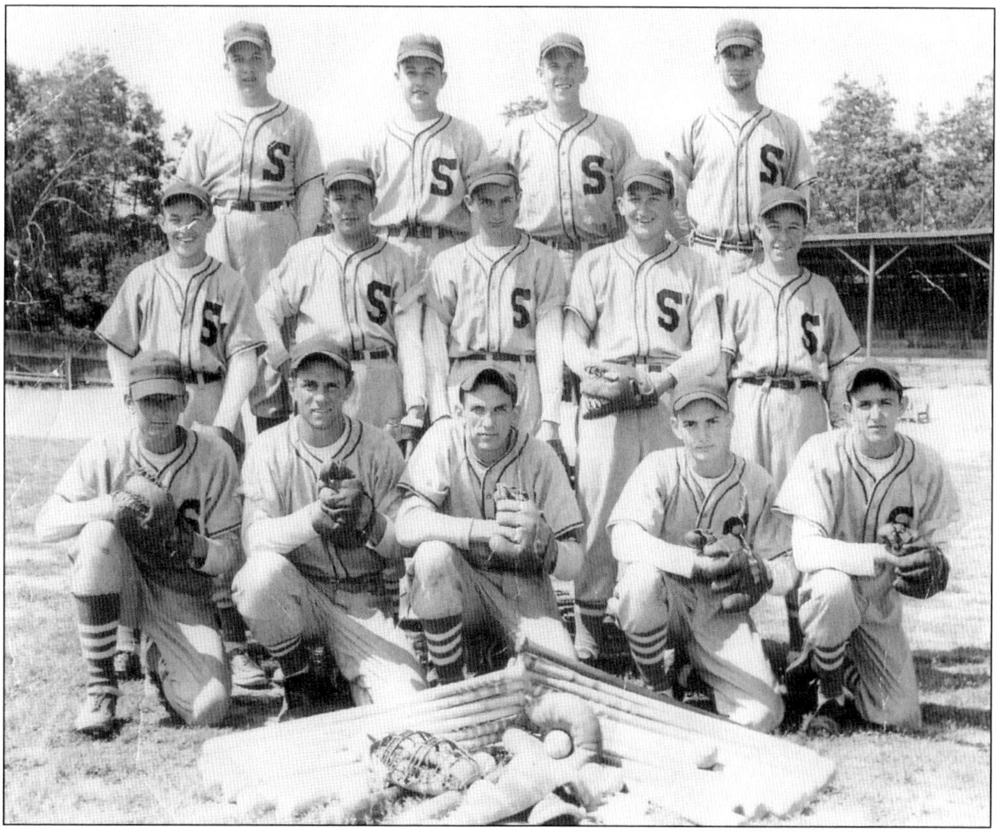

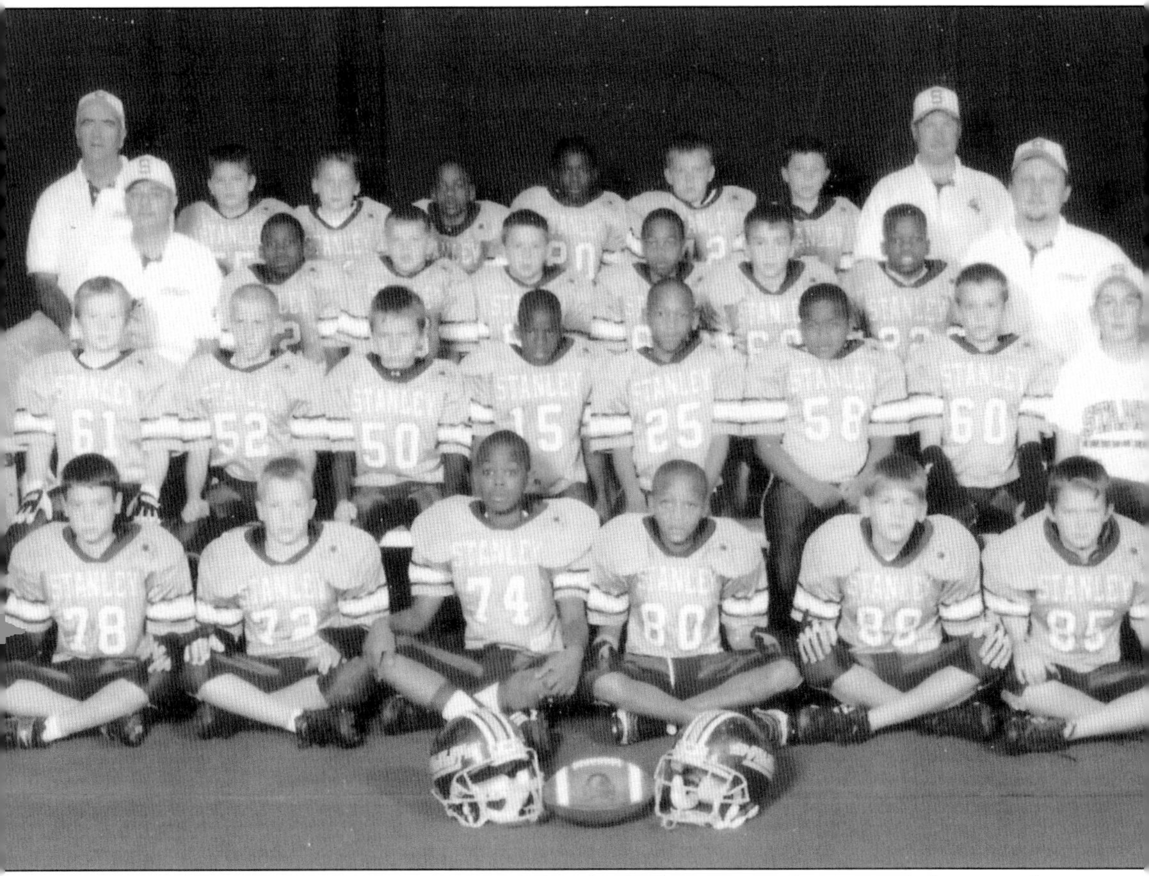

In 2002, Stanley's Pop Warner Little Scholars football team won the national championship in Orlando, Florida. In an expression of community pride, the young players were paraded down Main Street in white limousines. Players pictured are, from left to right, (first row) Triantafilos Scoumis, Christopher Trogdon, Quintin Smith, Diquivius Hatten, David Larson, and Tony Brogdon; (second row) Zachary Bumgarner, Michael Stewart, James Conn, Kevin Cathcart, Paul Brooks, Casey Wilson, Blayne Bowen, and J.R. Rudisill (manager); (third row) Mark Smith, (assistant coach), Preston Watts, Christopher Hovis, Jacob Wooten, Austin Shipp, Christopher Holland, Michael Adams, and William Crosby (assistant coach); (fourth row) John Rudisill (head coach), Jeremy Smith, James Guy, Darius Edwards, Justin Clark, Michael Harkins, Patrick Armstrong, and Doug Hawkins (assistant coach).

James Taylor "Buddy" Green, outstanding quarterback at Stanley High, led the Blue Devils to a 12-1 record in 1971, their only loss coming in the state playoffs. He also played on two Atlantic Coast championship baseball teams. Green went on to become a standout football player at North Carolina State University. He coached at North Carolina State, Louisiana State University, and Southern University, and is currently the defensive line coach at the US Naval Academy. Green was inducted into the Gaston County Sports Hall of Fame in 2013.

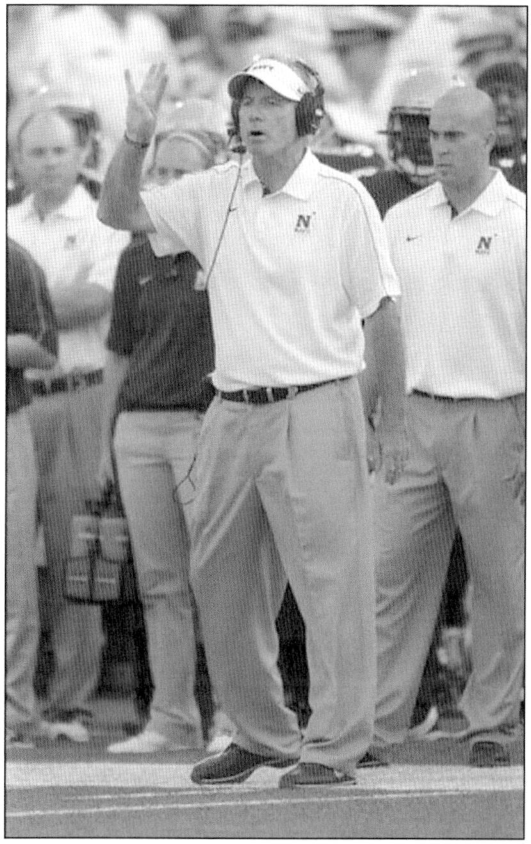

Stanley was proud to be the host of the Dixie Youth state championship baseball tournament at the brand-new Harper Park in 2013, with the Stanley team winning the state title. From left to right are Tyson Ensley, Jake Thomas, Zach Clark, Adam Rushing, Andrew Gall, Cody Chapman, Bryson Walker, Will Farnsworth, Carson Preston, Jack McCall, Riley Dunlap, and Savannah Baldwin; the three men standing behind the boys are coaches Bill Farnsworth and Jody Chapman, and head coach Jason Dunlap.

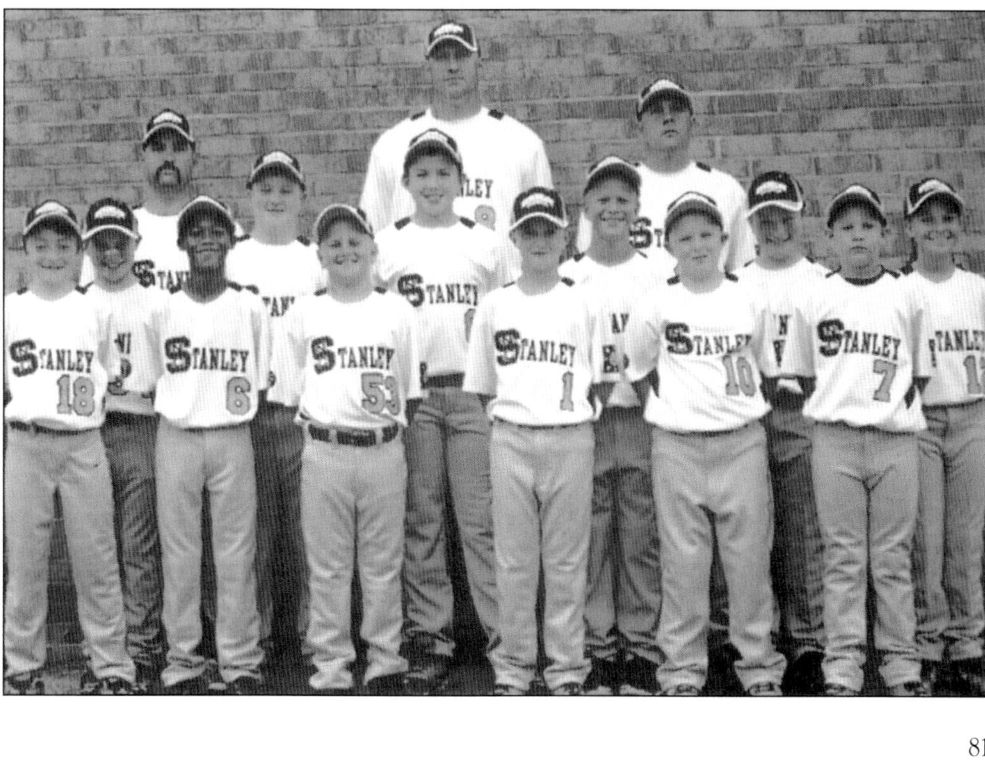

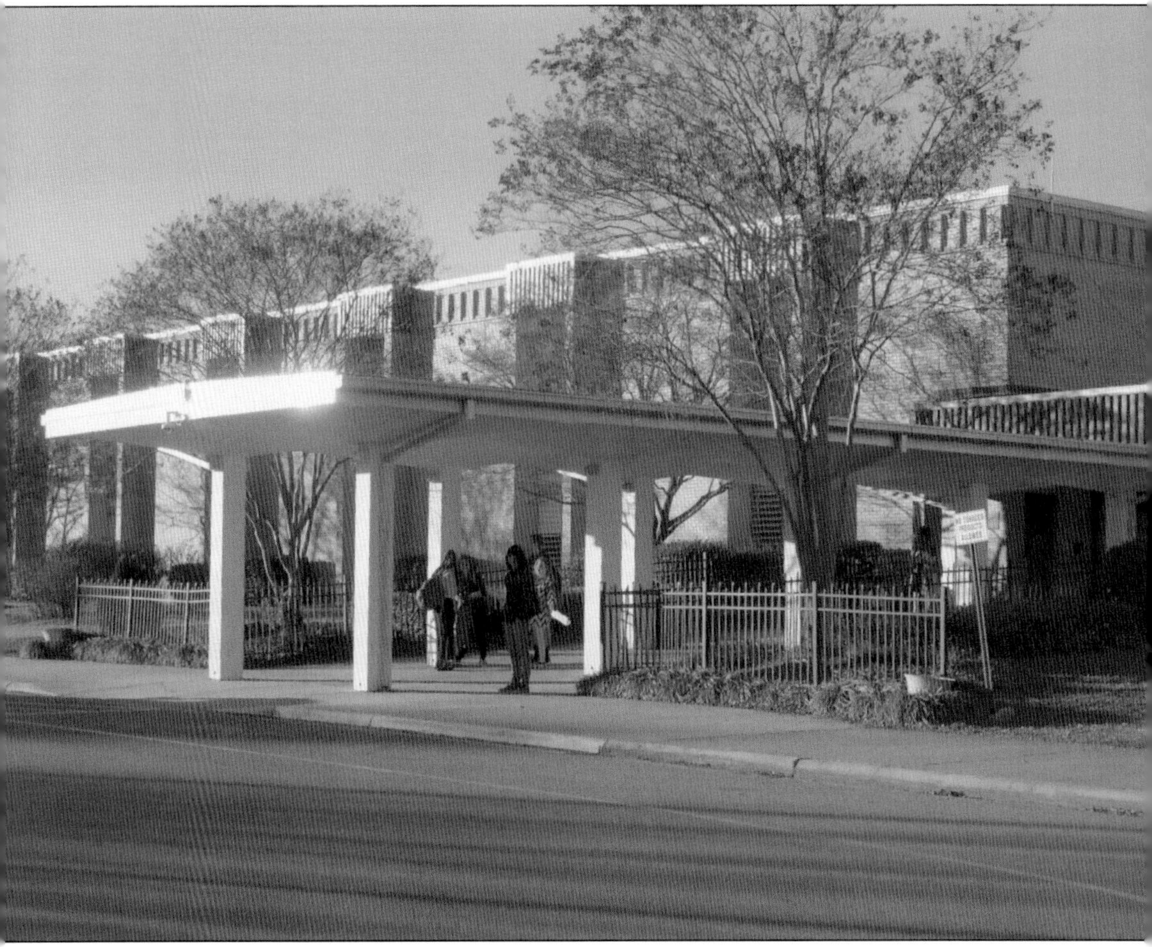

East Gaston High School opened in 1972 when high schools in the neighboring communities of Stanley and Mount Holly were consolidated. These longtime athletic rivals joined together as the Warriors. Richard M. Thompson was the first football coach, and the team achieved its first successful season. The women's basketball team, the Warriorettes, crushed all competition to win the first trophy for East Gaston as they captured the conference championship. In recent years, the school offers baseball, basketball, cheerleading, cross-country, dance, diving, football, golf, marching band, softball, soccer, swimming, tennis, track and field, volleyball, and wrestling. The school's sign proudly proclaims that it is the home of the Warrior wrestling team state champions—dual state—in 1990, 1991, and 1992 and state tournament champions in 1990, 2002, 2003, and 2004. East Gaston provides a comprehensive educational program with outstanding opportunities for students in academics, athletics, fine arts, career, technical education, and extracurricular activities.

# *Six*

# Churches and Organizations

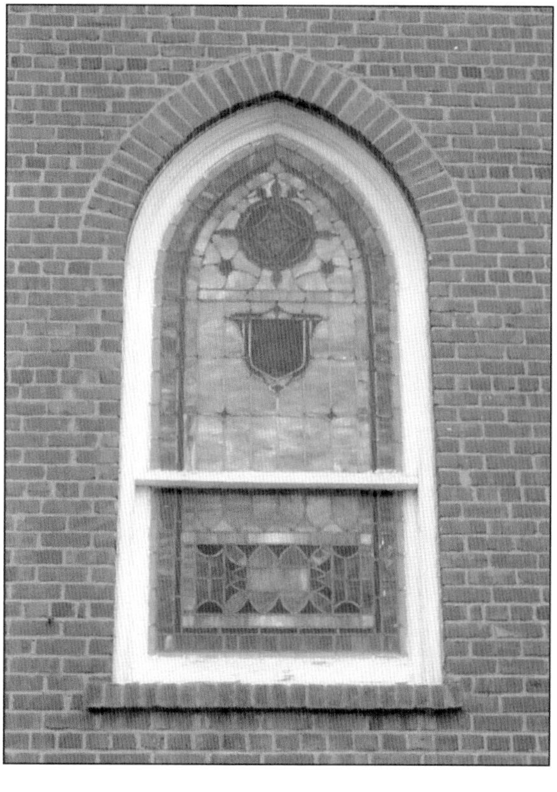

Stanley is fortunate to be the home of many churches, including Alexis Baptist, Christ's Lutheran, First United Methodist, First Baptist, First Presbyterian, First Community Pentecostal Center, Craig Memorial Baptist, Depot Baptist, First Free Will Baptist, the Fountain, Front Line Worship Center, Jehovah's Witness, Jesus is Love Holiness, Kings Tabernacle, Mount Pleasant United Methodist, New Life Baptist, New Road Baptist Church, Revival Tabernacle, Rock Hill United Methodist, Springfield Baptist, Stanley Pentecostal Holiness, and Trinity Full Gospel.

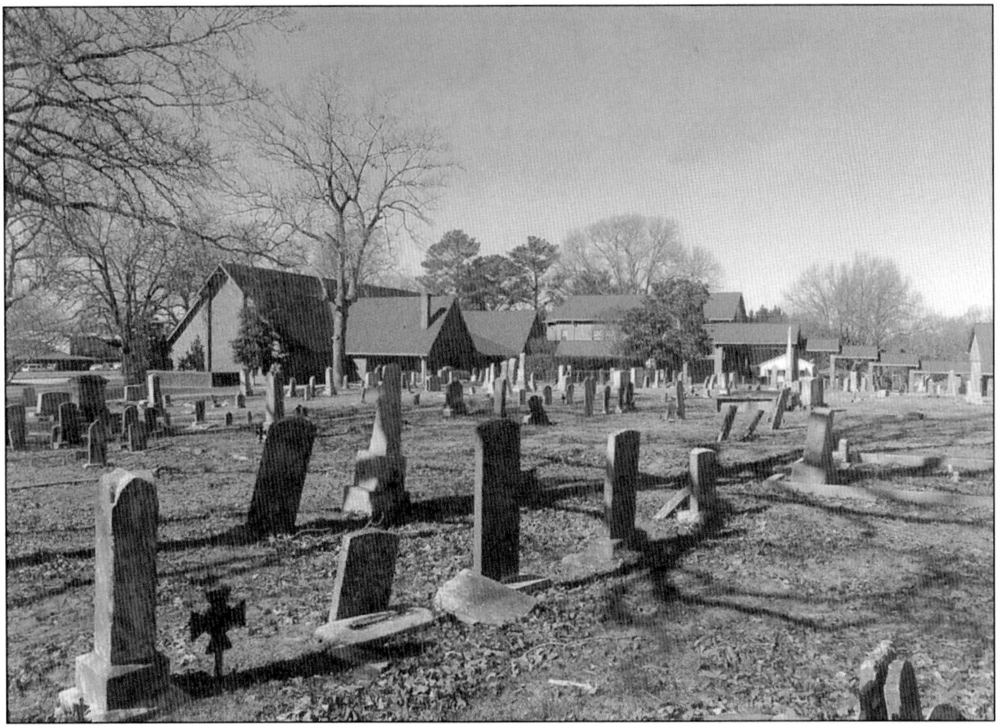

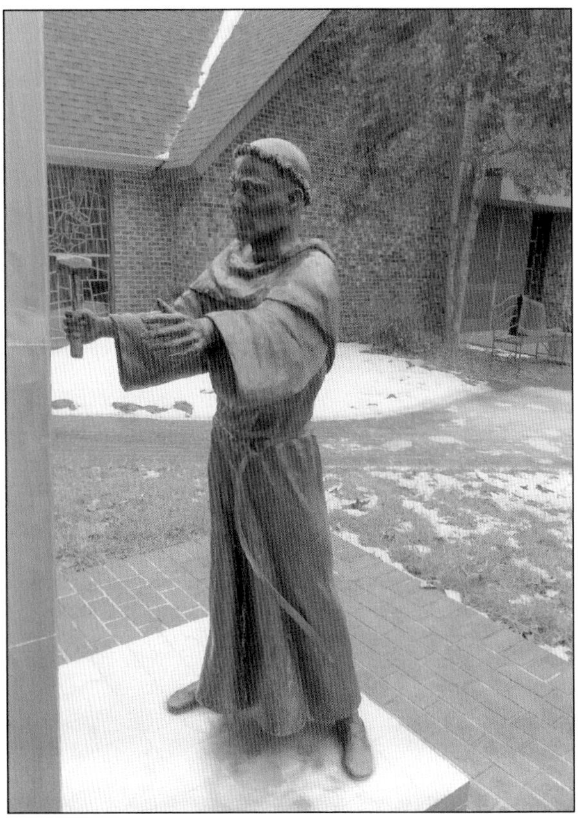

On the cornerstone of the first brick building of what was then called Chryst's Church was the founding date of 1841. Alexander Brevard's sons Robert A. and Ephraim provided land for building a Lutheran church in Stanley, and as was common at the time, it also served as a school. On September 14, 1969, the present church building, shown above, was consecrated. The cemetery at the church contains many of Stanley's founders. A committee has been formed to maintain and repair these historical gravesites. At left, the sculpture "Here I Stand" was dedicated in 2001 at Christ's Lutheran Church in Stanley. The stainless steel and bronze sculpture by Dr. Bailey Graham Weathers depicts Martin Luther nailing his 95 theses on the door of Wittenberg Cathedral in England, a key act in the Reformation.

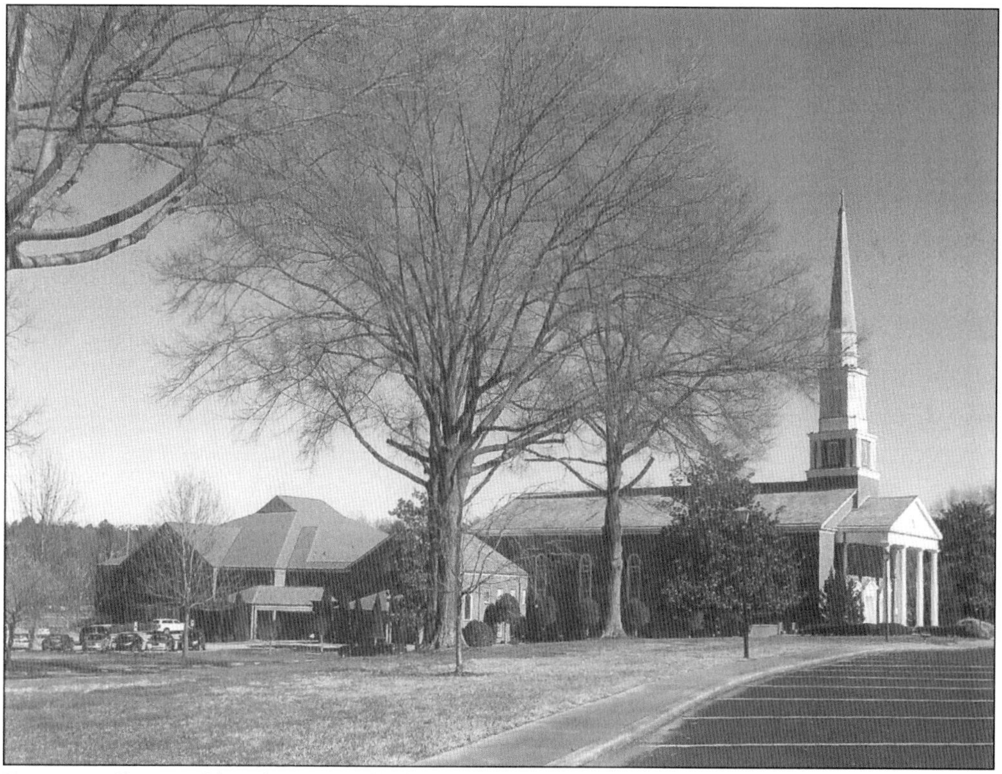

Bruington Baptist Church was established by Rev. Robert Bruington Jones in 1853 between the present-day towns of Mount Holly and Stanley. In 1885, the church bought property in Brevard Station and built the Little White Church. In the 1920s, a new brick building was erected on Main Street, but by the 1960s, the church needed a larger facility and bought property on Old Mount Holly Road. It was completed in March 1970, and the name was changed to First Baptist Church. In 2000, the church added a Family Life Center, which included a gymnasium, classrooms, kitchen, and dining room. The church is very active in mission projects, youth activities, community service, music programs, and education. Pictured at right is Rev. James Albert Snow, a minister in the 1940s. He established a fund to erect an educational building. He died in his rose garden beside the parsonage.

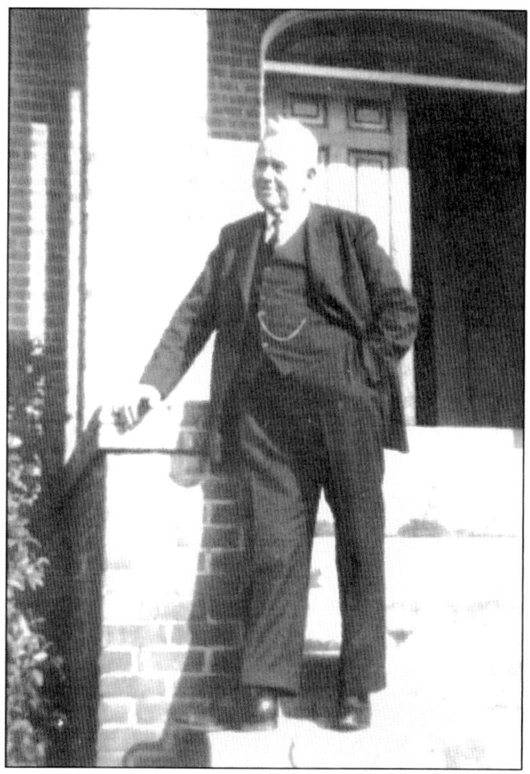

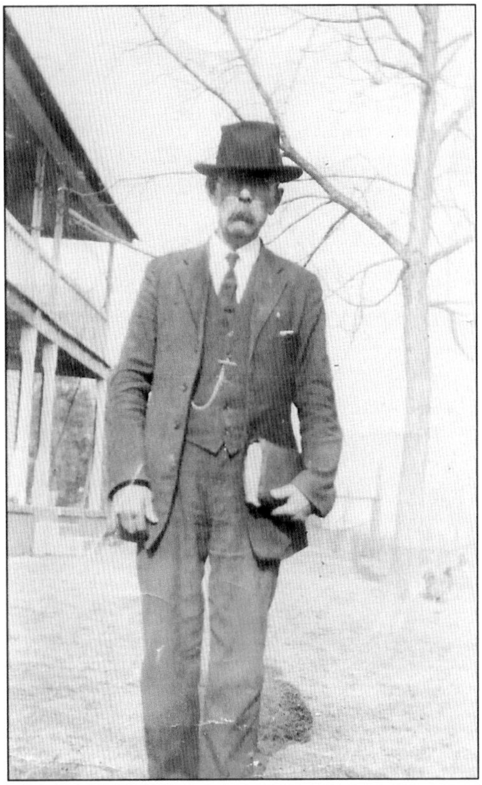

Rev. Lawrence Alexander McClure (1890–1966) was a minister of the gospel at Alexis Baptist Church during the 1930s and 1940s. His wife was Anna Helderman. Their daughter Robena married Daniel Thomas Long in 1931. McClure's grandfather James Henry McClure was a minister, and his father, William Bartlett McClure, was also an early minister at Alexis Baptist Church. (Courtesy of Traci Jenkins.)

An early American automobile is parked beside Alexis Baptist Church in 1915. Flowers adorn the gravesite of member and deacon William H. Abernathy, whose request to be buried by the church was honored and led to the beginning of the church cemetery. The church was organized in 1903 and was built on one acre of beautifully elevated land donated by Coleman Franklin Abernathy, situated in the center of his farm.

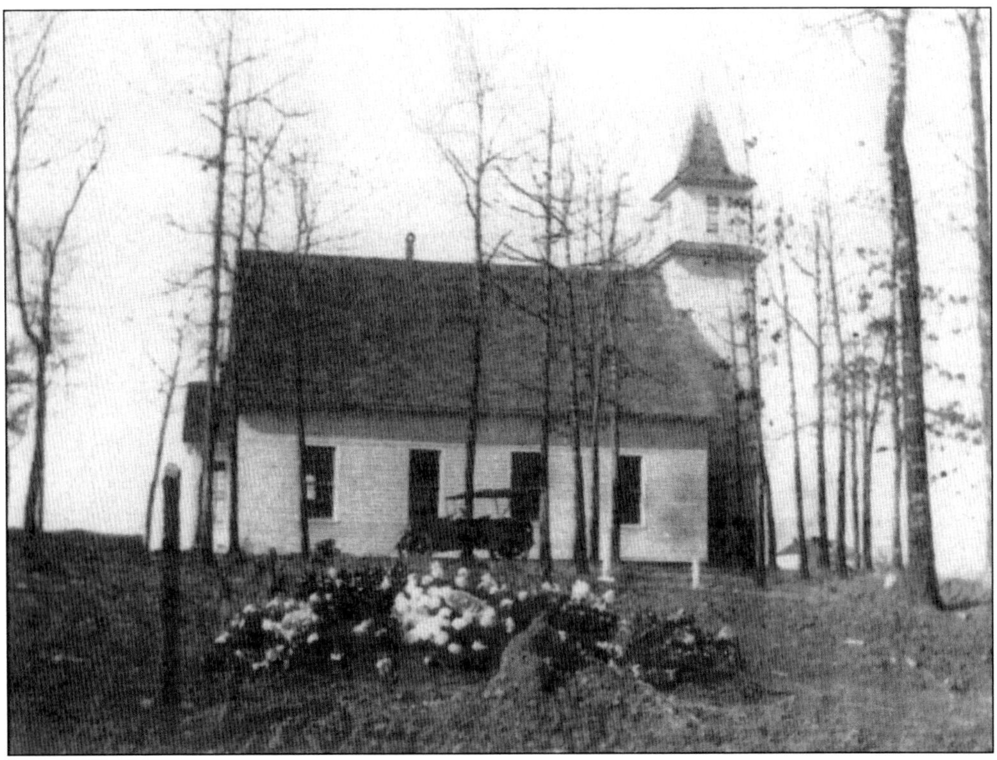

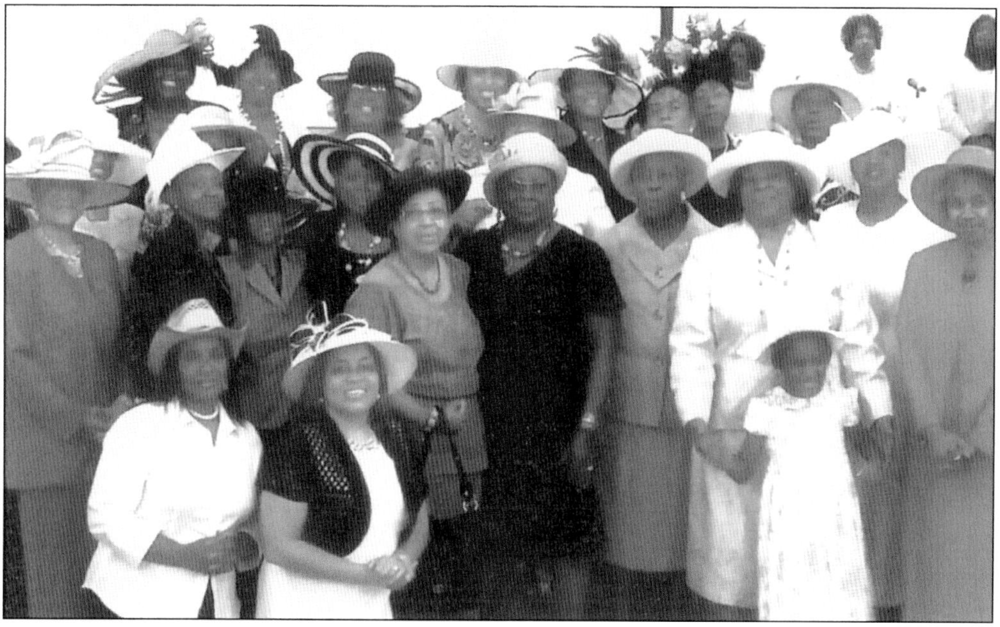

Springfield Memorial Baptist Church in Stanley has an annual Hat Day, when the women of the church don their prettiest *chapeaux*, as seen here. In 1863, twelve church members organized Galilee Baptist Church, which was later destroyed by fire. In 1874, Rufus and Susan Friday donated land for a new church. A log structure was built and named for Springfield, West Virginia, hometown of their pastor.

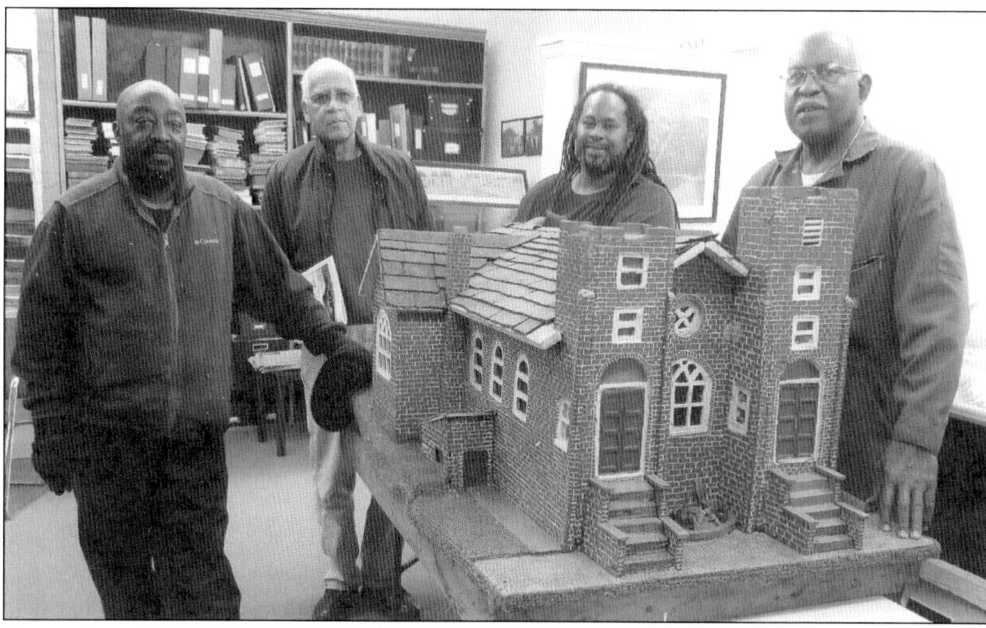

Everett Brown built an amazing replica of the old Springfield Baptist Church, which opens to display the interior. He was a member of this church, which was built in 1928. Brown became legally blind and, unfortunately, was killed on his way to attend church. Delivering the replica to Brevard Station Museum are church members, from left to right, Bruce Lynch III, Lionel Sanders, Wendall L. Williams, and Carlyle N. Friday Sr.

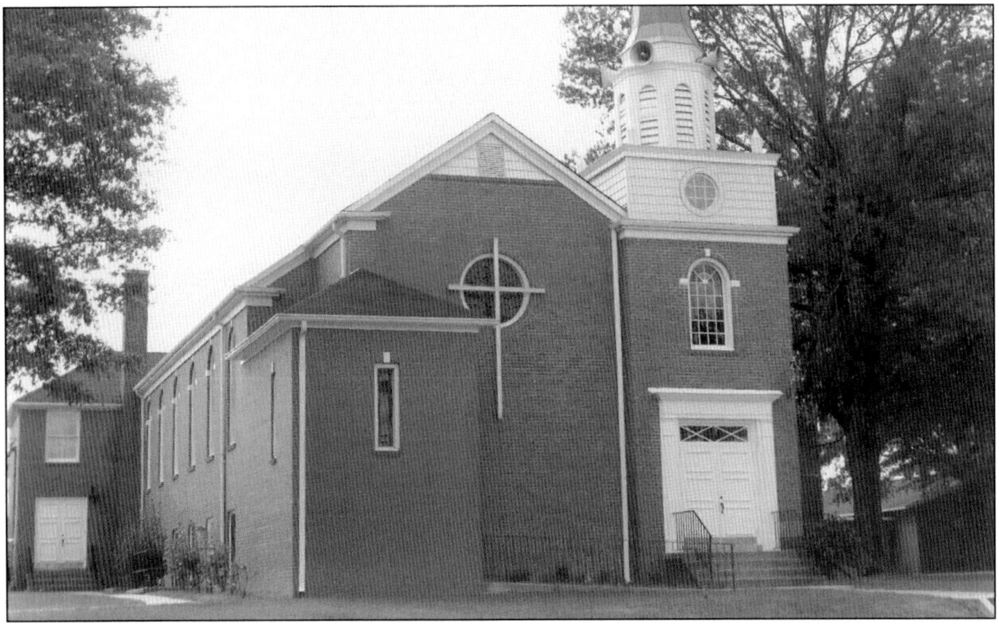

Stanley First United Methodist Church recently celebrated its 200th anniversary. In 1815, circuit preachers came several times a year to preach under a brush arbor. Some of the early families were Morris, Derr, Abernethy, Rankin, and Rutledge. By 1859, it was called the Stanley Creek Methodist Episcopal Church South. About 1880, the church had its first resident pastor, and a new church was built. Soon, educational institutions were started by the Western North Carolina Methodist Conference, and this area was chosen as a location for one of its schools. In 1940, the present church was built, and continuous additions have been made. In 1968, the Methodist church and the Evangelical United Brethren Church merged and formed the United Methodist Church. In 1995, ninety-three acres were purchased on Hickory Grove Road, and a large Family Life Center was built. The photograph below shows the church's bible school in 1955. Summer bible schools are still offered by many churches and provide religious study with crafts, refreshments, and games.

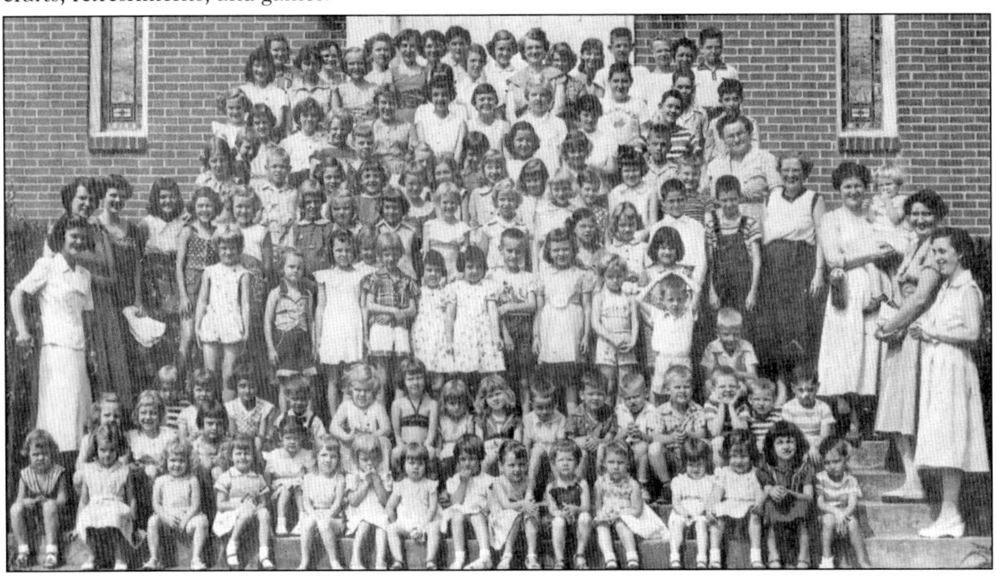

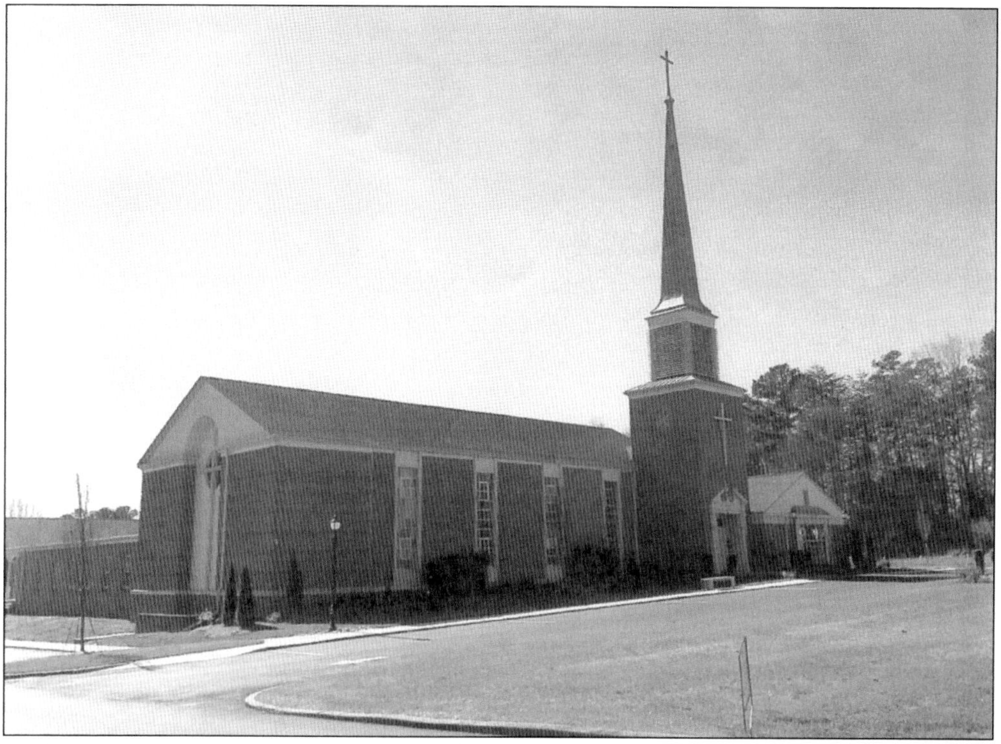

In 1891, Presbyterians in the area petitioned the Mecklenburg Presbytery to organize a church in Stanley. The first families were Robinson, Nantz, Smith, Rutledge, Pegram, Summerow, Humphries, Richards, and Abernethy. Rev. Jonas Barclay was the first minister, and was married to Edna Pegram in the first wedding at the church. A new church was built in 1928 in the shape of a cross. Decades later, plans were underway to build a larger church. The first services were held in the sanctuary in 1973. The church also runs a child development center for preschool children. In the 1970s, a member of the First Presbyterian Church offered $1,000 towards a rest home for the elderly. In 1983, the ground was broken for the Total Living Center, located adjacent to the church. The Total Living Center has expanded and become an asset to the entire Charlotte area. It is well known for its quality of care and medical expertise. Seated at right is resident Mildred Abernethy Hallman, assisted by Mary Doris Chapman (left) and Lola Ballard (right). (Right, courtesy of Carolyn Huskins.)

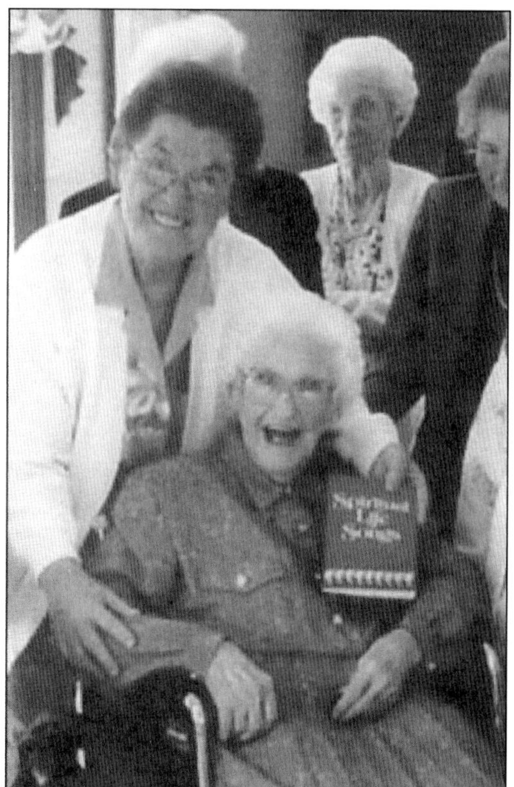

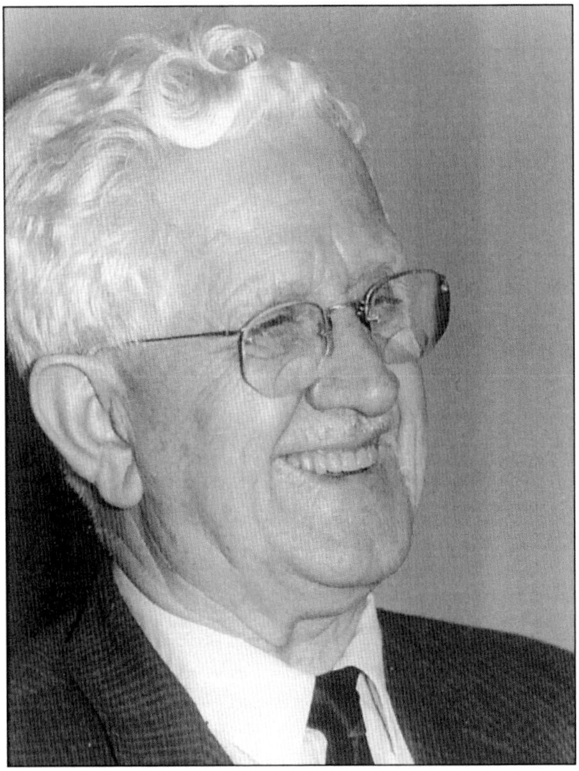

At age 26 in 1923, William McCulloch came to this country from Glasgow, Scotland, became a preacher, married, and settled in Stanley, where he pastored the small Brethren Church. He was admired by everyone in town, and was known as "Preacher Mac." After the death of his wife in the 1960s, he stated, in his Scottish accent, that he would like to visit his homeland. People in Stanley contributed money for him to return to Scotland.

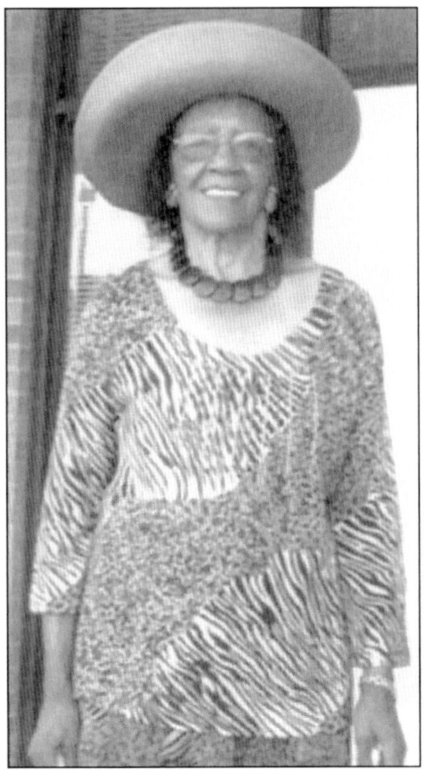

In 2013, Elizabeth Forney was honored as the oldest female member of Springfield Memorial Baptist Church. Forney, born September 1, 1924, has outlived two husbands: John Jeffries Jr. and Charles Forney. She is the mother of four children (Richard, Felicia, Bill, and Sherron), seven grandchildren, and five great-grandchildren. She has been a member of her church since childhood, serving willingly anywhere needed and singing in the choir. (Courtesy of Lois Brown Barnett.)

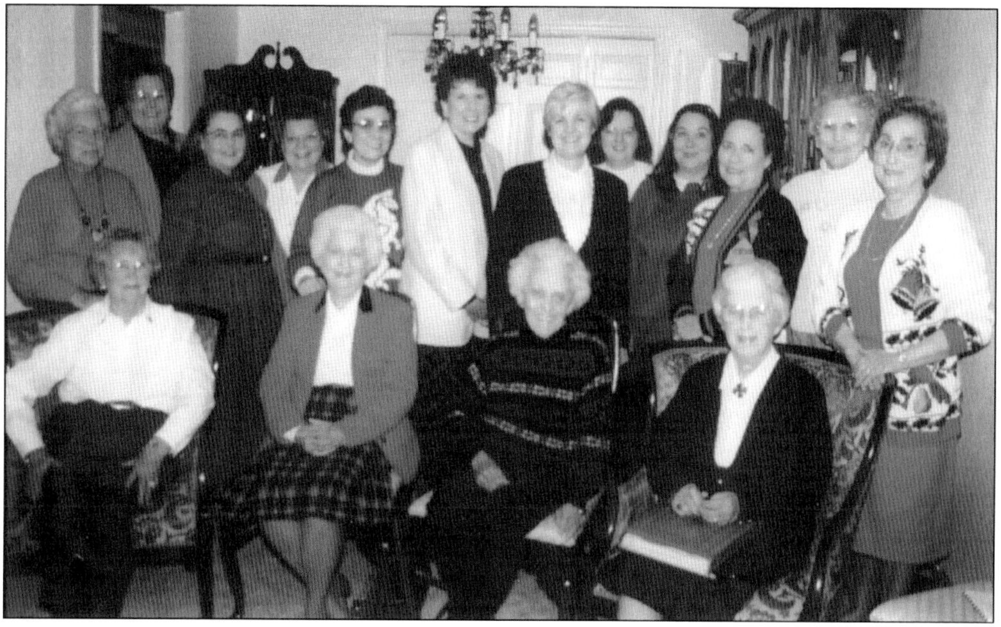

The 16 Friends Book Club was established in 1946 by Lois Craig, and its first meeting was held at her home. The club's object was to broaden their mental outlook. The membership has changed often over the years, but all agree that the purpose of the club was achieved. The ladies have enjoyed reading and hearing reports on numerous best sellers and especially sharing close friendships with one another.

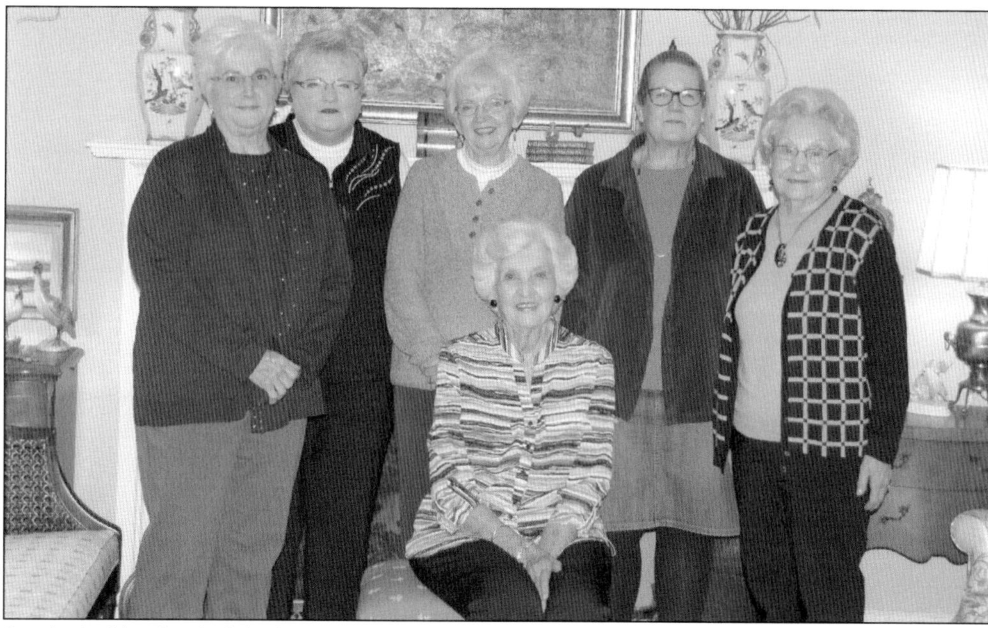

Stanley's oldest book club, the Beacon Book Club, was established in 1931. Lula McCorkle organized the club, and the 1931 officers were Myrtle Wallace, Beulah Craig, and Marguerite Hacker. There were 14 charter members. The club continues to evolve today and remains an active group of women who seek to enrich their lives through having lively book discussions, attending author lectures, concerts, theater, and other cultural activities. (Courtesy of Kitty Smith Saunders.)

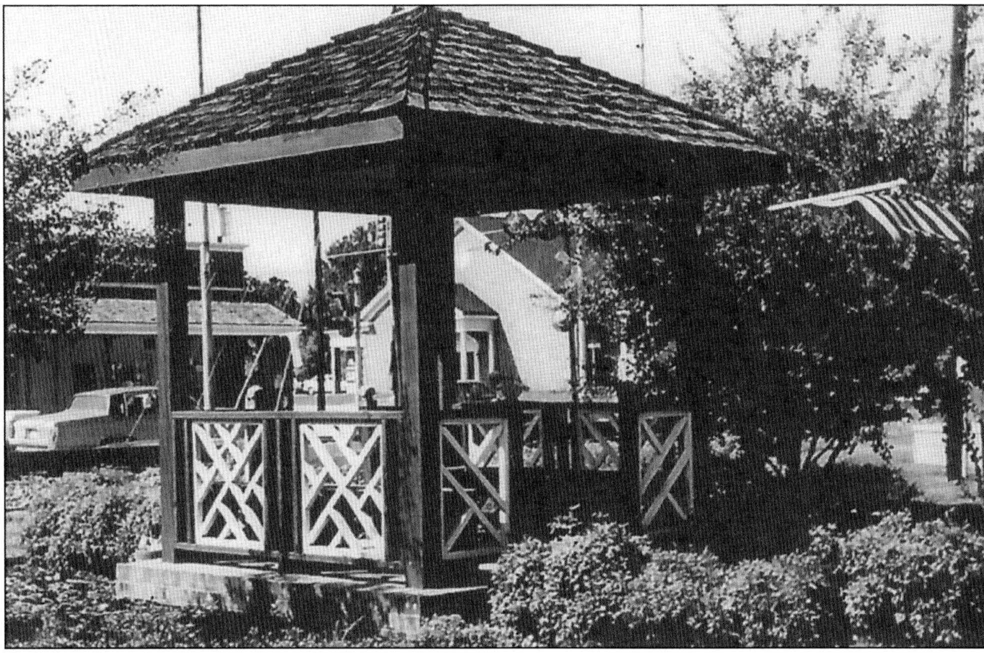

The Grow and Show Garden Club began in 1969, with Kathryne Homesley Caliendo as president. With an intention of refurbishing the look of downtown, the club decorated with Christmas wreaths and lights. They initiated, designed, and planted a green space alongside the railroad. In the early 1980s, after demolition of the old railroad depot, a gazebo was built in the green space.

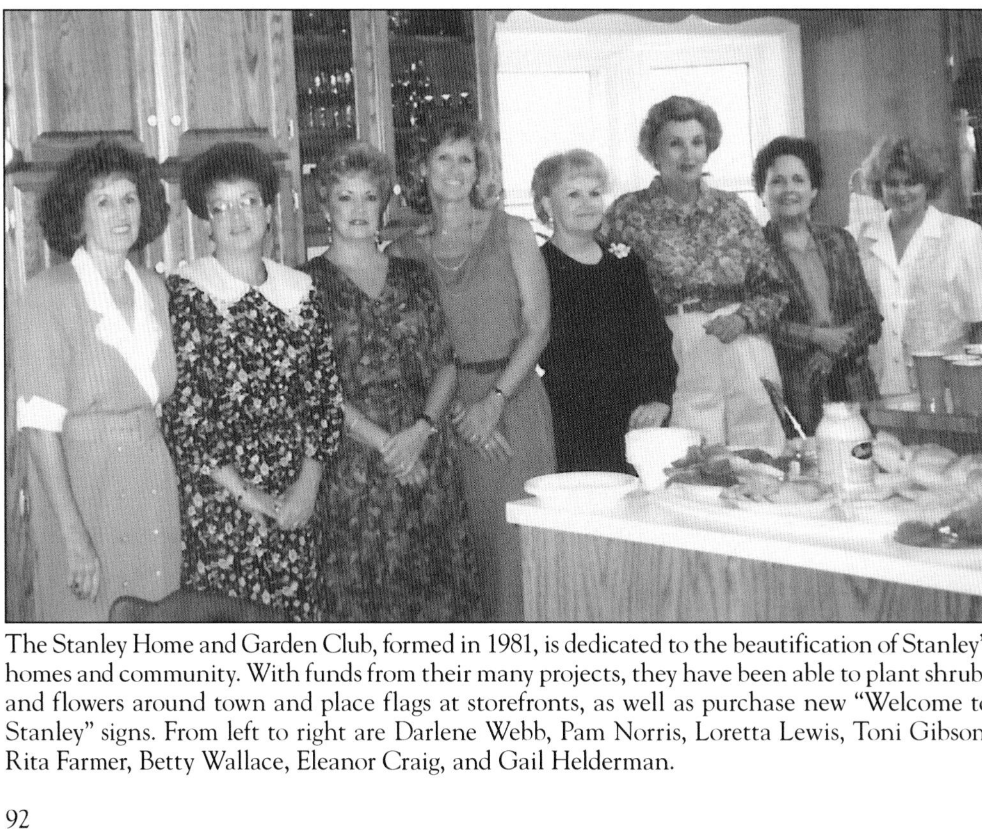

The Stanley Home and Garden Club, formed in 1981, is dedicated to the beautification of Stanley's homes and community. With funds from their many projects, they have been able to plant shrubs and flowers around town and place flags at storefronts, as well as purchase new "Welcome to Stanley" signs. From left to right are Darlene Webb, Pam Norris, Loretta Lewis, Toni Gibson, Rita Farmer, Betty Wallace, Eleanor Craig, and Gail Helderman.

Pictured here are three members of the former Stanley Junior Woman's Club; from left to right are Martha Murphy, Louise Newton, and Doris Skidmore. The club helped with various community projects. To fund those efforts, they organized a sale of lovely spring and summer hats. The ladies are shown here modeling several as they admired the others the club had for sale.

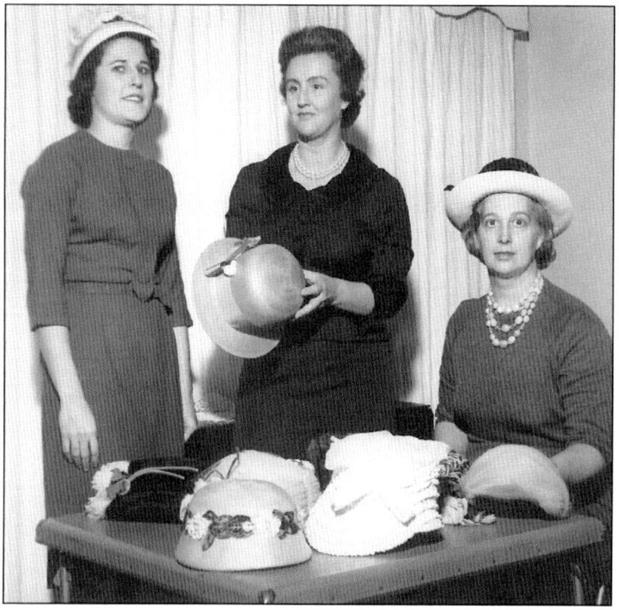

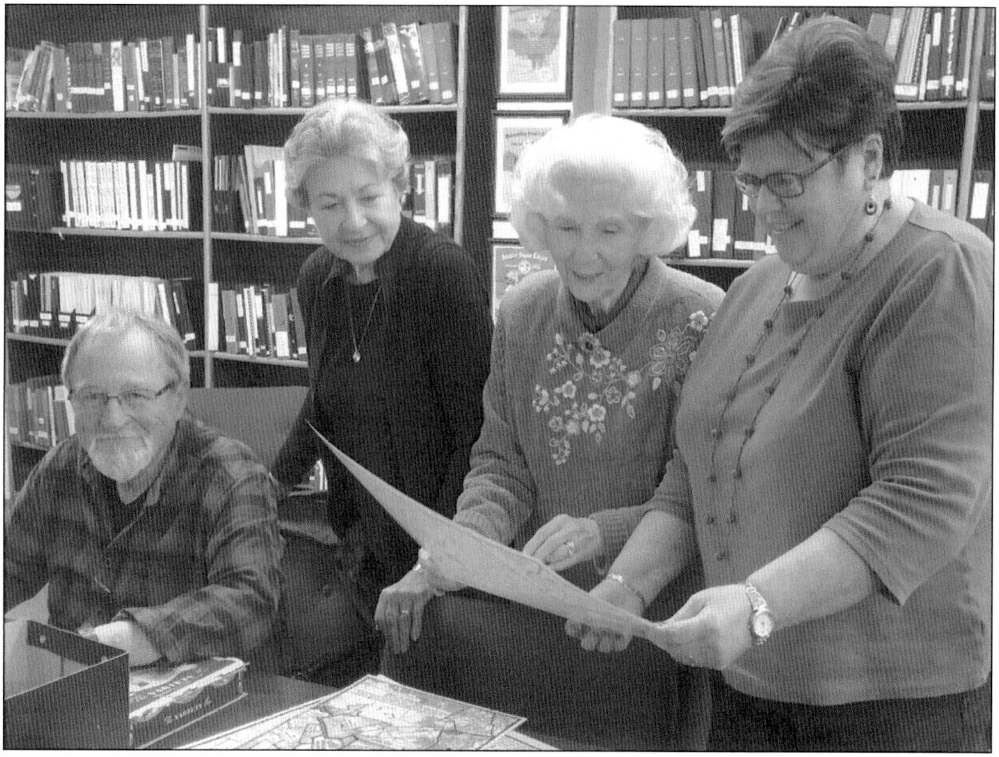

Volunteers at Brevard Station Museum examine a map of the Stanley/Dallas area drawn by William Hoffman, using the deeds of early settlers' properties. The museum was started in April 1991 to preserve the history of Stanley. In 2004, the museum moved to 112 South Main Street where historical artifacts, photographs, and documents are carefully displayed. The research area contains many family histories. Pictured from left to right are William Carangelo, Joyce Joy Handsel, Ruth Campbell Wood, and Freida Long Robinson.

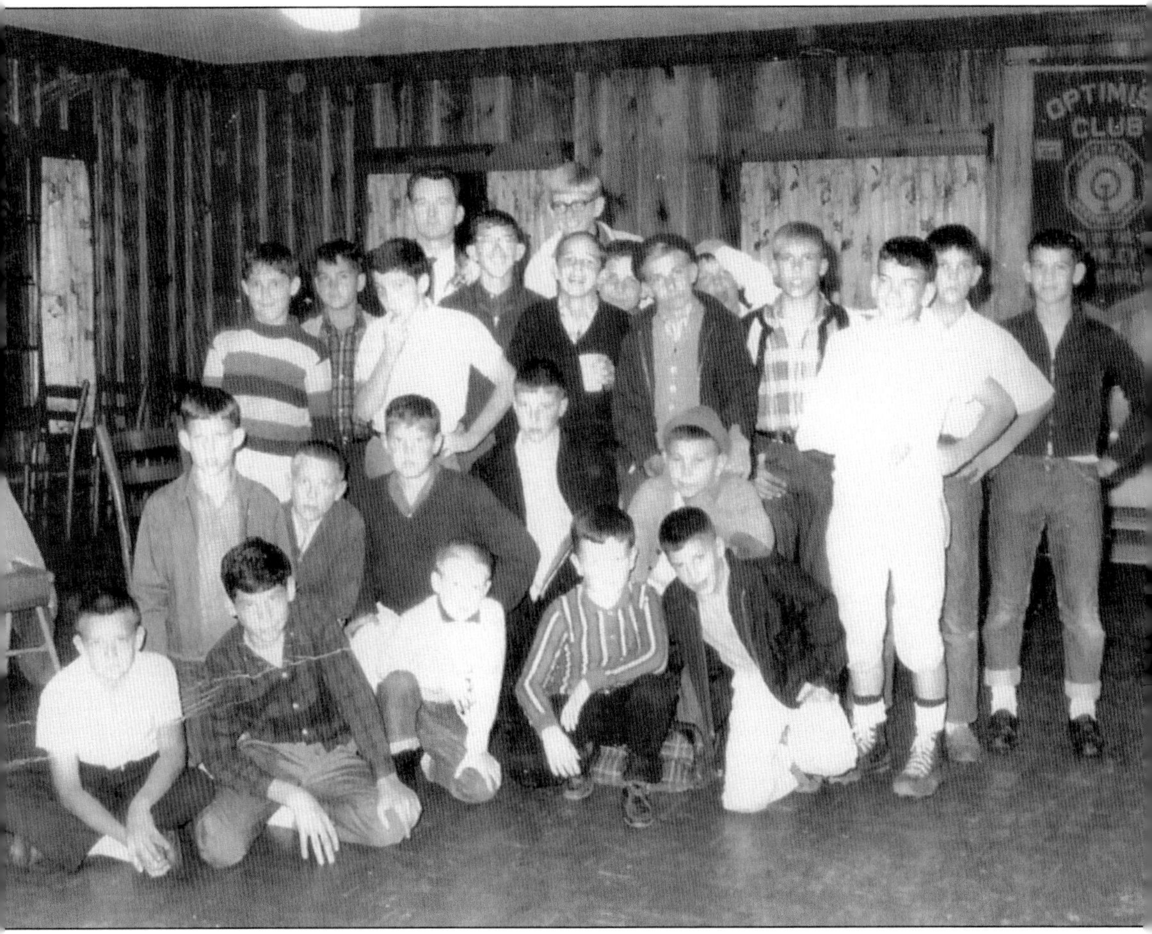


The Optimist Club of Stanley was chartered on April 30, 1959. The club's objective is to conduct positive service projects for children of the community, and it has sponsored many sports activities. Pictured is the Optimist Club football team of 1966. From left to right are (first row) James Brooks, Ronnie Winchester, Dean Coley, Randy Skidmore, and Eddie McGinnis; (second row) Billy Withers, Terry Vernon, Mike Williams, Roger Stepp, and Jimmy Bumgarner; (third row) Eddie Bailey, Jack Moore, Randy Cloninger, Don Calvert, Joe Bentley, Tim Brown, Terry Canipe, Buddy Green, Randy Morrison, Buddy Oates, Rick Evans, and David Miller; (fourth row) Don Bumgardner and Rod Rudisill.

The Lions Club, known especially for its service to the blind, has been in existence in Stanley since 1944. The first president was Dr. Bailey Graham Weathers Sr. Among their many accomplishments, the club has generously given annually to statewide projects to help the eyesight research at Duke Hospital, Wake Forest University, and the University of North Carolina. For the club's 50th anniversary, a pin was designed depicting the gold prospector for whom Stanley is named.

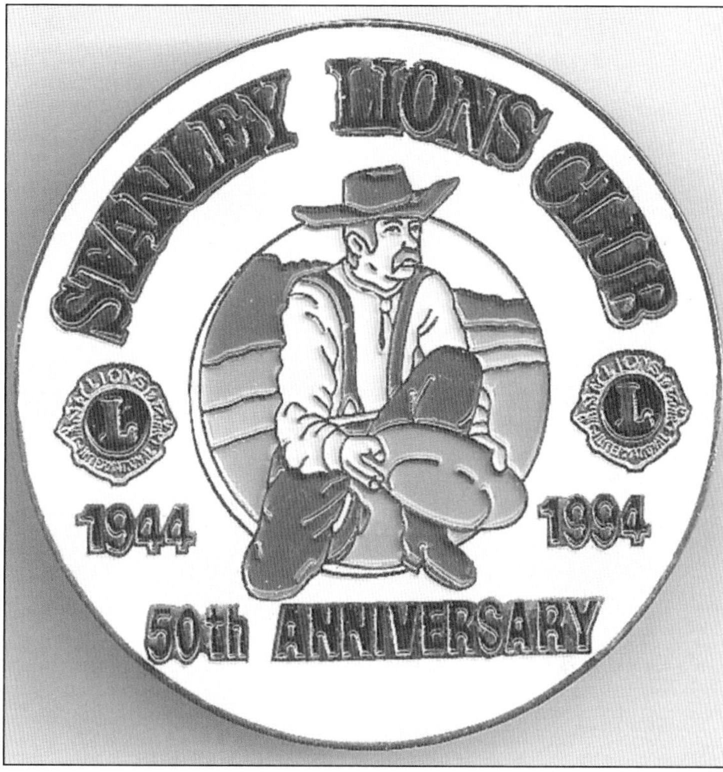


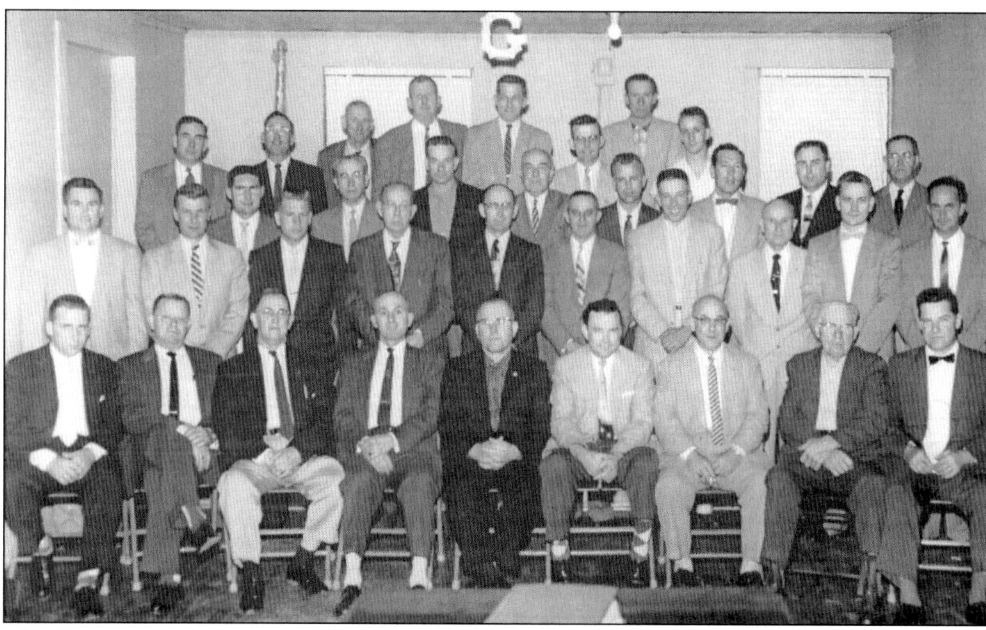

The charter for the Masonic Lodge in Stanley was issued in 1958, and each year, its membership continued to increase. In April 1974, the membership changed the name of the lodge from McClurd Lodge 713 to Stanley Lodge 713, and a new structure was built in 1976. The Stanley Masons have been involved in many charitable projects, including the Oxford Orphanage and the Masonic and Eastern Star homes.

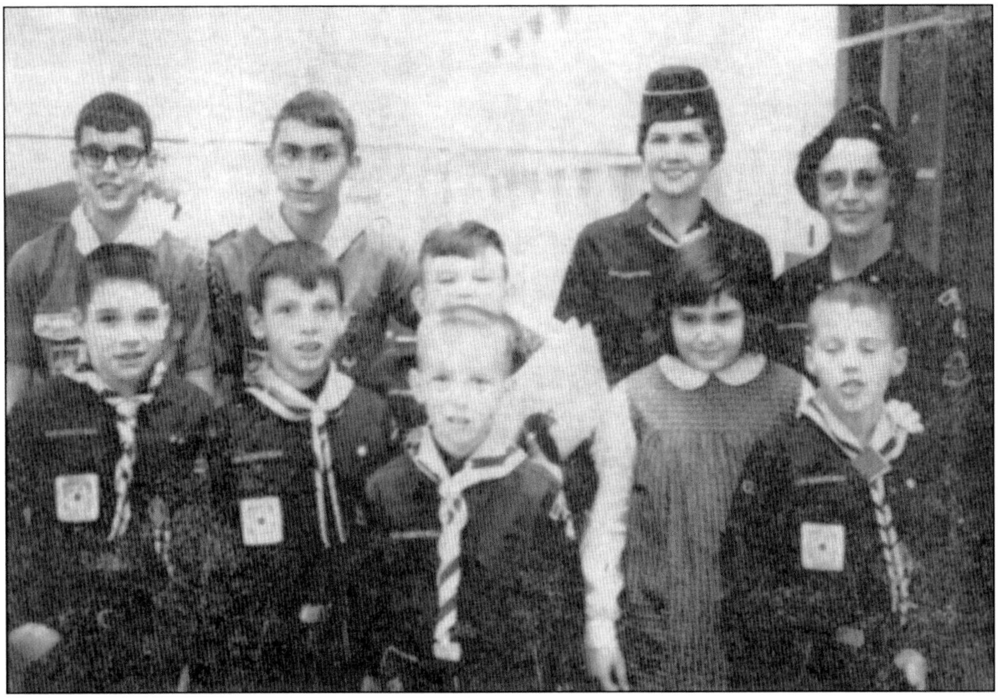

Boy and Girl Scout groups were formed in Stanley in the 1920s. Early leaders were Edith Mason, Marguerite Hacker, William G. Hawley, "Gump" Hornbuckle, Walter Carpenter, and Luther Abernathy. By 1943, Stanley Methodist Church took responsibility for the scouting programs. In the 1966 photograph above of Troop 49 are, from left to right, (first row) Frank Carlton, unidentified, Sonny Reavis, Sue Carlton, and Randy Mason; (second row) Steve Haynes, Ted Morris, Tracy Withers, Shirley Haynes Gunn, and Kathryn Black. Pictured below are the members of this troop at their Christmas party in 2015.

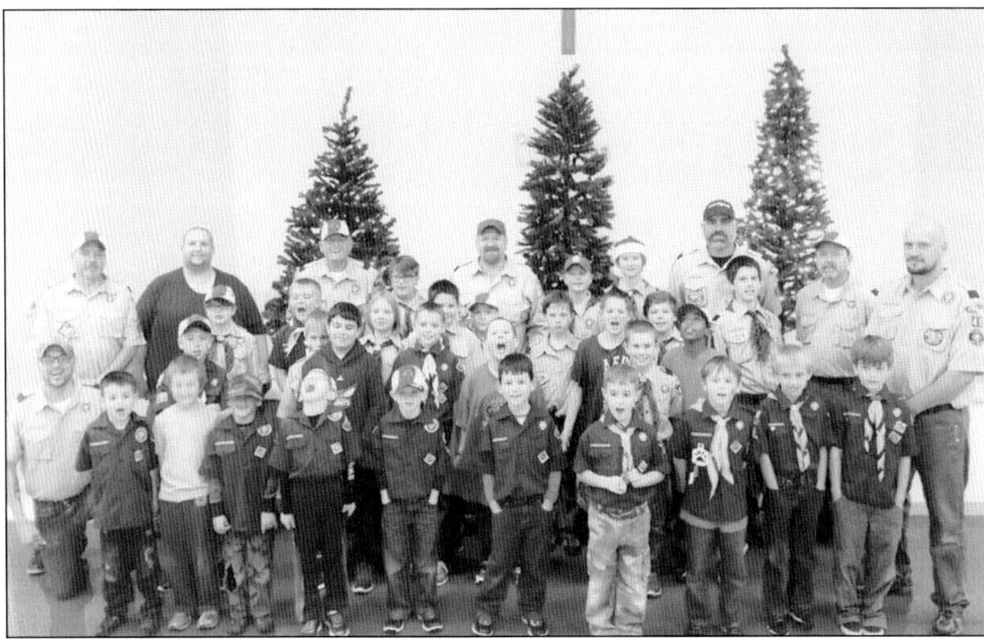

# *Seven*

# People and Events

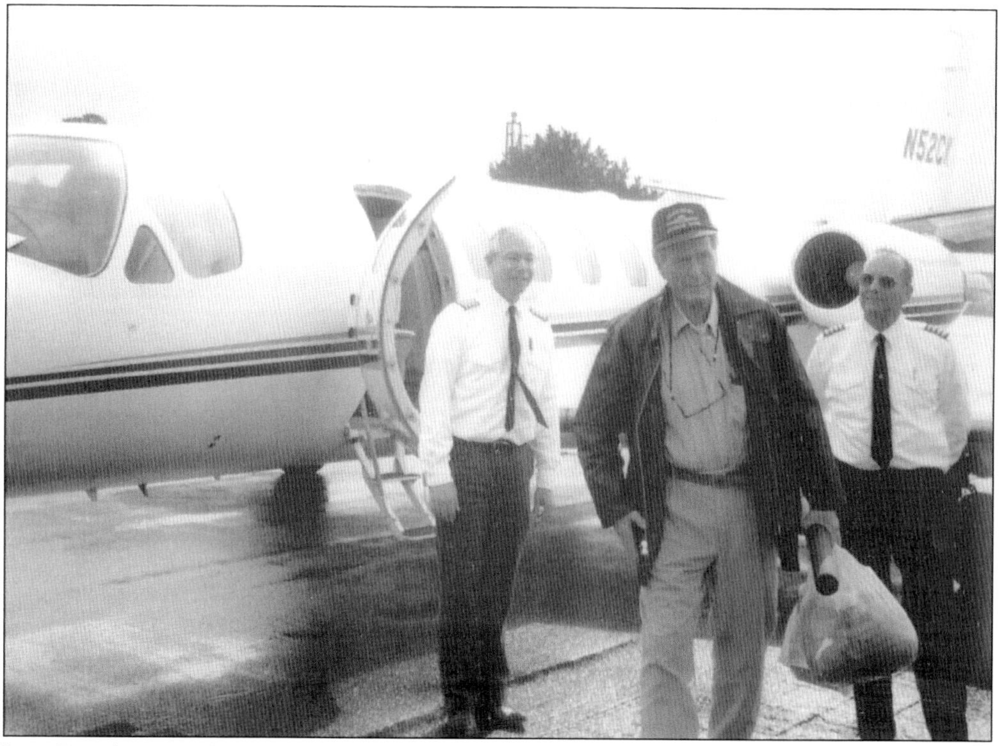

Jerry Davidson Weathers grew up in Stanley as the son of Dr. and Mrs. Bailey Graham Weathers Sr. After schooling, he became a commercial pilot. He flew many prominent people and dignitaries, including former president George H.W. Bush. After retiring as a pilot, Weathers continued in the industry as a flight instructor. Pictured here are, from left to right, unidentified, President Bush, and Weathers.

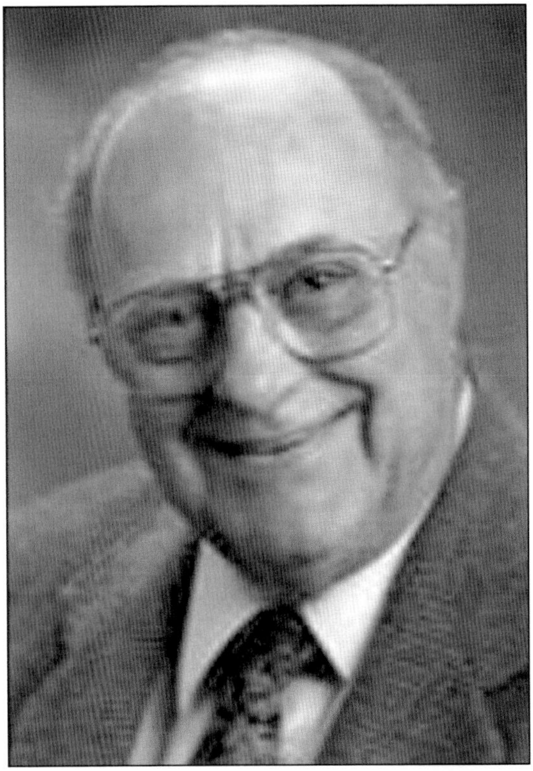

Dr. Bailey Graham Weathers Jr. was a man well educated and interested in numerous subjects, including classical piano. He was a physician and produced prolific art creations, verifying that he was an extraordinarily dedicated and talented individual. His paintings and sculptures are displayed in various facilities here and abroad. Many books make mention of his life, including *La Revue de Moderne*, *The International Who's Who of Intellectuals*, *Men of Achievement*, and *Personalities of the South: Outstanding and Distinguished.* His creations can be found in numerous states and in the Smithsonian Institution. The Brevard Station Museum in Stanley displays bronze busts of police chiefs Ralph Handsel and Donnie Davis sculpted by Weathers. Below is Weathers's sculpture *Queen Charlotte*, located at the entrance to the World Trade Center at East Fifth and North College Streets in Charlotte, North Carolina.

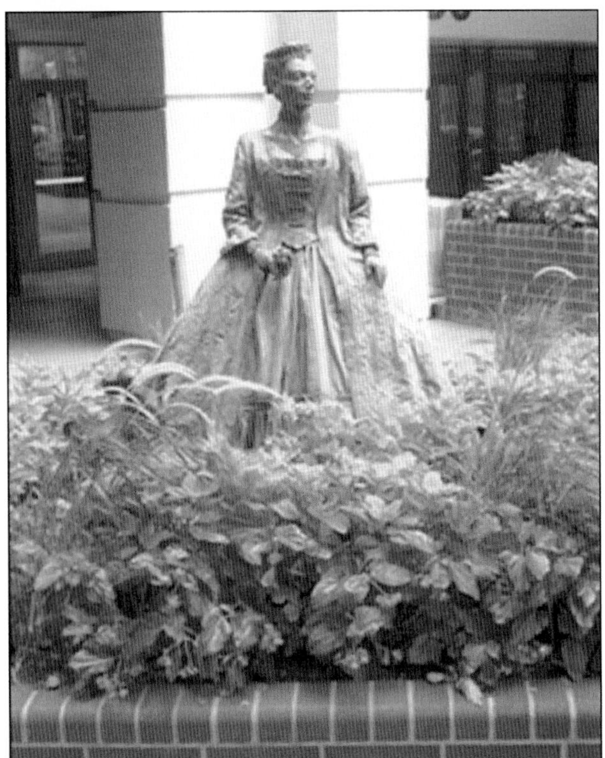

Robert Fulton Craig, born in 1877, and his wife, Martha Cobb, came to Stanley around 1918. He became one of the proprietors of Lola Manufacturing Company. While in that capacity, he and the mill supervisor, William Hornbuckle, invented a new type of dyeing machine for the textile industry and became the founders of Gaston County Dyeing Machine Company. Robert Fulton Craig was a town alderman from 1919 to 1921. He died in 1946.

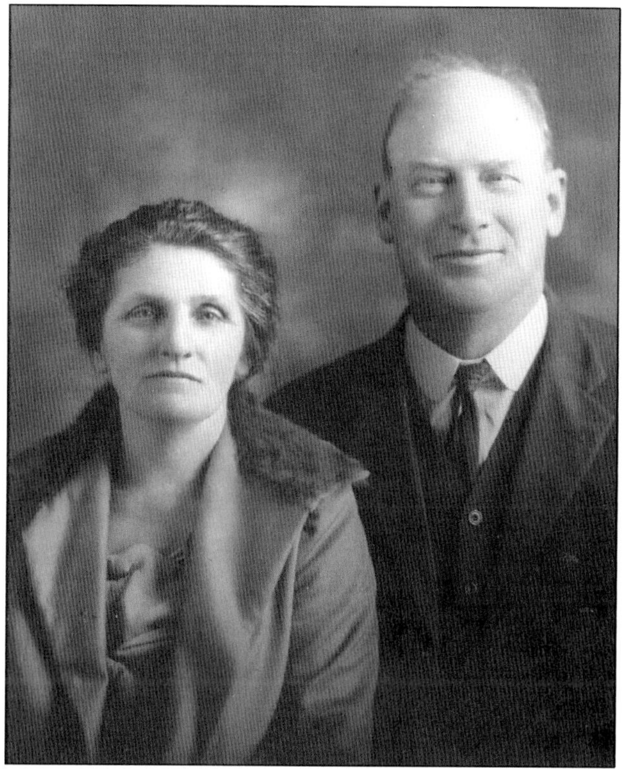

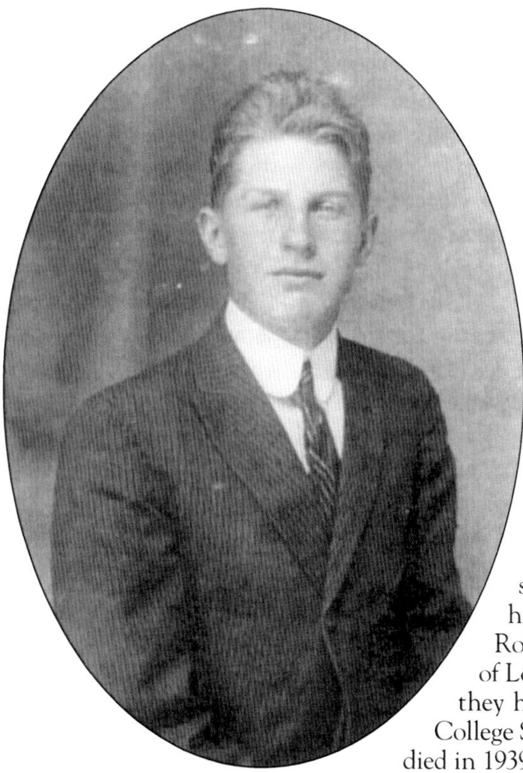

Though Inzie Eugene Craig was a fourth-year student at Wake Forest University studying law, he returned home at the urging of his father, Robert Fulton Craig, to serve as vice president of Lola Mills Inc. He married Essie Clemmer, and they had eight children. The family lived on East College Street, where Essie taught piano lessons. Craig died in 1939 at age 42.

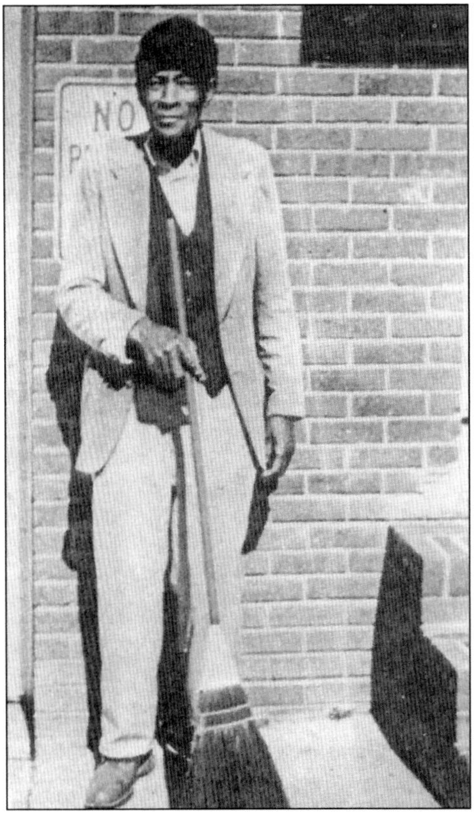

John Roseboro worked for the town of Stanley fir nearly 50 years until the age of 84, cleaning the streets and sidewalk in front of the business district. Roseboro said that he had worked for five Stanley mayors. In all the years that he worked for the town, he never missed a day of work, except one week a year to take his wife to Tuckers Grove Camp Meeting. He was chosen one year to be grand marshal in the annual Christmas parade.

Tony Parker is showing his fine horse. Parker grew up in Cramerton, North Carolina, but moved in his adulthood to Stanley, where he owned and operated Trinity Tire Company for many years. He and his family continue to live in Stanley.

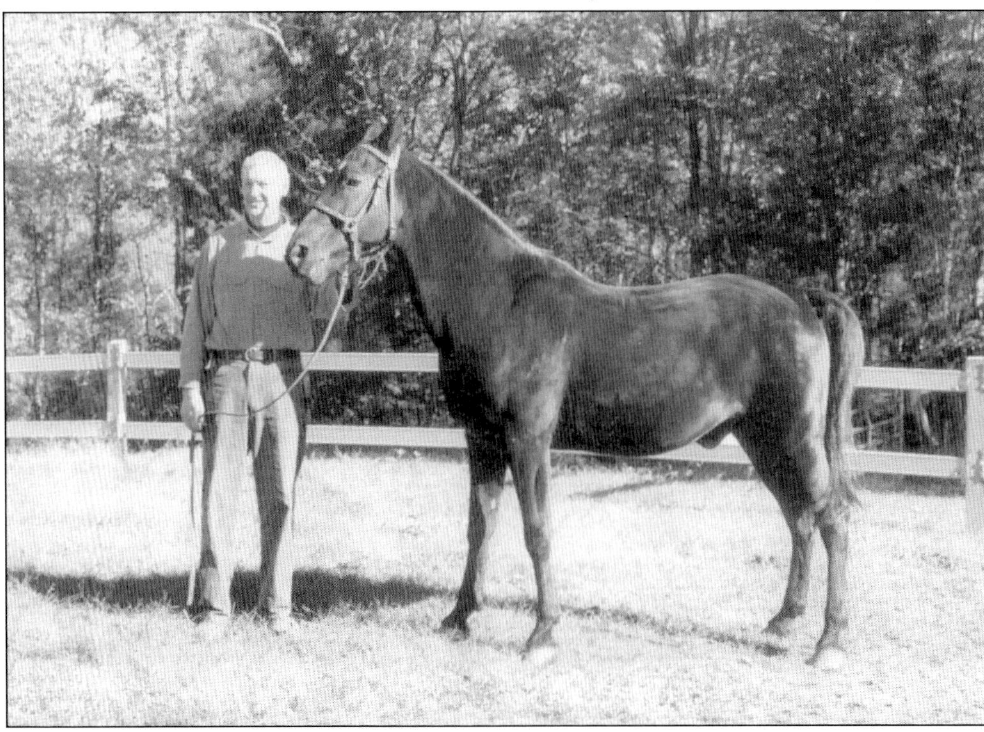

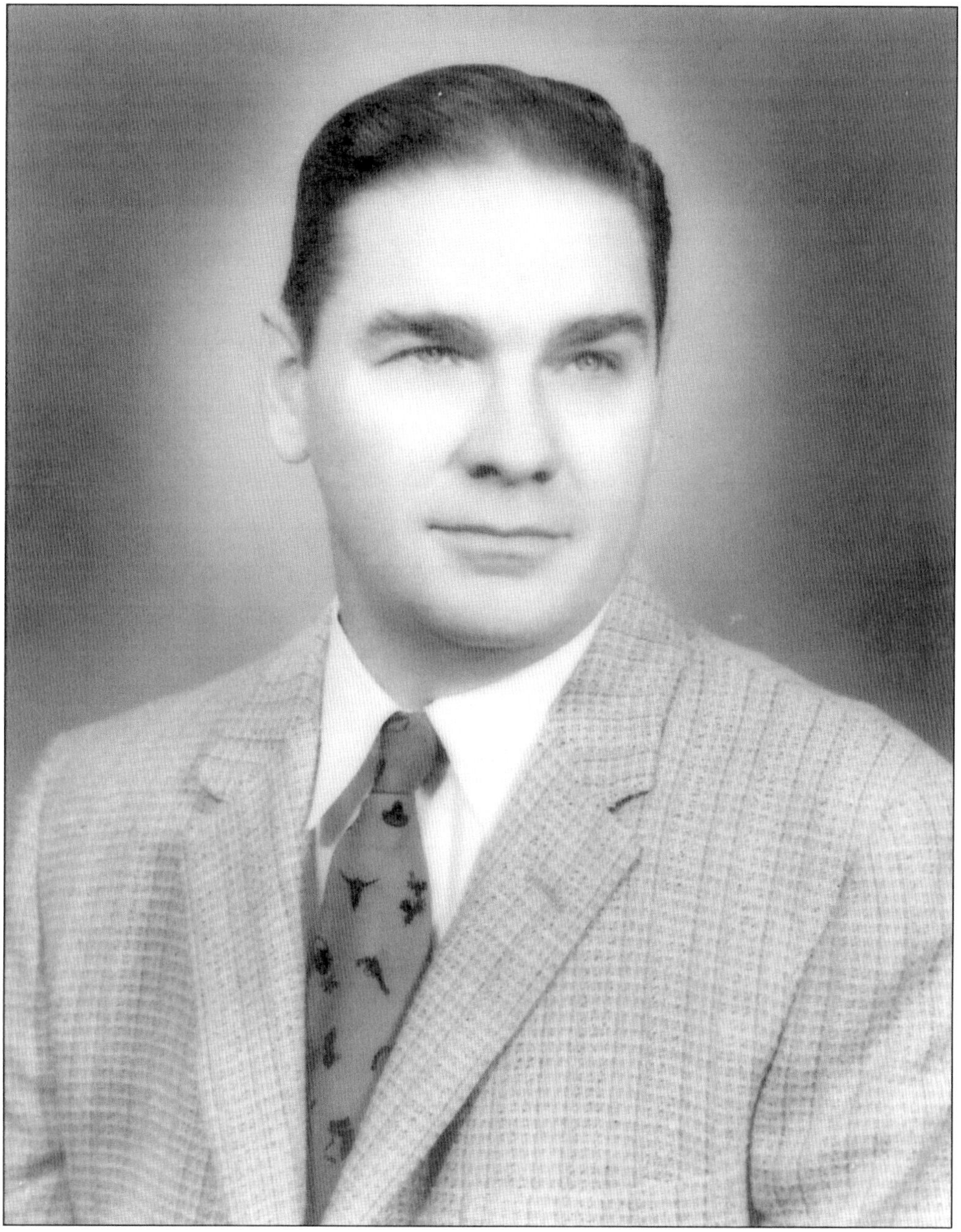

Education held a place of utmost importance to Ray Palmer Craig. He received his degree to become a pharmacist, a vocation he worked in for several years. He then returned to Stanley to work with his father, Robert Fulton Craig, at Gaston County Dyeing Machine Company. Education continued to rank high with Craig, as he became a member of the local Stanley School Board. He then went on to be one of the organizers of Gaston College and was the very first chairman of the board of trustees of the college. A Gaston College structure, the Ray P. Craig Arts and Sciences Building, is named for him. In addition, he was on the board of directors for the Schiele Museum in Gastonia. Craig was married to Lois Hogan, and together they had three children: daughter Beverly and sons Barry and Michael. (Courtesy of Michael Craig.)

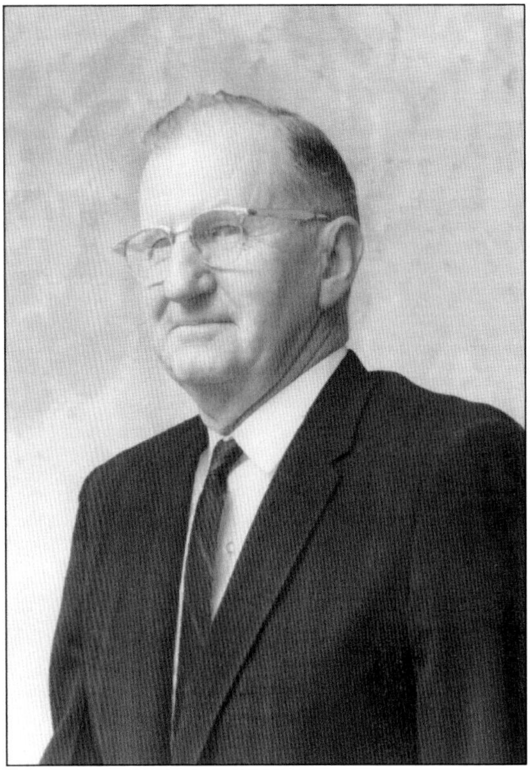

Edgar Stewart Dellinger was the grandson of one of Stanley's first families. He was an unofficial historian, recounting stories about the beginnings of the town passed down to him from his pioneer grandmother, Adeline McLurd. Dellinger operated an insurance business in Stanley for many years and is remembered for his quiet benevolence. He and his wife, Ruth McLean, had three daughters: Rosemary Easton, Judith Johnson, and Elizabeth Miller.

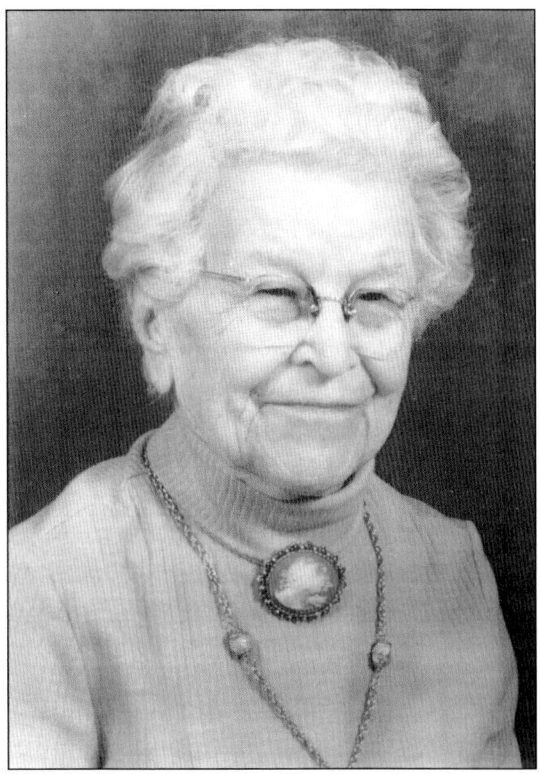

Born in 1885, Alice Pegram Mason Rhyne attended school in Stanley and then went on to the Normal School to become a teacher. She taught school at the Stanley Creek Institute, a Methodist Church Conference School. Rhyne was instrumental in preserving the history of Stanley. Many friends and relatives today cherish the quilts she handmade for them. One of her most esteemed accomplishments was maintaining a library in her home.

Hubert Maxton Craig Sr., son of Martha Cobb and Robert Fulton Craig, was president of Gaston County Dyeing Machine Company. Craig served two terms on the town council and five terms as the mayor of Stanley. He built the first housing development in Stanley for the returning World War II veterans who were guaranteed US government low-cost home loans, thereby contributing to the economic well being of Stanley. In the early 1950s, Craig developed the Jackson Park subdivision.

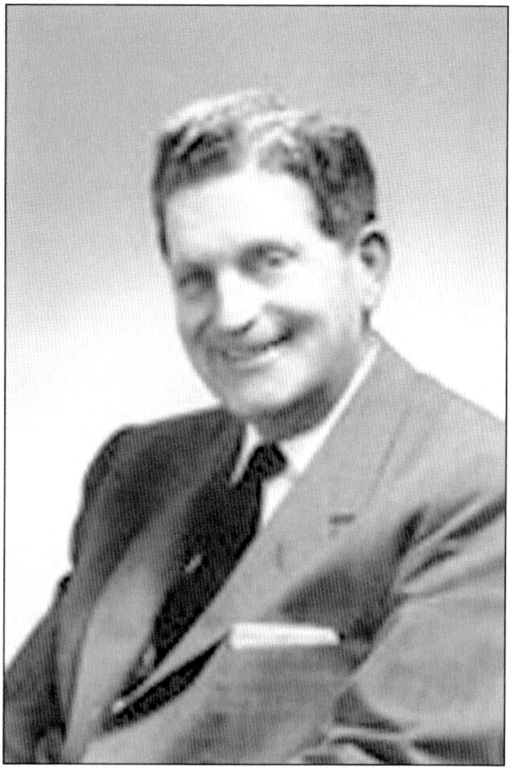

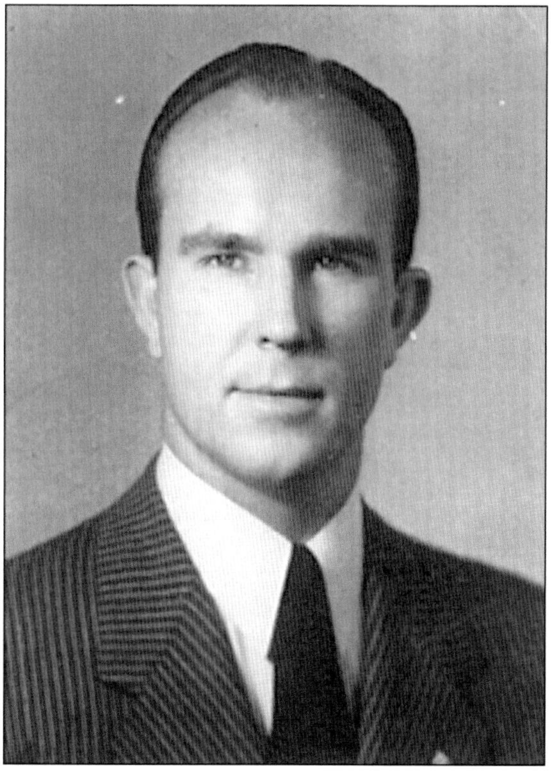

In 1952, Dr. Joseph Claude "Jake" Fesperman opened his family medicine practice in Stanley after serving in the Navy during World War II. He attended Duke University and graduated from Bowman Gray Medical School. This much-beloved doctor made house calls, delivered at least 2,500 babies, and was very active in community affairs. Fesperman was married to Kathleen Trexler and they had two sons, Dr. Joseph Fesperman and William Mark Fesperman.

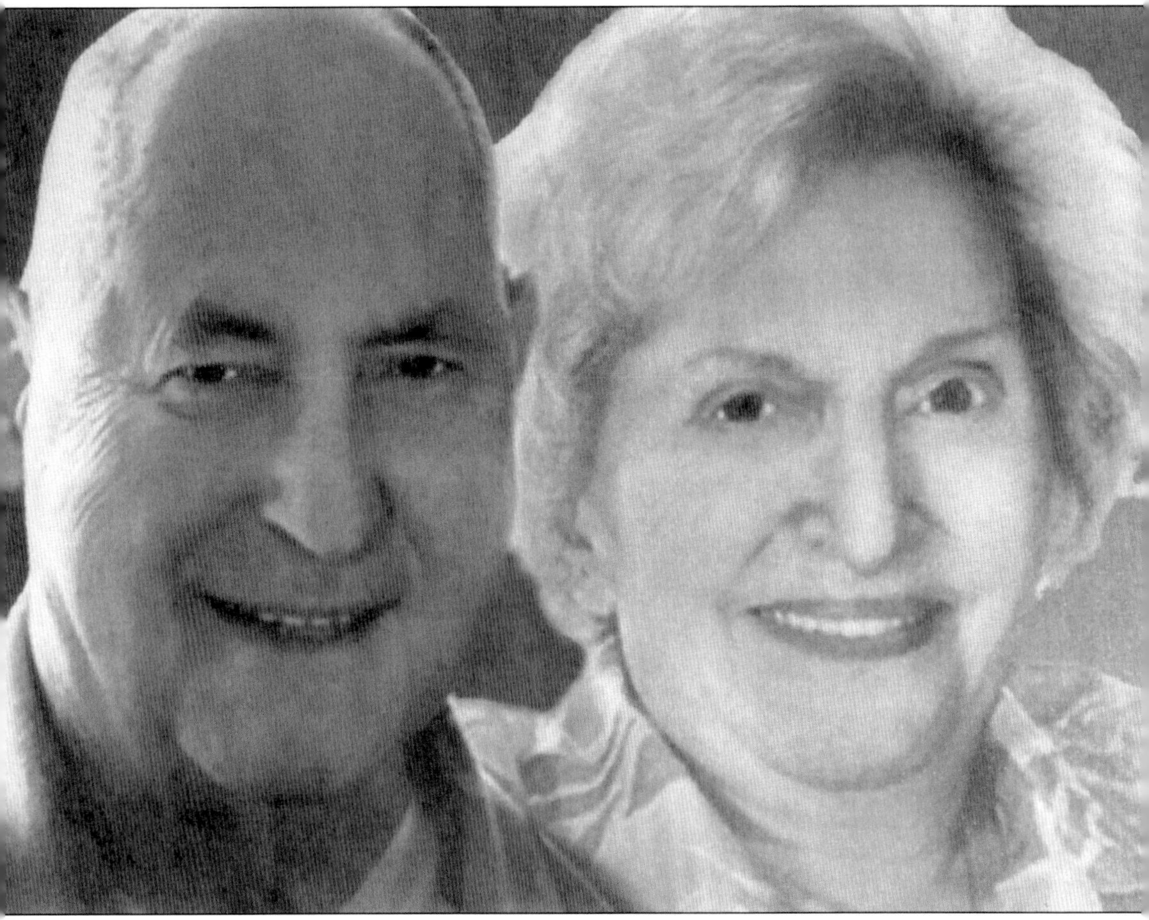

Ronald and Katherine Harper moved to Stanley after living in Charlotte for 54 of their 57 years of marriage. Both highly successful entrepreneurs, they founded three international corporations that were involved in the flexographic printing industry. Their legendary philanthropy includes an endowment to Central Piedmont Community College; a substantial contribution to Appalachian State University, where a building is named for Katherine Harper; and a $1 million donation to Clemson University. There is a Harper Endowment at California Polytechnic State University, Fox Valley Technical College, and Dunwoody College of Technology. The Harpers were instrumental in establishing printing programs in several high schools in the Charlotte area, along with a foundation to establish a Teacher's Education Fund. After moving to Stanley, they contributed to a park on Blacksnake Road, named Harper Park in their honor. Contributions also went toward the purchase of the town clock and the food bank and school supplies programs at two of Stanley's churches. A donation was made to Brevard Station Museum to help in a much needed renovation program. In 2010, the Harpers contributed a $2 million matching fund to enable all Gaston County Schools to have a SMART board in each classroom in the county.

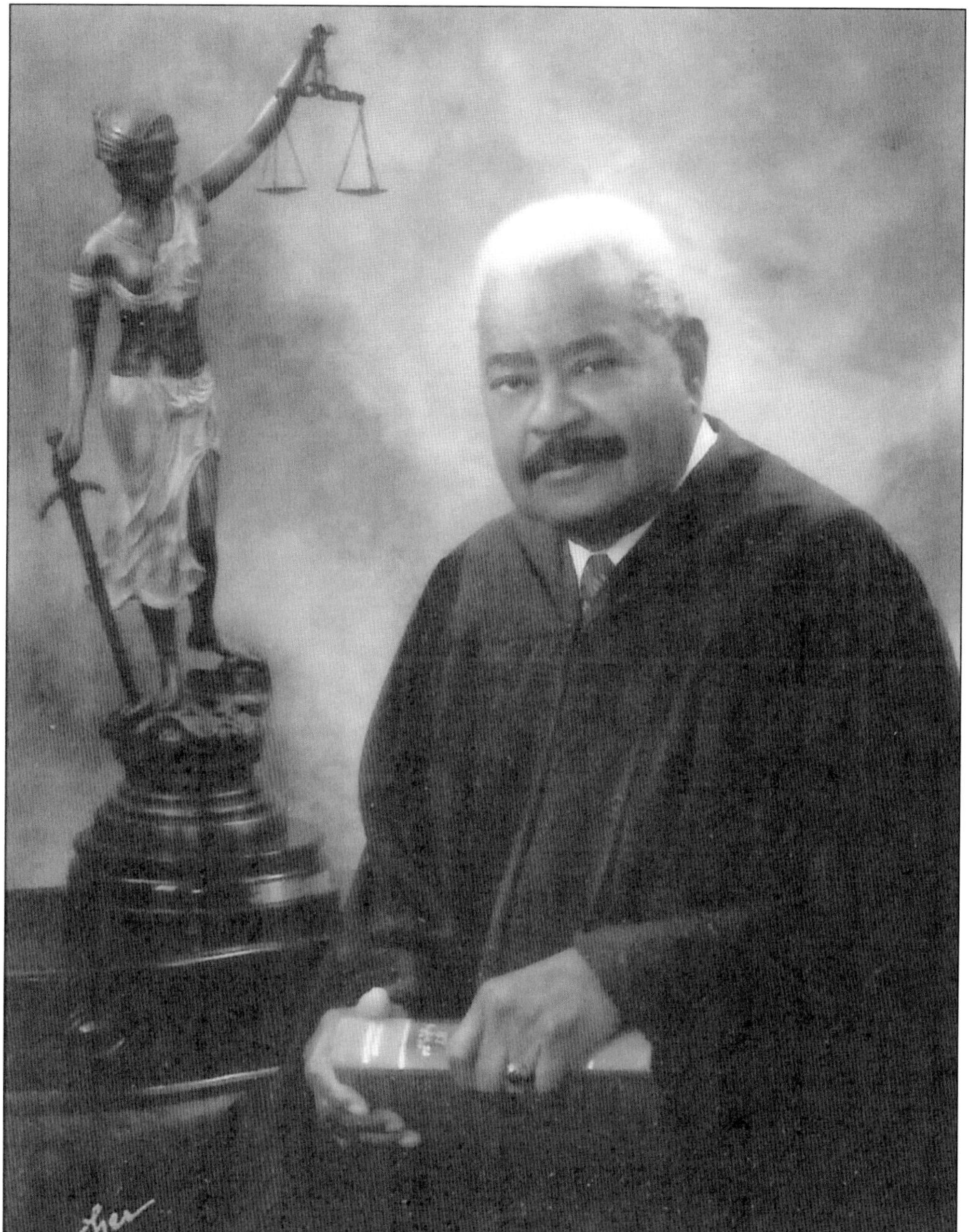

Judge James Albert Lineberger, born in Stanley in 1930, was the only child of Archie and Viola Lineberger. He attended Springfield Elementary School in Stanley and graduated from Highland High School in Gastonia, North Carolina. Lineberger served with the US Army and became a captain during World War II. He was chairman on the boards of many civic organizations in Philadelphia, Pennsylvania, where he settled after earning a law degree. There, Lineberger had a private practice for eight years. In 1992, he took a seat on the bench as judge for Court of Common Pleas, Criminal Division, First Judicial District of Pennsylvania, until his retirement on December 31, 2005.

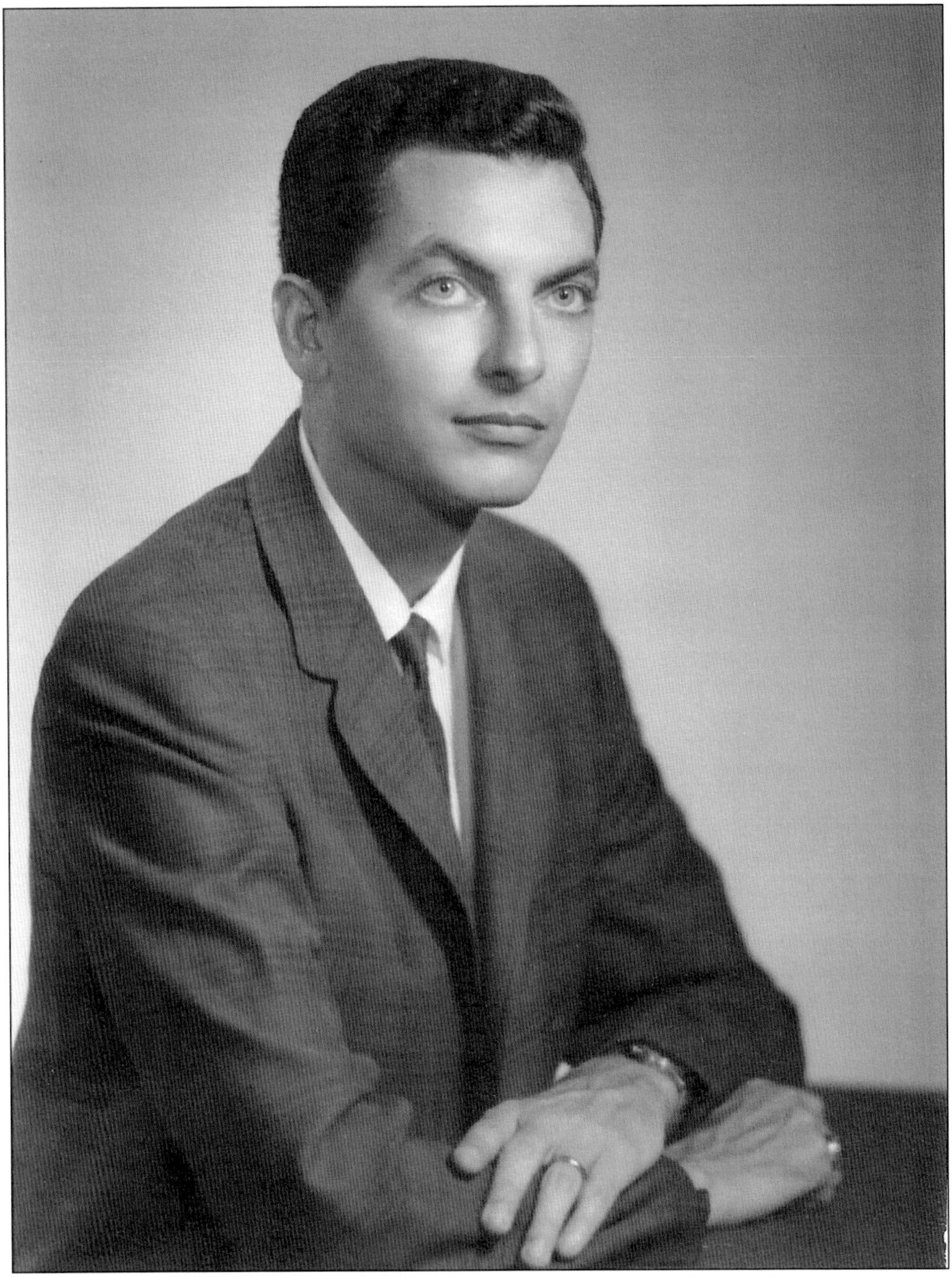

Hubert Maxton Craig Jr. was president/chairman of Gaston County Dyeing Machine Company, H.M. Craig Metal Company, and Craig Realty and Development Company. Craig served as director on the boards of First Citizens Bank, Public Service Company, and American Textile Machinery Association. In the 1970s, through Craig Realty, he developed and enhanced the shopping district in Stanley, changed the facade of the buildings, and added a roof over the sidewalk. Craig served in the North Carolina House of Representatives from 1967 to 1968. He was also a member of the North Carolina Ports Authority.

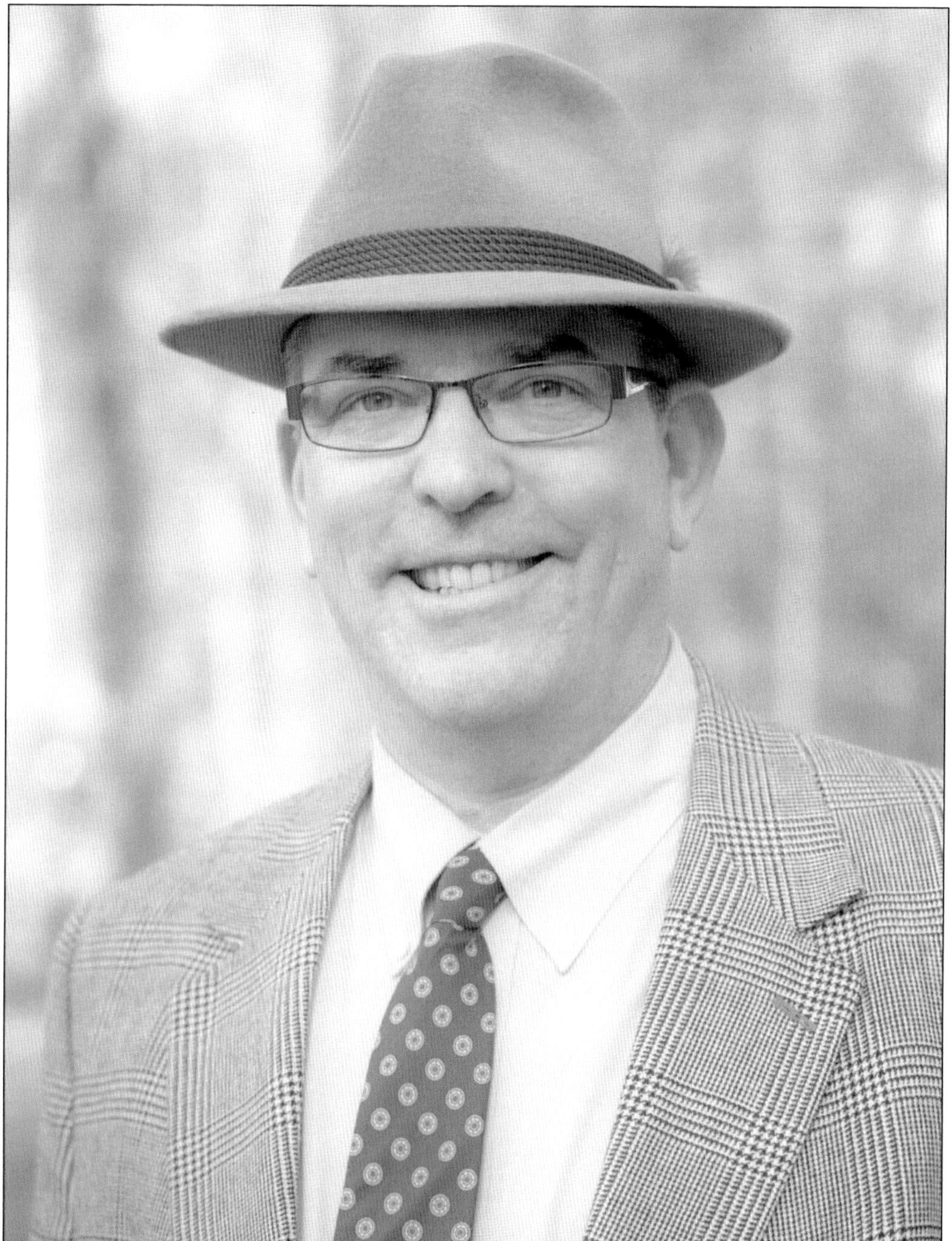

Richard E. Rankin Jr., PhD, is headmaster of Gaston Day School in Gastonia. He and wife, Sarah Park, reside on the old Rankin property. He has written five nonfiction books including *Margins of a Greater Wildness: Nature Essays About Stanley Creek and Beyond*. He is the past president of the Catawba Land Conservancy and was instrumental in the donation of 506 acres as the Stanley Creek Forest, ranked as a state-level significant natural heritage site. Other private land donations have since increased its size to approximately 1,250 acres known as the Stanley Creek Natural Area.

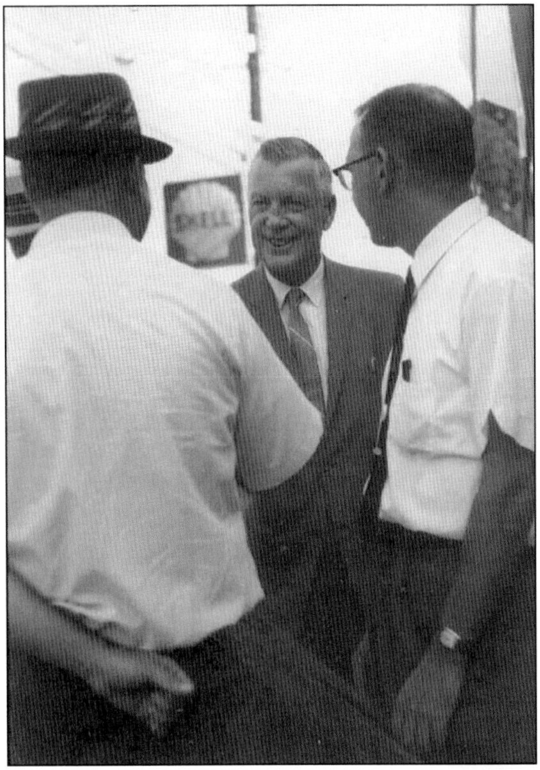

Daniel Killian Moore was governor of North Carolina from 1965 to 1969. Sometime during his campaign, he visited Stanley. Conversing with him in the photograph are Jack Moore and Charles Rhyne. After his tenure as governor, which at that time was one term, Moore was appointed to the North Carolina Supreme Court, where he served until retirement.

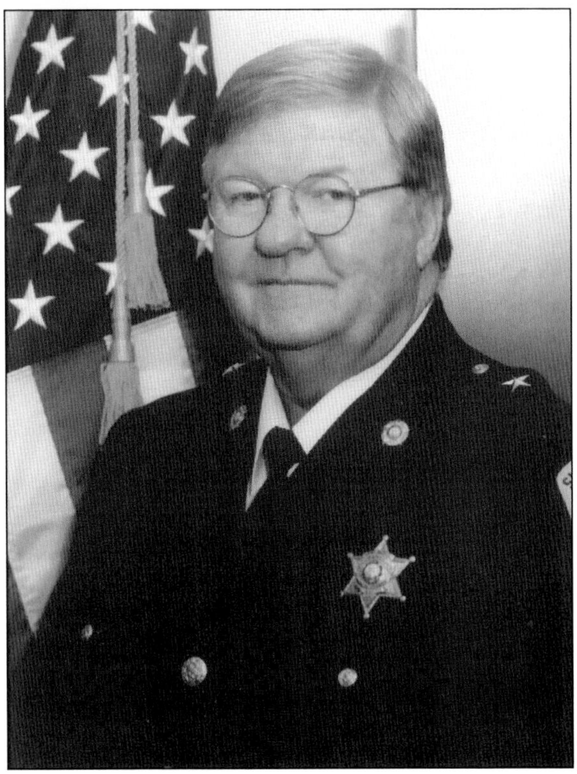

Leroy Russell served as sheriff of Gaston County from 1982 to 2004. He moved to Stanley with his family when his father came to work at Carother's Funeral Home. Russell also served as a member of the Gaston County Law Enforcement Association. A talented man, he was a licensed funeral director, a county magistrate, an employee of Gaston County Schools, a driver's license examiner, a police officer, and a proud US Air Force veteran.

On December 15, 1989, North Carolina senator Terry Sanford sent a letter to Daisy M. Brown Floyd of Stanley, congratulating her on receiving the 1989 Black Achievement Award. The senator commented on her dedication to improving the quality of life in her community and her concern for others and expressed that this was an example for all of us to follow. (Courtesy of Lois Brown Barnett.)

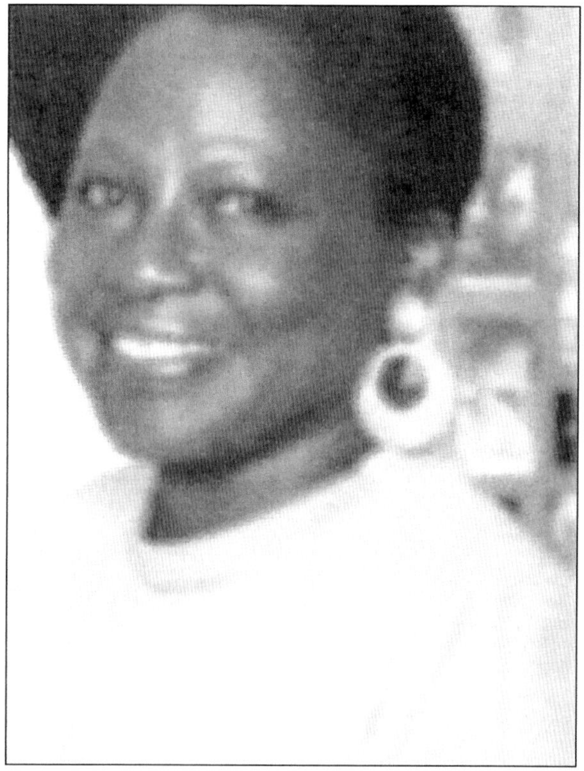

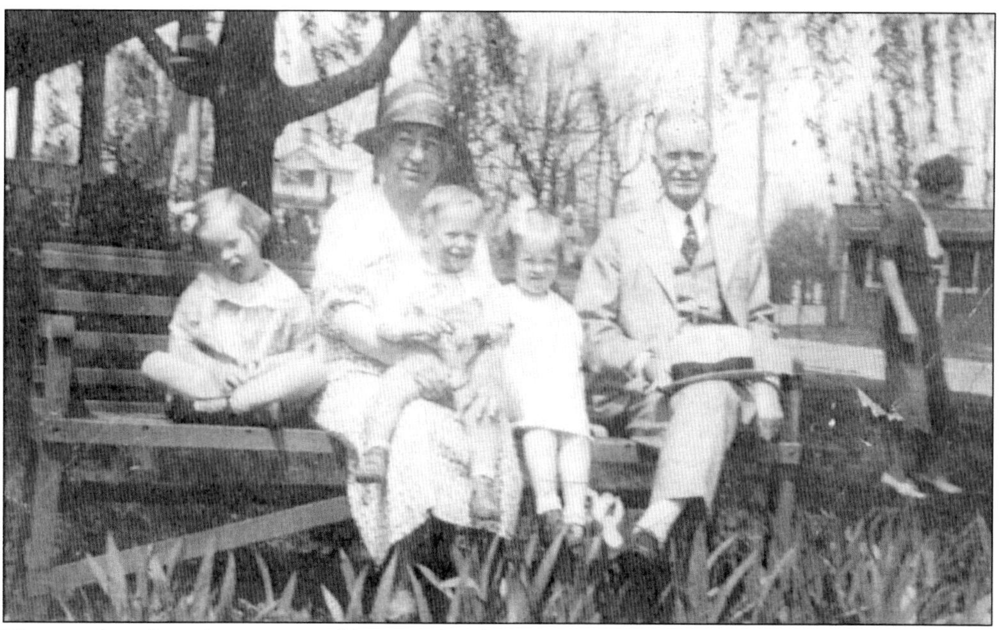

Thomas Lee Saunders was an alderman for the town of Stanley from 1941 to 1945. His wife, Mary, was the daughter of Julius and Sara Gaston, some of the first settlers in the community of Brevard Station. From left to right are Margie Saunders (granddaughter), Mary Gaston Saunders (wife), Joe Saunders (grandson), Jean Saunders (granddaughter), Thomas Saunders, and Louise Cornwell.

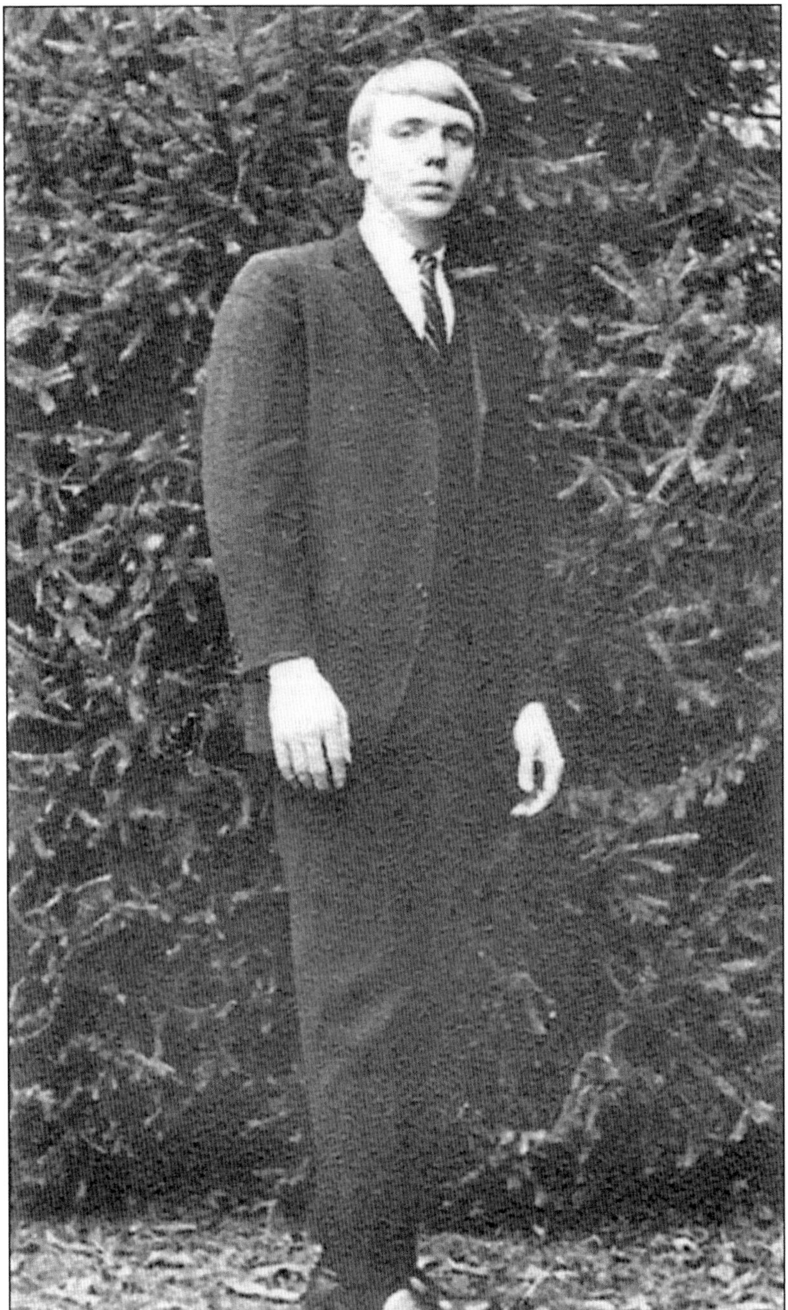

Stanley native William Barry Smith received the Professional Achievement Award from the Western Carolina University Alumni Association in October 2008. He is a 1967 graduate of Western Carolina with a bachelor's degree in business administration and an MBA degree from Tulane University. Smith managed Pfizer Pharmaceutical Company operations in 10 countries as regional director for southern Africa before his retirement. Brevard Station Museum is currently privileged to have him as chairman of its board of directors. In this 1967 photograph, Smith is pictured in his college years when he was listed in *Who's Who in American Colleges.*

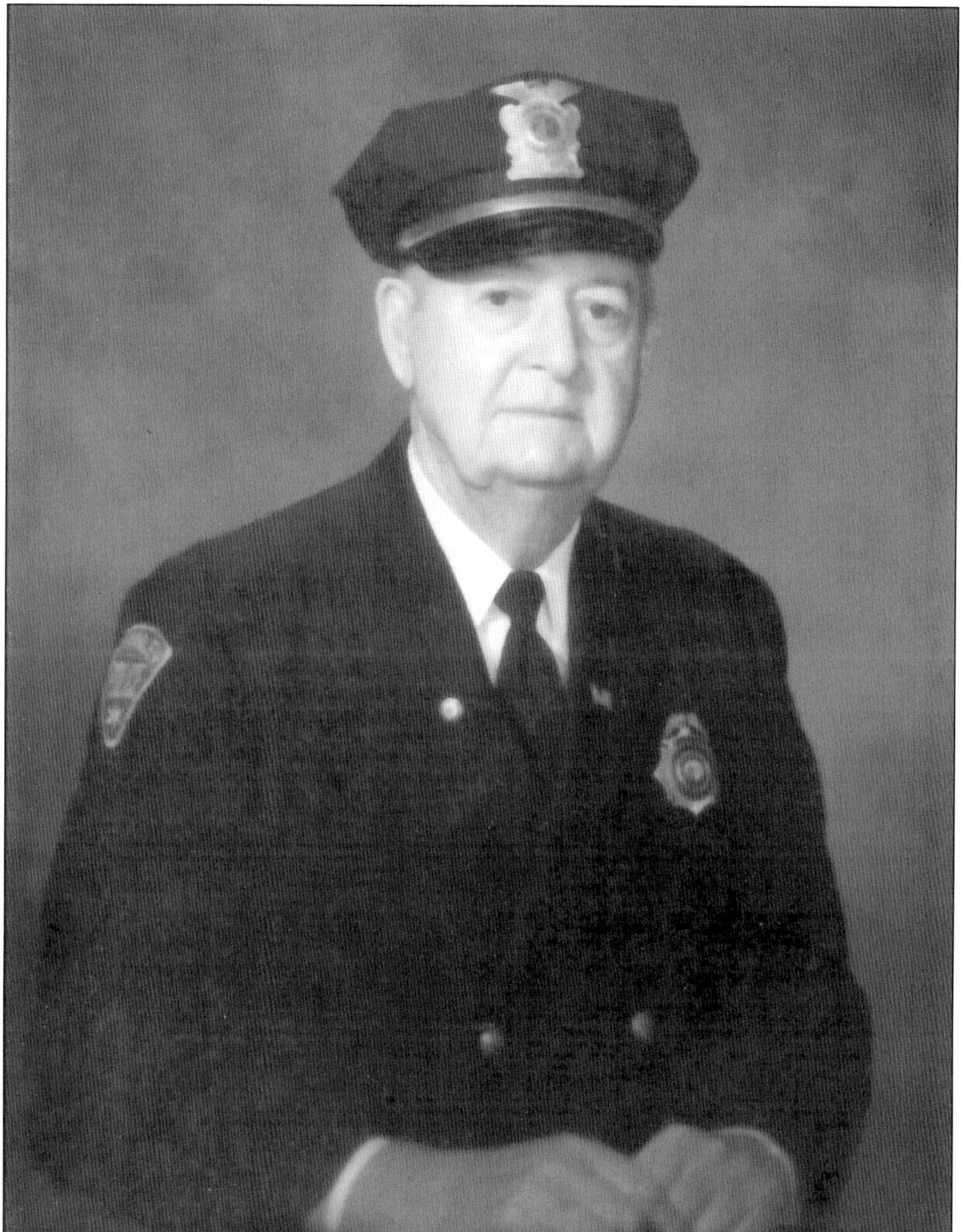

From a very young age, Ralph Handsel wanted to be a policeman. Hearing there was a need in 1932 for a deputy in Stanley, he applied and was hired. In 1941, he was made chief of police and also chief of the fire department. Until 1951, he drove his own car on police work. He was selected Man of the Year by town council in 1968, and in the 1970s, the town was said to have one of the lowest crime rates around. In 1988, at the age of 81, Handsel was recognized as the oldest police chief in the United States and received congratulations and appreciation from Pres. Ronald Reagan. He retired at the age of 82. A bust of the chief, sculpted by Dr. Bailey Graham Weathers Jr., is on display at the Brevard Station Museum.

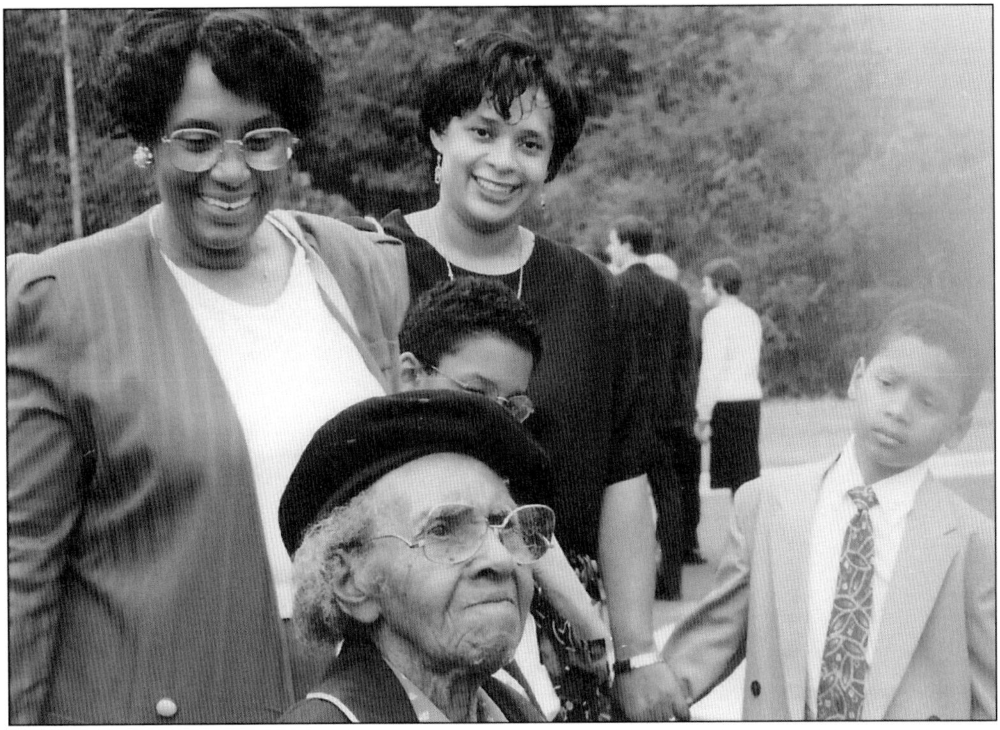

When Highway 27 was being built through Stanley in the 1920s, twelve-year-old Stowe Cannon got a job helping to get water and sand for the workers. One day, when going to the spring for water, he passed the home of Theodore Abernethy. The older gentleman, whom everyone referred to as "Uncle Dorry," had been born into slavery. As time passed, Abernethy did not see the boy return from the spring and went to investigate. He found the boy unconscious, overcome by heat, and took him home, where he was cared for and recovered. Cannon never forgot the incident that he felt saved his life, and in 1990, he made arrangements to commemorate Theodore Abernethy's heroic act. Descendants of "Uncle Dorry" gathered with other folks in town for the ceremony at Springfield Baptist Church Cemetery where a monument was placed in Theodore Abernethy's honor. Speeches were made by Cannon, by his grandson Glenn McGuire, and by Abernethy's 92-year-old daughter, Zettie Friday, shown seated above. Also pictured, from left to right, are Odessa Coulter, Teresa Coulter, and two great-great-grandsons of Theodore and Zettie Friday.

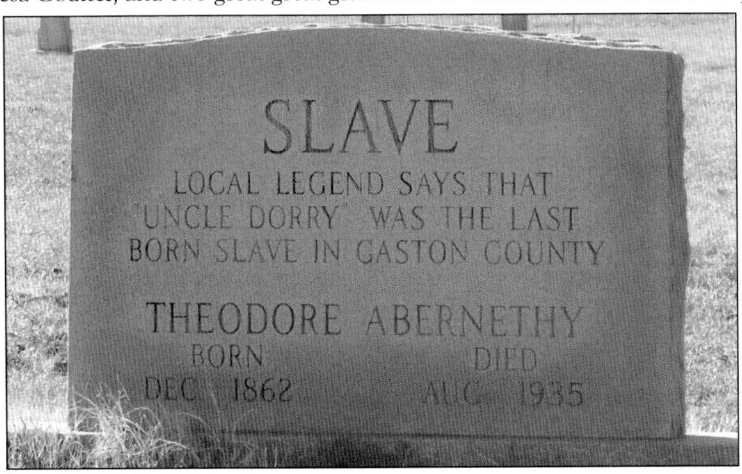

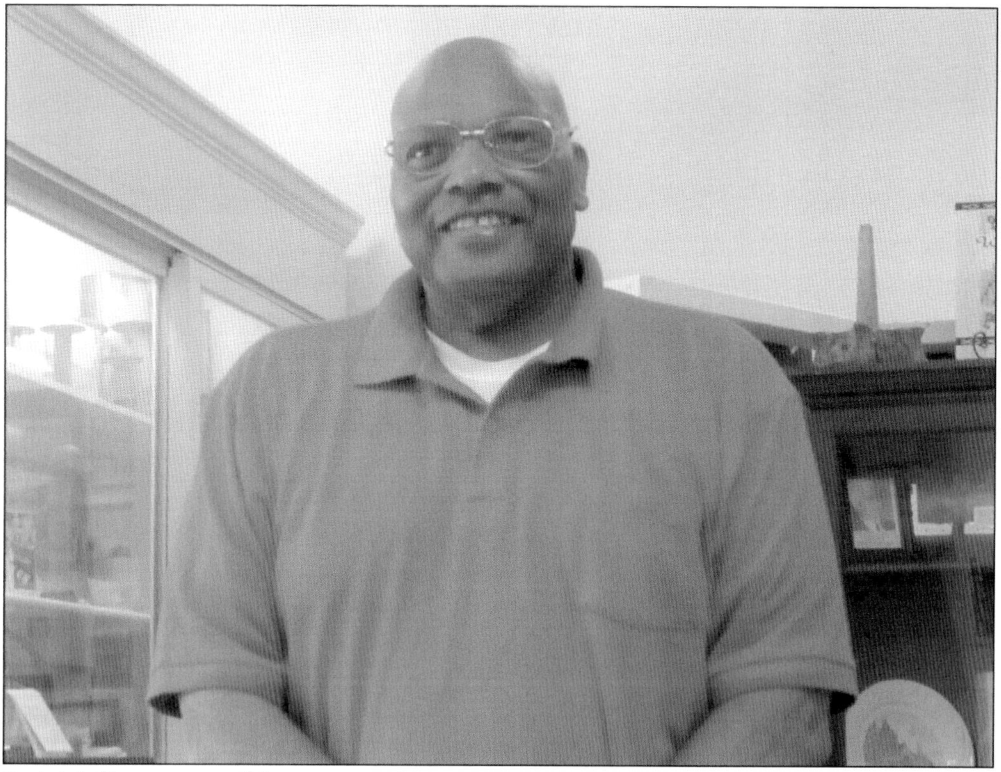

Rudolph Young is a well-known genealogist and history enthusiast. He has written a number of books relating to the history of African Americans in Gaston and surrounding counties, including *Inside the Circle of the Large Leaf Magnolia—1830 to 1900*. A retired veteran of the Army and the Air Force, Young also serves as president of Trans Catawba African American Genealogical Association and periodically does volunteer work at Brevard Station Museum.

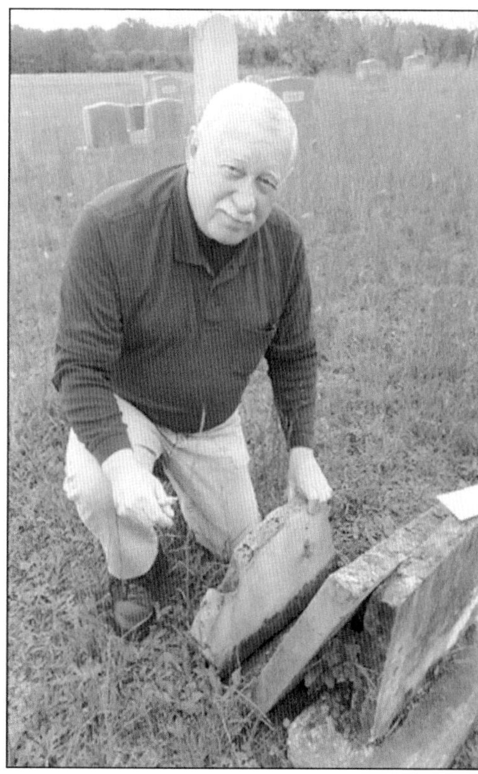

Terry Waldrop is the author of the three-volume series *Old Gravesites Revisited in Gaston and Lincoln County, North Carolina*, and many websites. What started as a hobby has turned into a wealth of information for genealogists and historians. He has helped families locate old and abandoned cemeteries and catalogued authentic names, locations, dates, and the art displayed on timeworn tombstones.

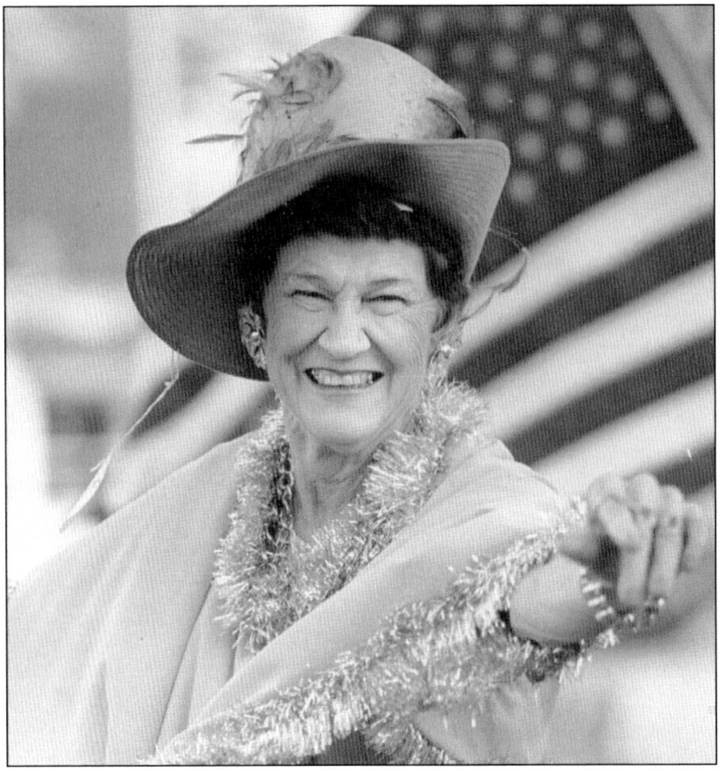

Grace Garrison Maxwell, born September 5, 1912, to Tom and Alice Friday Garrison, was always interested in music and sports, playing basketball at Stanley High School. She started imitating Minnie Pearl, of Grand Ole Opry fame, at age 65, calling herself "Ginny Girl." Grace formed the Snowflakes and the Goofy Girls, made up of women all in their 80s. They spent many hours entertaining senior citizens in nursing homes and churches.

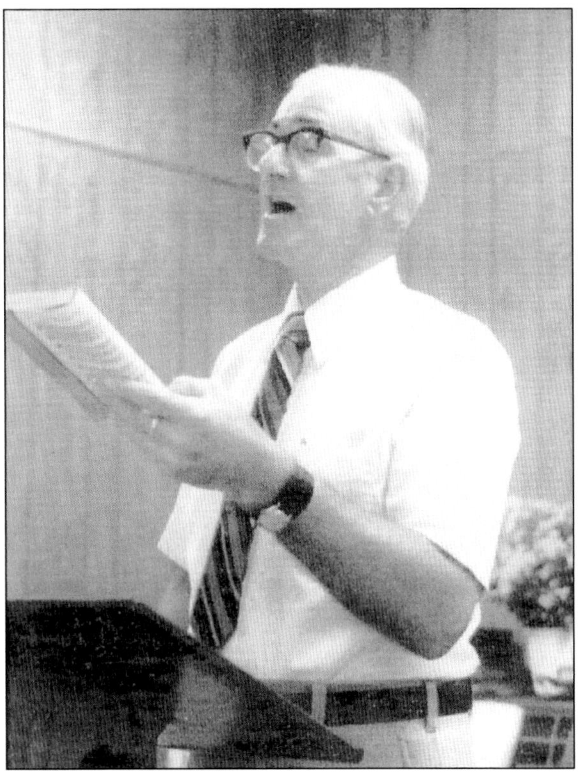

Dan Long was a remarkably talented man who sang as a young man on the radio. A friendly fellow who never met a stranger, he was also a gifted story teller. Long sang in the group Golden Heirs at First Presbyterian Church. Using cow bones and a unique combination of a washboard, cowbell, and bicycle horn to make music, he entertained the residents in many nursing homes.

# *Eight*

# COMMUNITY LIFE

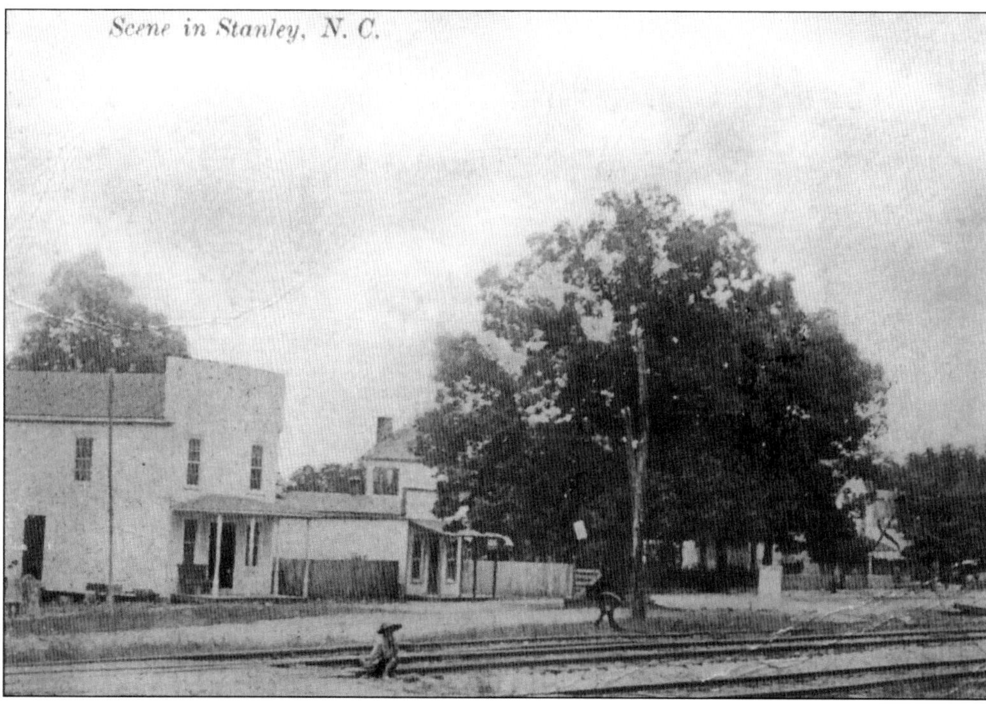


This postcard illustrates what the early businesses looked like around the beginning of the 20th century in Stanley. The view is looking north to south, and the town buildings are on the east side of the railroad tracks. The child sitting on the tracks is Earnest Cannon.

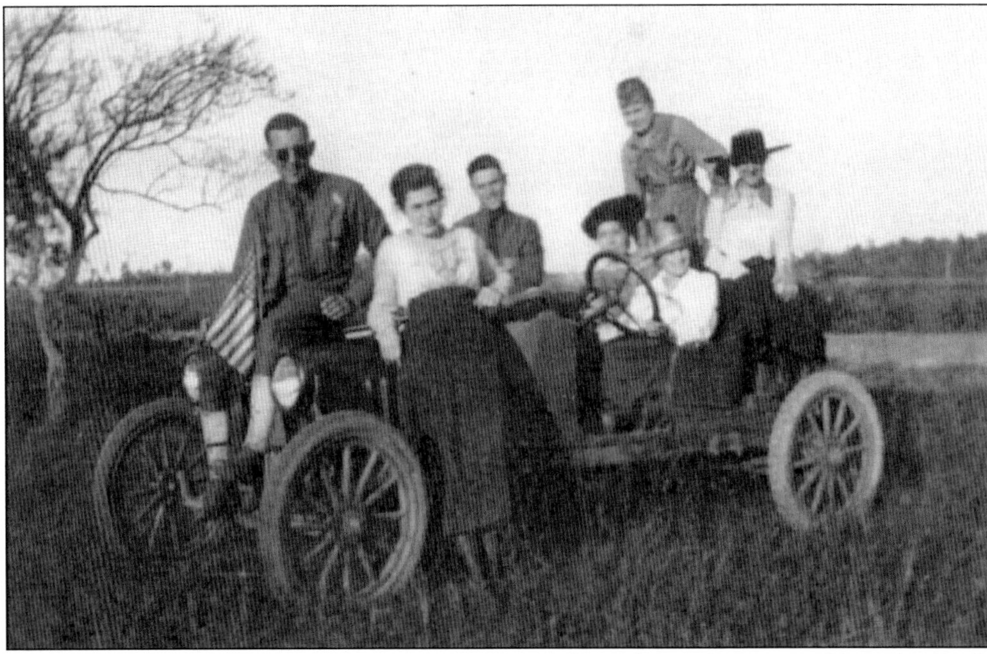

This group of young people seems to be enjoying a ride in this early "convertible." The World War I uniforms of the young men attest to the fact that they are in service, and the flag points to the fact that all are patriotic. From the smiles, they appear to be enjoying the outing. Could they possibly have planned a picnic in this nice open field?

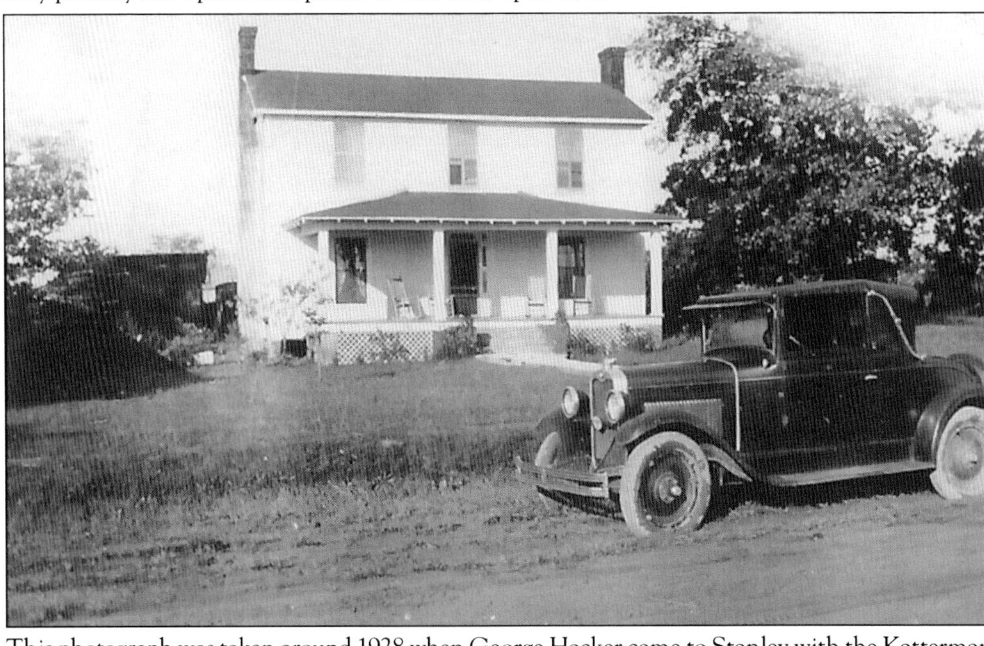

This photograph was taken around 1928 when George Hacker came to Stanley with the Katterman and Mitchell Silk Mill. The Hacker family lived for a while in the Alexander home (pictured) on the corner of Main and West Chestnut Streets. Notice that a portion of Main Street was unpaved. Hacker drove the company's 1928 red Chevrolet Cabriolet seen here until he bought his own 1930 Hudson.

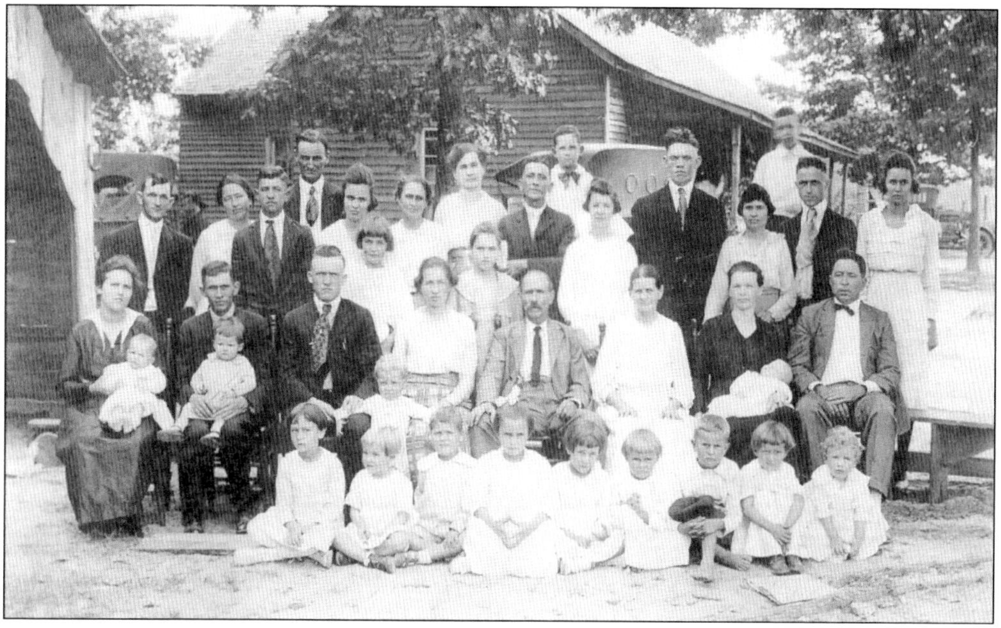

Early model Fords were the preferred mode of transportation for the Spargo family to travel to their reunion at the Jonathan J. Spargo residence in 1919. The children were all dressed in their Sunday clothes, and the little girl's favorite haircut appears to have been the Dutch boy style. A horseshoe hangs on the garage with the ends pointing up, which was said to keep the luck from running out.

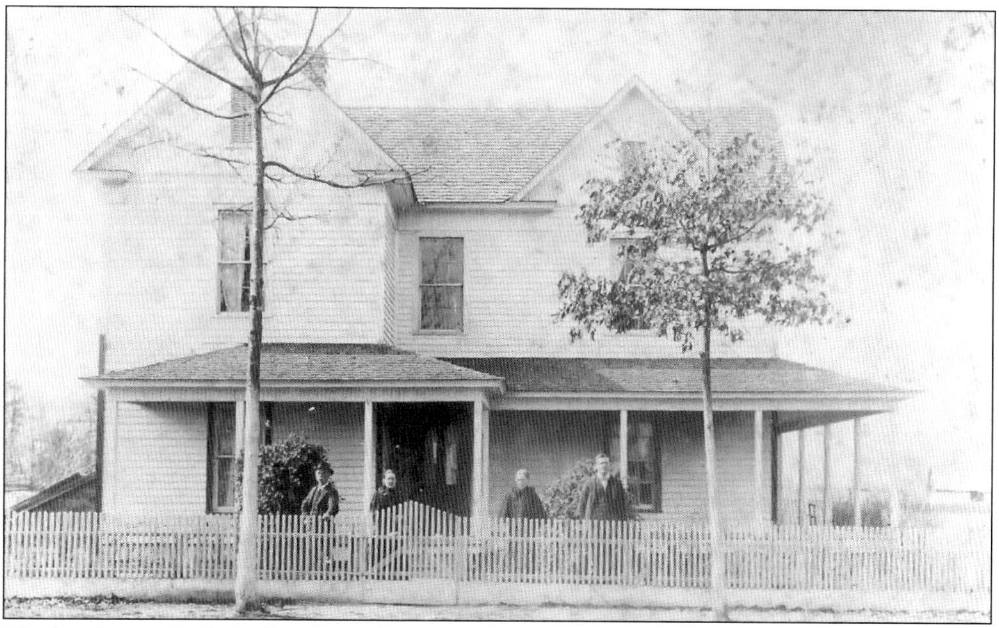

The Lineberger-Rutledge house was built around 1890 by Augustus Lineberger for his new bride, Ella Abernethy. The house stood on Main Street and is said to have been one of Stanley's finest. Later, it was sold to Wade and Lou Suggs Rutledge and stayed in the Rutledge family until it burned in the late 1980s. From left to right are Robert Laban Abernethy, Julia Abernethy, Ella Lineberger, and Augustus Lineberger.

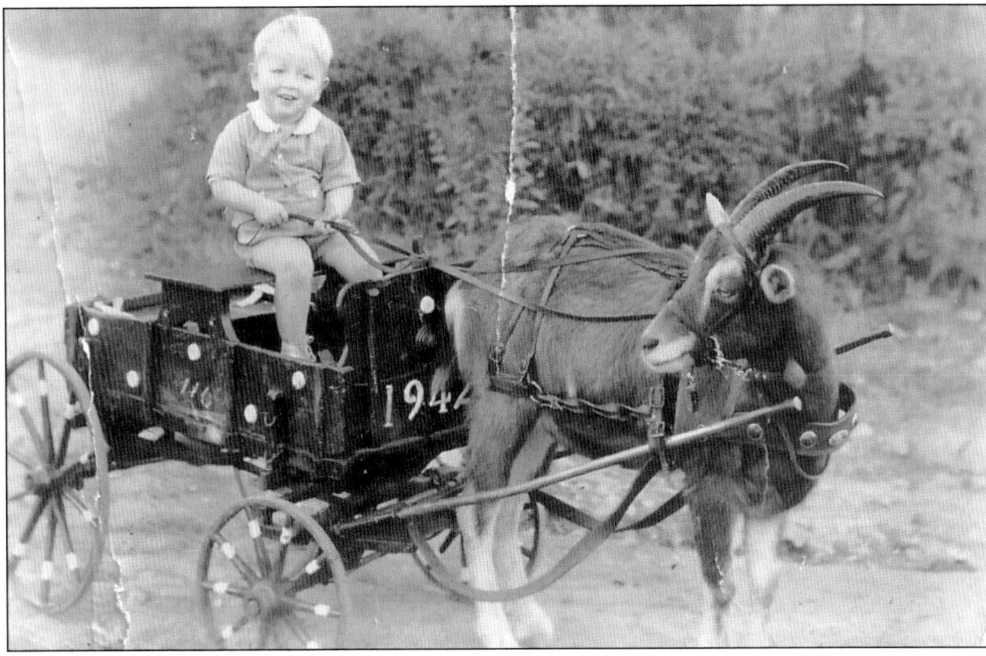


Steve Morris is shown riding on a goat cart on this postcard in 1942. Traveling photographers used these cute props as a way of promoting business. Steve is the son of William Morris and Sarah Virginia Broome. William was a World War II veteran who served in Europe with the 135th Engineer Combat Battalion.

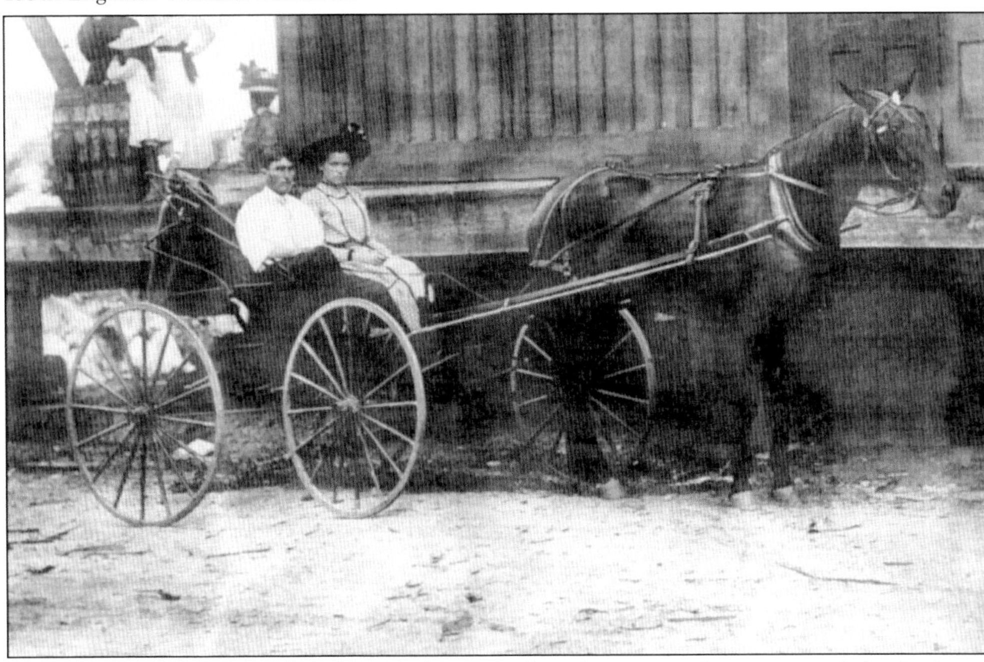

In July 1910, the people of Stanley Creek gathered in the center of town around the Seaboard Railroad Depot for the annual Picnic Day Celebration. In the horse-drawn buggy are Ivy Friday and Walter Stroupe. Friday later married Odel Lutz, and Stroupe married Bessie Robinson. (Courtesy of Elsie Lutz Dellinger.)

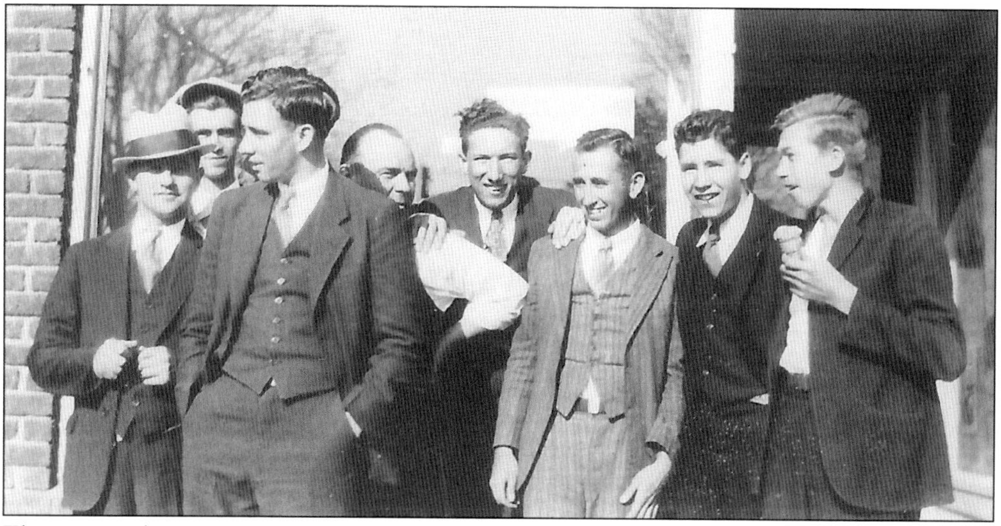

This group of men seems to be enjoying getting together downtown in the 1940s. From left to right are Raymond Spargo, Judson Vipperman Lineberger, Ralph Wallace, Forney Goodson, Doyt Morris, J.B. Rhyne, Heath Bumgardner, and David "Pete" Rhyne. They all are wearing their Sunday "go to meeting" suits and ties. Rhyne especially seems to be enjoying his ice-cream cone as Doyt Morris smiles broadly for the camera.

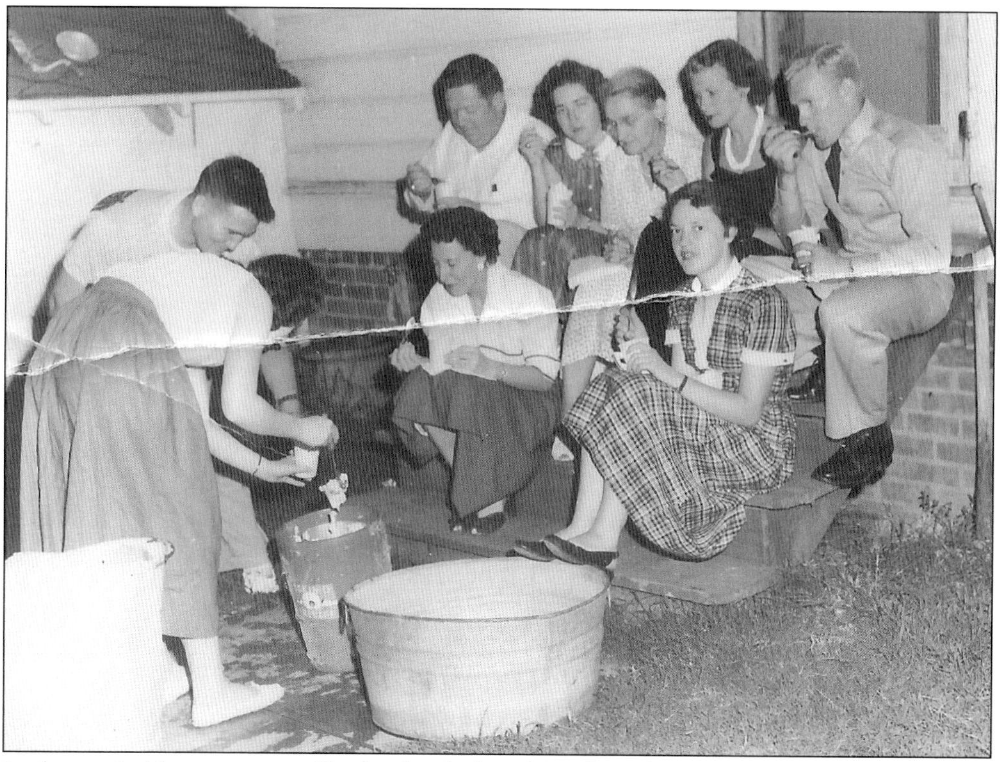

In the good old summertime, Hawley family friends' and neighbors' thoughts turned to getting together for some delicious ice cream. This group seems to be enjoying the rewards of their labor. With some ice, salt, and cranking, the milk, sugar, and eggs turn into a cold, refreshing treat. If one churning was not enough, it did not take that long to make another.

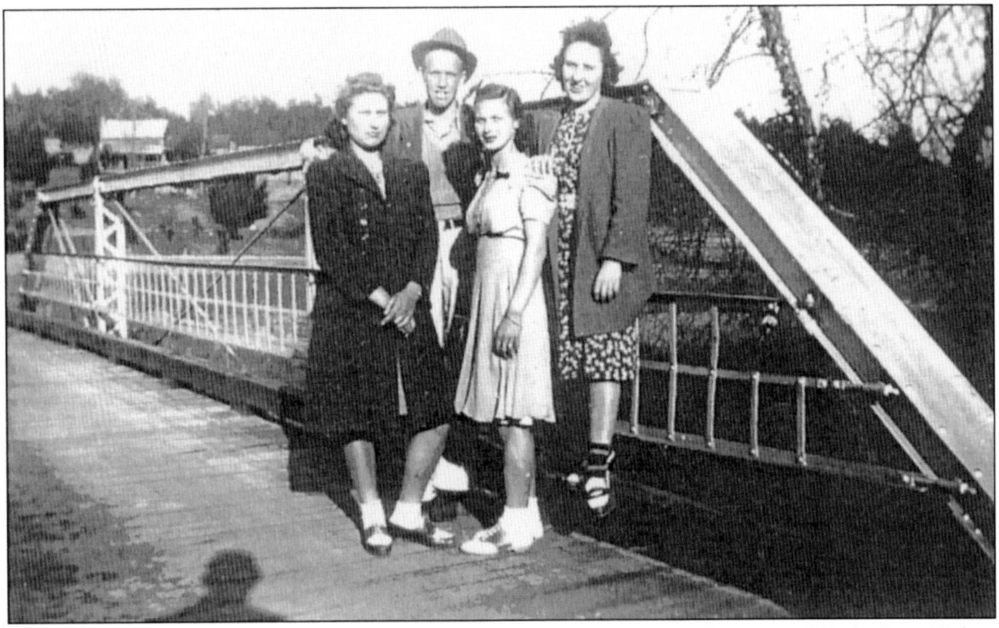

Standing on Stanley Creek bridge are, from left to right, Juanita Walker, Tom Black, Sara Helms Grissop, and Mary Cloninger. In the background is the Valentine Derr home that served as the post office from 1856 until 1861, when the post office was moved into the Brevard Station Depot. The Derr home had cubbies on the back porch for mail waiting to be picked up. The house stood until the 1960s.

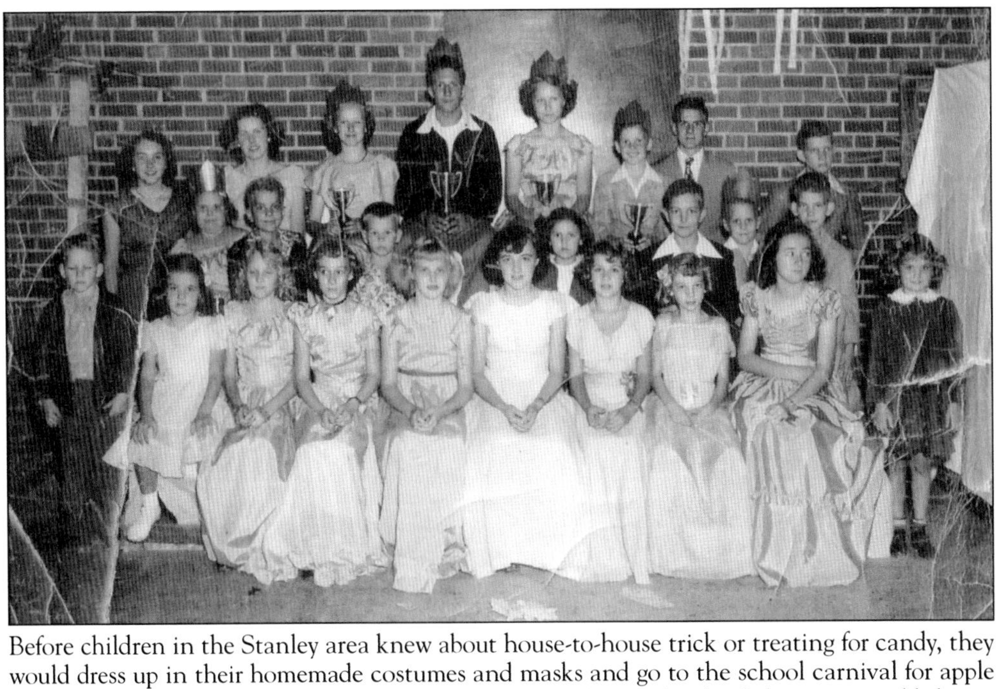

Before children in the Stanley area knew about house-to-house trick or treating for candy, they would dress up in their homemade costumes and masks and go to the school carnival for apple bobbing, climbing a greasy pole, dart throwing, and more fun. Each school classroom would choose a girl and boy to vie for the Halloween queen and king. This photograph of the contestants was taken around 1946 or 1947.

Pictured in the foreground from left to right are Mayor Glenn Rhyne, Jim Rutledge, Chief Ralph Handsel, Luther Benton, John Roseboro, Lee Smith, and Arthur C. Taylor. In the background are George Derr, Alfred Rhyne, and Martha Sue Taylor among various unidentified persons. City officials ceremonially pour illegal liquor down the drain. Someone had been caught by local police driving through town with the forbidden "white lightnin'. " (Courtesy of Barbara Rankin Brakebill.)

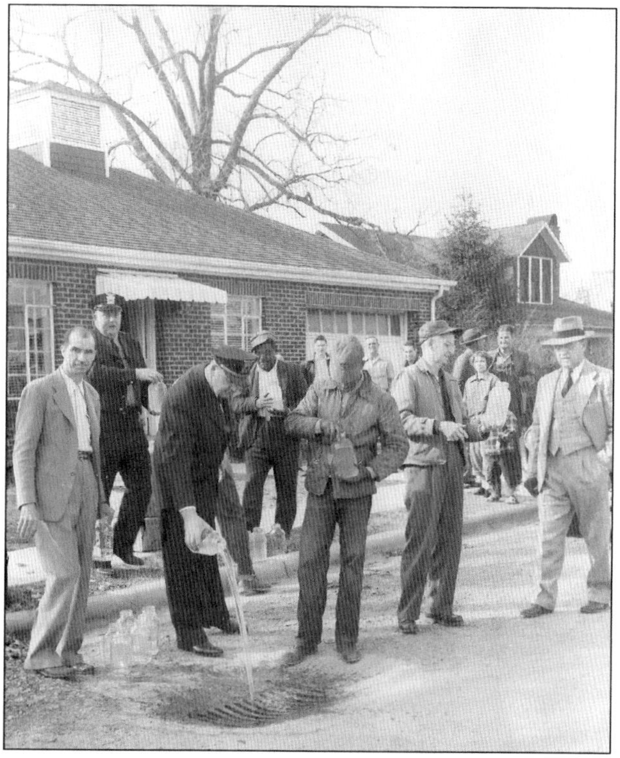

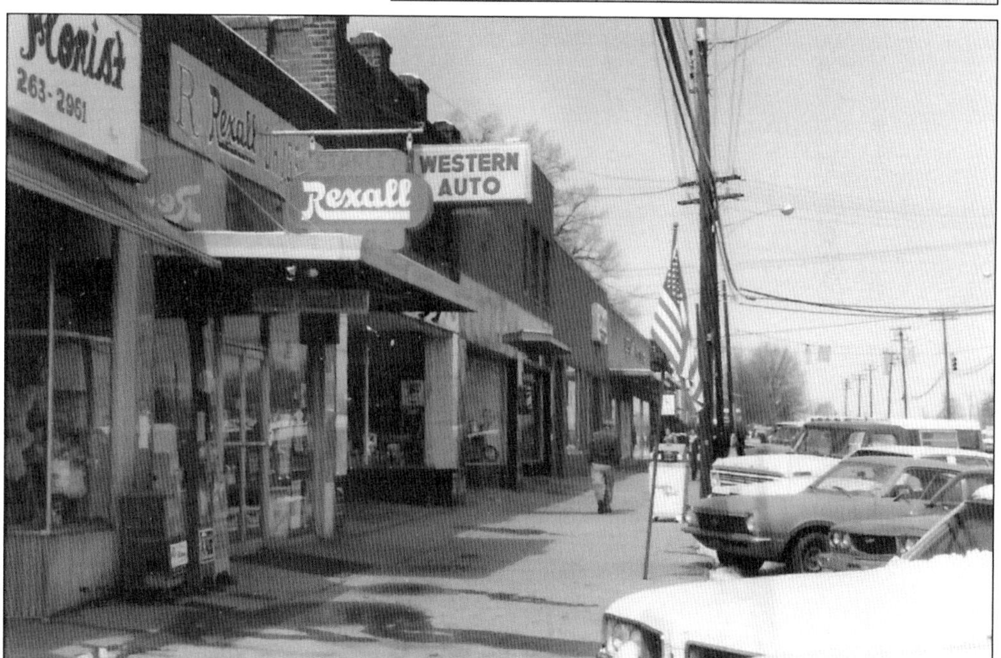


This Stanley streetscape in the 1960s shows Main Street filled with many retail stores. This photograph illustrates the diversity of the business operating in the town of Stanley. The cars parked in front speak to the fact that the establishments were well frequented. Unfortunately, as malls opened in the area, more and more people abandoned the downtown shops.

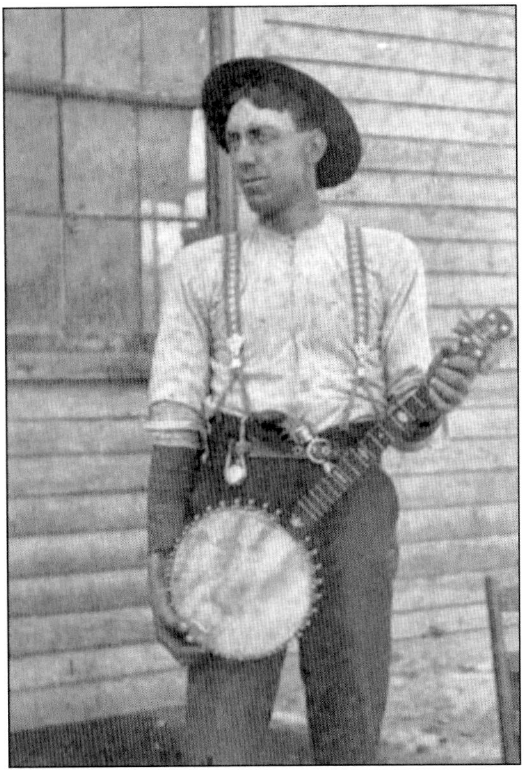

William Gaston Matthews lived to the age of 104 and farmed most of his life, except for a few years when he worked in a local mill. Matthews was six feet six inches tall, "with a hand so big he could carry two 200-pound bags of fertilizer, one under each arm," as told by his nephew William Matthews. As this photograph would indicate, William Gaston Matthews also enjoyed playing the banjo.

This group of folks in the Alexis community enjoyed getting together to sing. From left to right are Dan Long, Dorothy Shelton, Spencer Shelton, J.D. Lowe, and Louise Hager (the piano player). Long actually broadened his talent by singing with other groups and entertaining at nursing homes.

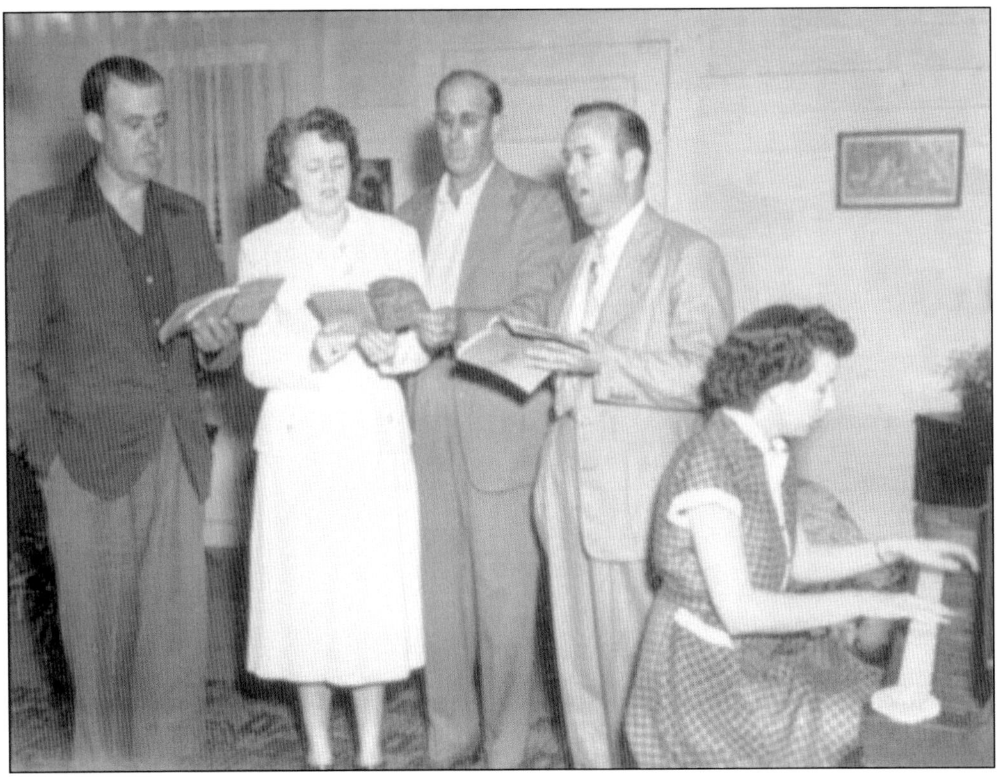

This young man is returning a book he borrowed from the Stanley Library. Originally, the only lending library was the bookmobile that came to town occasionally. Then Allie Rhyne kept some books in her home to make them more accessible to everyone. Many folks can remember going to "Miss Allie's" for a book to enjoy before the library was built in 1960 as a branch of the Gaston County Library system.

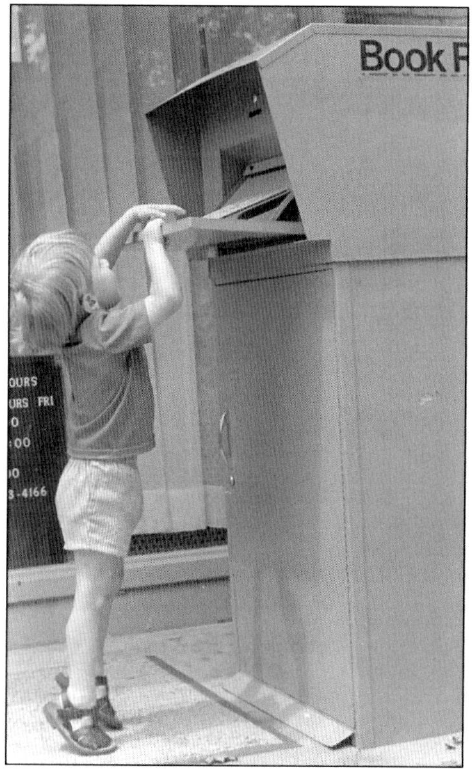


Family and friends of the bride and groom are gathered outside the church to congratulate Annette Handsel and Billy Joe Noles on their wedding day in 1959. Behind the just married couple are, from left to right, Faye and Ralph Handsel and Forest Armstrong. Greeting them are, from left to right, Michael and David Watts, Rachel Armstrong, Earlene and Terry Handsel, Nancy Jamison, Alease Armstrong, Patricia Ritchie, Bernice Thompson, Marie Sitton, Doyt Abernathy, Frances Noles, and Clarence Armstrong.

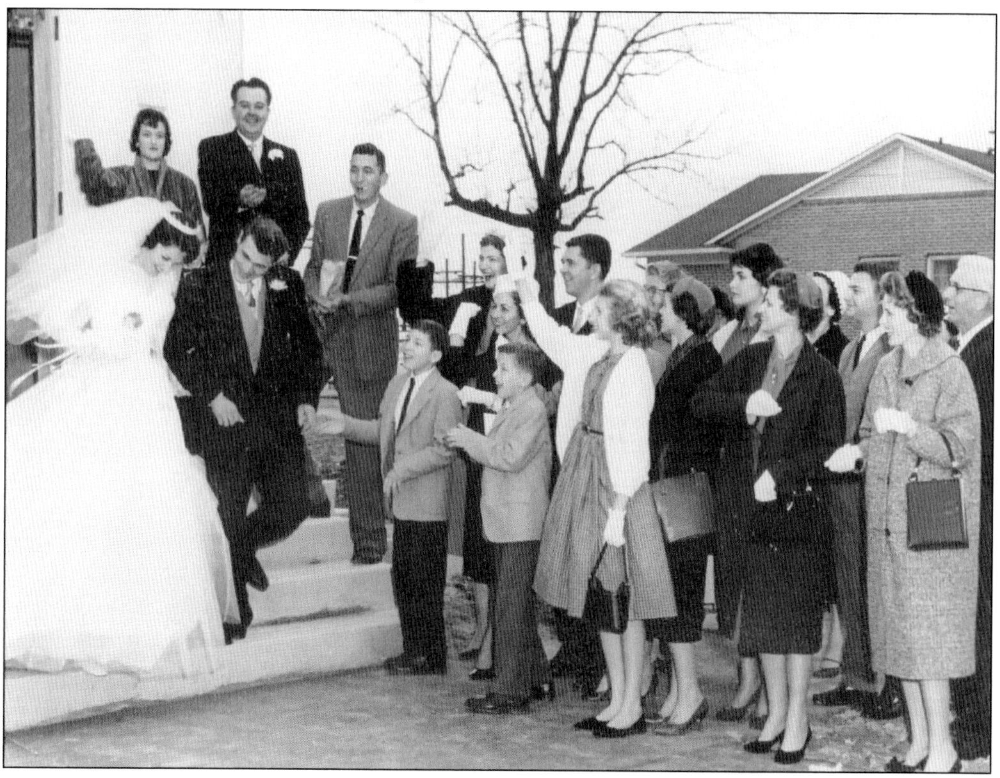

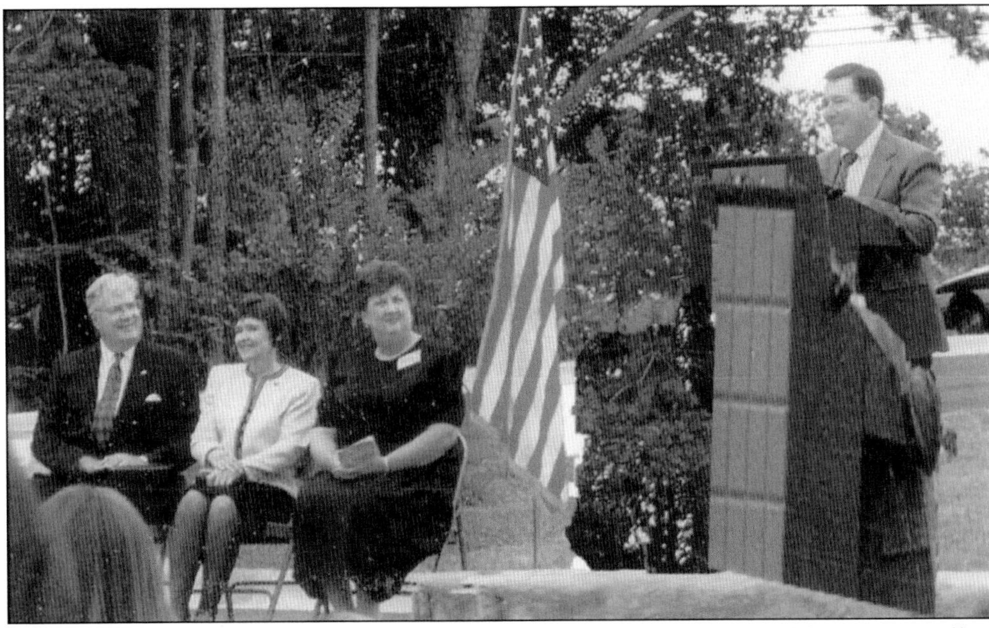

Citizens gathered on Sunday, September 29, 1996, to celebrate the opening of the new post office, with speeches by local dignitaries. From left to right are James S. Forrester (North Carolina senator), Sue Myrick (US House of Representatives, 9th District), Gail Brotherton, (Stanley mayor), and Frank Guida (Stanley postmaster). A few days later, a time capsule was buried on the grounds, to be opened in the year 2046.

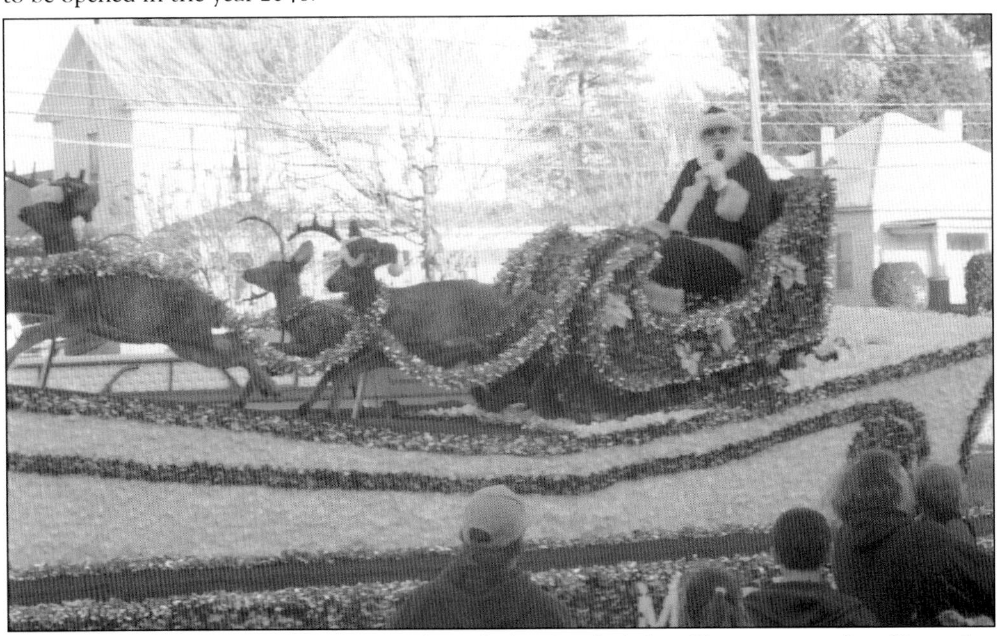

Dr. Bailey Graham Weathers Sr. was grand marshal in Stanley's first Christmas parade in December 1974. The parade is pleasantly anticipated by the community. It always has a diversified lineup with bands, dancers, fire trucks, horses, classic cars, and celebrities. The most popular celebrity is the fellow with the reindeer, Santa Claus, who is always the last to appear. The children especially wait impatiently to hear Santa's "Ho ho ho."

Preparing to enjoy the playground area at Harper Park are brother and sister Cooper and Haleigh Park. Neighborhood children have quickly made the park a favorite place to visit, keeping the playground equipment busy. The picnic area is used by families for many special occasions. The ballfields and walking track provide entertainment and exercise for anyone interested. Named for philanthropists Ronald and Katherine Harper, the park is a fine asset for Stanley.

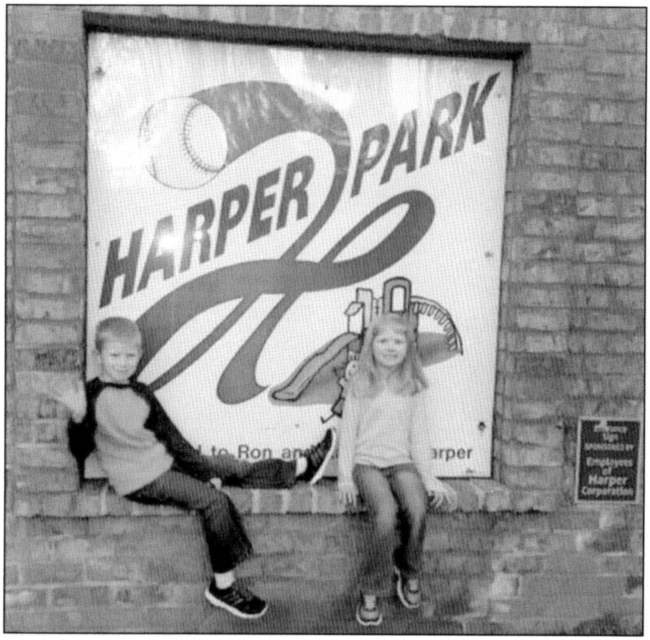


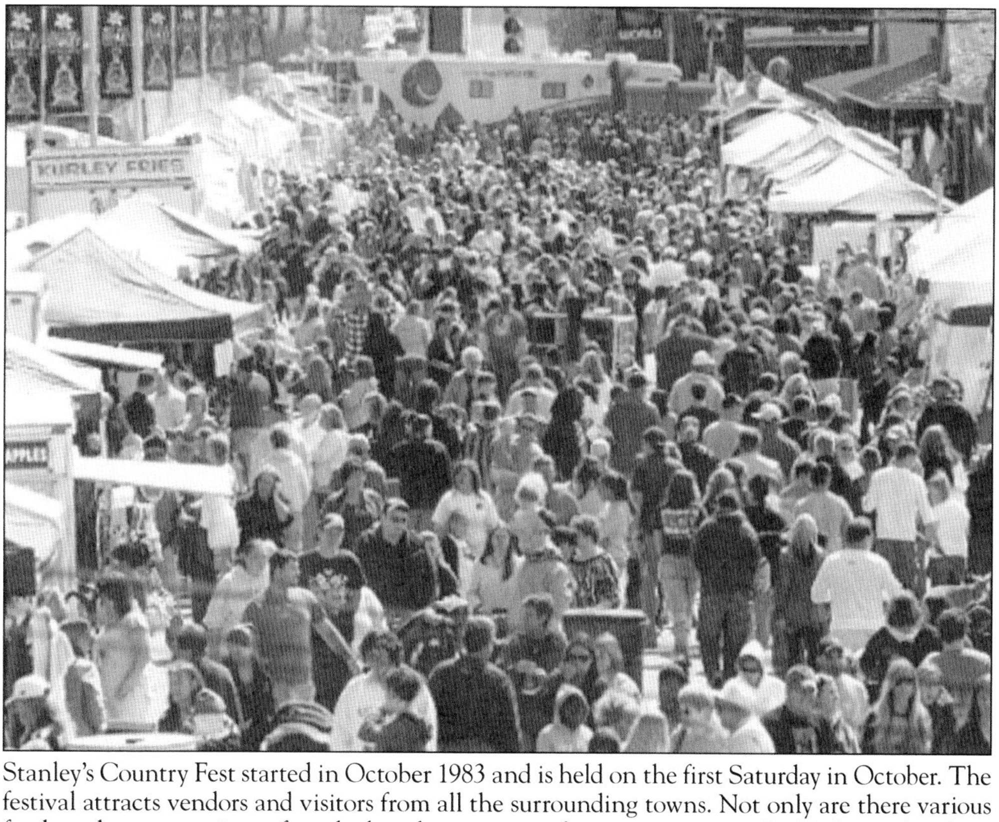


Stanley's Country Fest started in October 1983 and is held on the first Saturday in October. The festival attracts vendors and visitors from all the surrounding towns. Not only are there various foods and numerous items for sale, but there is music for entertainment. On Friday night, there are carnival rides for the children. Country Fest always attracts a large turnout and is one of the many times Stanley lives up to its motto as "A Friendly Place."

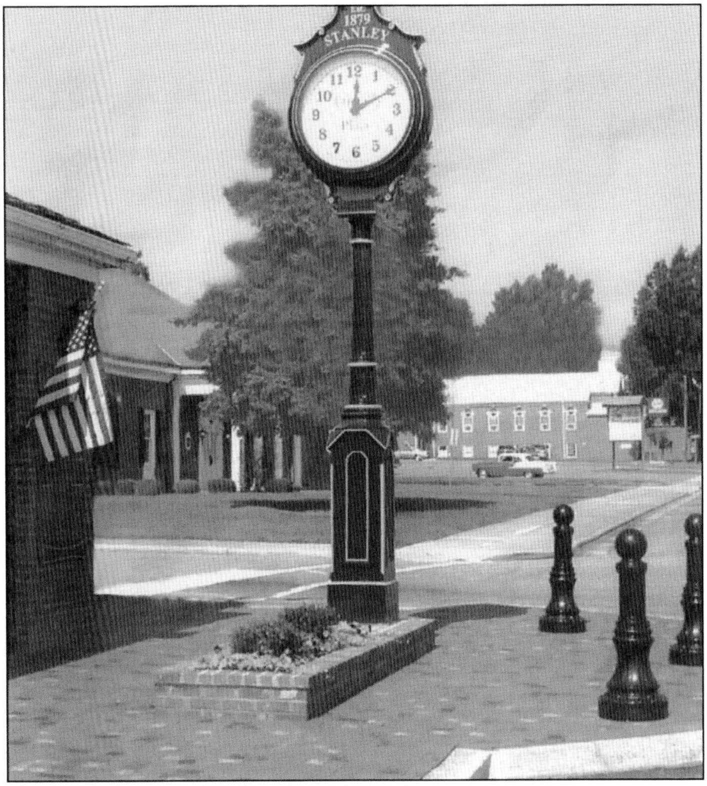


The new town clock was dedicated on September 26, 2009, by North Carolina District 108 representative John Torbett. The plaque on the wall at left lists the sponsors who paid for the clock as part of a revitalization of the downtown area. Ginnie Guida Tofaute, the mother of Mayor Frank Guida, unveiled the plaque. On October 3, approximately 15,000 people viewed the clock during Country Fest. (Courtesy of James Flanders.)

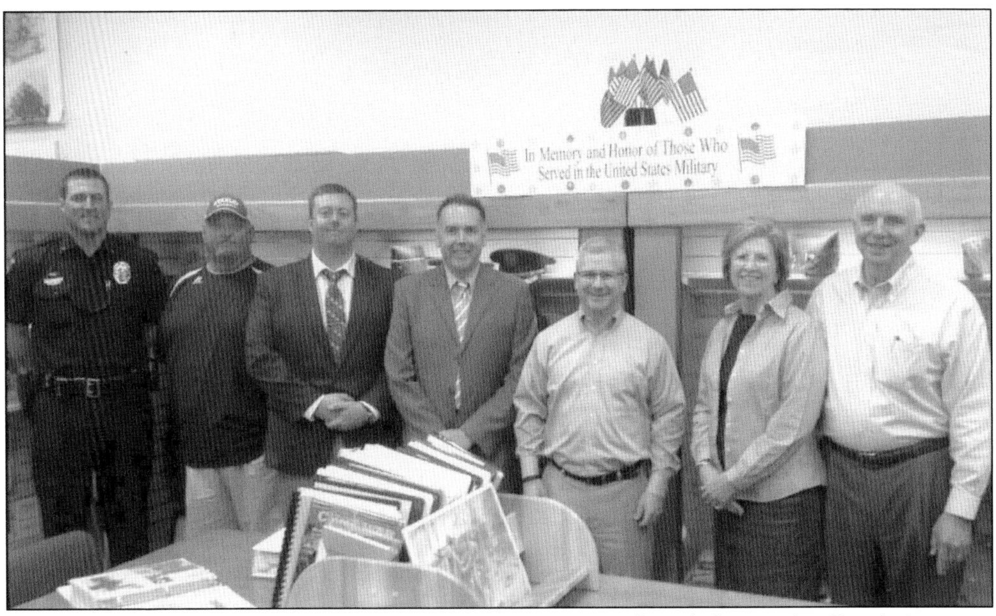


On a 2014 tour of Stanley's Brevard Station Museum are, from left to right, Derek Summey (Stanley police chief), Tug Deason (recreation director), Andrew Quinley (mayor), Heath Jenkins (town manager), Patrick McHenry (US congressman), and Pat and Barry Smith (museum board of directors members). The museum is dedicated to preserving the history and heritage of Stanley and its people.

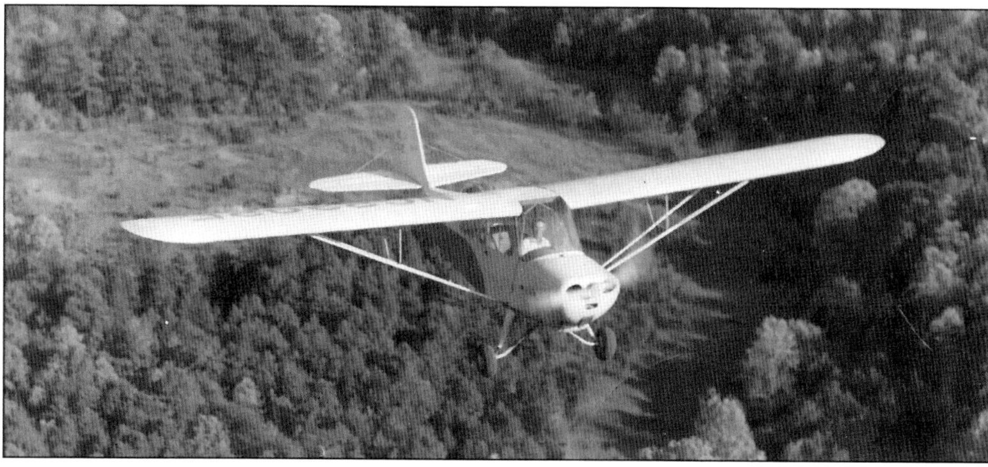

William Garfield "Bill" Hawley Jr. joined the Navy during World War II and became enamored with airplanes. After the war, he took flying lessons and, with a partner—Rich Mauney from Mount Holly—operated a private airport. The two pilots took many aerial photographs of Stanley and Mount Holly. Many people in Stanley went to the airport to get a ride with Hawley in his airplane. (Courtesy of Peggy Hawley.)

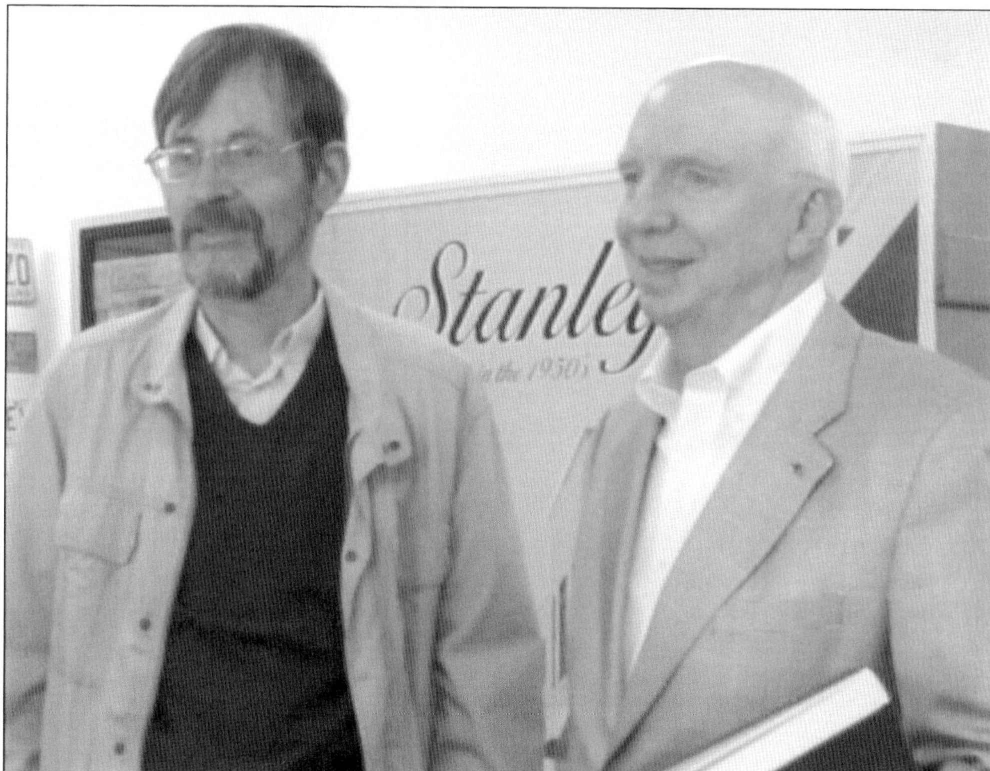

In this photograph is Régis Pluchet (left), the third great-nephew of André Michaux, and William Barry Smith, a third-great grandson of Peter Smith, in Stanley's Brevard Station Museum. Michaux discovered the Magnolia macrophylla while at the home of Peter Smith. Pluchet, of Le Mans, France, was invited to this country to visit Michaux's Charleston Garden site. His extensive itinerary included a visit to Stanley, the place where his ancestor first encountered the magnolia.

Consistent with our mission to preserve history on a local level, this book was printed in South Carolina on American-made paper and manufactured entirely in the United States. Products carrying the accredited Forest Stewardship Council (FSC) label are printed on 100 percent FSC-certified paper.

MADE IN THE USA